Usability: The Site Speaks For Itself

Kelly Braun

Max Gadney

Matthew Haughey

Adrian Roselli

Don Synstelien

Tom Walter

David Wertheimer

Published by glasshaus Ltd,
Arden House,
1102 Warwick Road,
Acocks Green,
Birmingham,
B27 6BH, UK

Printed in the United States
ISBN 1-904151-03-5

Usability: The Site Speaks For Itself

Cover Image

The title of the cover image is "Head", by Don Synstelien.
It is a statement on immersing oneself into mass entertainment.

To find out more about Don's illustrations, visit his personal site at *http://www.synstelien.com*
or send an e-mail to *don@synstelien.com*

glasshaus

web professional to web professional

© 2002 glasshaus

Trademark Acknowledgements

Credits

Authors

Kelly Braun
Max Gadney
Matt Haughey
Adrian Roselli
Don Synstelien
Tom Walter
David Wertheimer

MC

Molly E. Holzschlag

Additional Material

Molly E. Holzschlag
Victoria Hudgson

Reviewers

Devin Lunsford
Martyn Perks
grant Aaron Richmond
Dean Rose
Kevin Vanourney

Indexer

Bill Johncocks

Proof Readers

Bill Johncocks
Chris Smith

Commissioning Editor

Bruce Lawson

Lead Editor

Chris Mills

Technical Editor

Devin Lunsford

Managing Editor

Liz Toy

Project Manager

Sophie Edwards

Production Coordinator

Pip Wonson

Layout

Rob Sharp

Layout Design

Liz Brown
Deb Murray

Cover

Dawn Chellingworth

The Authors

Kelly Braun

Manager, Usability Engineering team, eBay.com

Thanks to my husband Ed for his support on my many endeavors.

Max Gadney

Head of Design, BBC News Online

Thanks to the News and Sport Design teams for their talent and conscientiousness. Thanks to the Technical team whose intelligence and wit could power a large planet. Thanks to the journalists and our bosses whose faith in the benefits of good design is an example to all in the industry.

Matt Haughey

Creator, metafilter.com

Thanks to Bruce, every MetaFilter member, the WebDesign-L and A List Apart communities. I dedicate this to my wife, Kay and all my friends who have helped me.

Adrian Roselli

Vice President of Interactive Media, Algonquin Studios Founder member, evolt.org

I need to thank all the members, writers, subscribers, lurkers, and others on the evolt.org lists and sites who've made me a better developer just by challenging me every day. I also need to thank the original founders who let me write this chapter on all our behalfs. I just hope they like it.

I'm also terribly grateful to my partners and staff at Algonquin Studios for playing the role of guinea pigs to the evolt.org designs, and later for my sleepy mornings when I was up too late the night before writing this chapter. I thank cattle for steak.

Don Synstelien

Creator, SynFonts.com

Special thanks to: Bruce and the whole glasshaus team, whose editors reviewed my original chapter and gave me the feedback and suggestions that I needed to finish it and make it much better that it would have been with my efforts alone.

Thanks also to my most excellent friends and cohorts in crime, Chris MacGregor and Leif Wells, who always challenge me and inspire me to do better. And to my many other friends who read and re-read the chapter for me so that I could understand if what I was writing made any sense at all.

A thousand thanks to my customers and fans – if I didn't have them, SynFonts wouldn't exist. They are the real driving force behind every useful change that I make to the site.

Most of all, thanks to my wife Annie, because she puts up with the increasingly strange work schedule required in order to keep my many projects going.

Tom Walter

Executive Creative Director, eBay.com

I would like to thank Don Donoughe, who opened the door for me into this business, Jim Vandegrift, who let me stay once I came in, John Avilla, who helped me branch out into new creative realms, and especially, Maria Lee, whose exhibited great faith and confidence in me.

I dedicate all of this to my wife, Beau, who opened my eyes to see what was possible, and my three children, Auden, Raleigh and Taggard, who opened my heart more than I thought possible.

David Wertheimer

Design Director, Economist.com

Thank you: everyone at Economist.com, colleagues past and present, for making the site a success. Andrew Rashbass and Asahi Pompey for their proofreading, approvals, and patience. Bruce Lawson for approaching me with this project. Rachel Bernstein and Sherri Trager for their professional assistance. My family for, well, everything. And thanks and a back tickle to Amy for her endless encouragement and enthusiasm.

Molly E. Holzschlag

Coined "one of the greatest digerati" and deemed one of the Top 25 Most Influential Women on the Web, there is little doubt that in the world of Web design and development, Molly E. Holzschlag is one of the most vibrant and influential people around. With over 20 Web development book titles to her credit, Molly is also a popular columnist and feature writer for such diverse publications as Macworld, PCMagazine, IBM developerWorks, WebReview.com and Builder.com. She is an engaging speaker and teacher, appearing regularly at such conferences as Comdex, Internet World, CMP's WEB shows, and Web Builder.

As a steering committee member for the Web Standards Project (WaSP), Molly works along with a group of other dedicated Web developers and designers to promote W3C recommendations. Currently, she is serving as the Associate Editor for Digital Web Magazine. Molly also acts as an advisory board committee member to numerous organizations, including the World Organization of Webmasters.

Thanks to my co-editor, Bruce Lawson, who provided terrific insights and supportive assistance as we worked on this book. Chris Mills helped kept things rolling along nicely. Many thanks to Bruce, Chris, and all of glasshaus for the creative opportunity.

Bruce Lawson

Bruce became Brand Manager of glasshaus a year ago, with the modest aim of making it the premier source of information for web professionals. He began his career in 1988 as a computer programmer (VAX Fortran!) and UI designer. Since then he has variously been a musician, actor, theatre director, tarot card reader in Istanbul, volunteer pharmacist in Calcutta, movie extra in Bombay, Elvis impersonator in Las Vegas, kindergarten teacher in Bangkok, and arrested for spying in Moscow.

I thank Molly, and the glasshaus team, all those web professionals who have given me advice and help (especially those I met in Seattle and San Francisco), and those who post on the lists where I lurk (particularly evolt and webdesign-L).
I'm grateful to all the authors, and – in the case of the big corporate sites – the authors' bosses who OK'd their inclusion in this book. Thanks. Even to the lawyers ;-)
I dedicate this book to my wife, Nongyow, and our children, Marina and James, without whom life would merely be existence.

Picture Credits

Front cover

Don Synstelein

eBay™ Chapter

eBay™ screenshots by permission of eBay Inc.
Tom's daughter, Audie, by Tom Walter – cute or what?
Kelly's daughter, Josie, by Kelly Braun – tooooo cute!
Other photos Pip Wonson and Bruce Lawson.
Thanks to Dulcie Emery for lending us the sketching toy. You can have it back now.

SynFonts Chapter

Splash page from *http://www.synstelien.com/desktops.html*.
Stratosphere Las Vegas by Don Synstelien.
Usable things photographed by Don Synstelien, except
Chris Mills using the international banking system by Bruce.

BBC Chapter

Segway picture from *http://www.segway.com*.
Other photos by Pip and Bruce.

Economist Chapter

iPod picture courtesy of Apple.
Other photos by Pip and Bruce.

evolt Chapter

Photo of Adrian Roselli courtesy of Mark Dellas.
Usable things photographed by Adrian, except
for Bruce's daughter Marina with towel, photographed by Bruce.
And the blurring is deliberate. Honestly.

MetaFilter Chapter

Splash Page of electric light parade and man in lift by Matt Haughey.
TiVo picture – © 2002 TiVo, Inc. All Rights Reserved.
Powerbook courtesy of Apple.
Matt in Sydney courtesy of Matt Himself.
Thanks to Volkswagen for the car picture.

Preface

What is this book?

This book is not 20 infallible rules of great information architecture. Neither is it a bunch of sites critiqued from a one-size-fits all perspective that says every web site is used by the same people, in the same way, for identical purposes.

This book is about web usability of the sites you've seen on the front cover, from the designers of those sites.

The authors discuss their initial designs, their audience, how they got feedback on the sites, how they made design tweaks to meet the unique needs of that group of users. These are real life experiences – a snapshot of a point in time. As the web evolves, as broadband becomes the norm and more people come on-line, these sites will evolve. That's what makes them usable; a constant attention to the needs and expectations of site's audience.

Who is this Book for?

It's for every web professional who wants new perspectives on real-world usability from their peers.

It's for designers who care about the audience but have been put off by Usability Experts' emnity to visual design, and it's for developers who want to think beyond the code and consider the client's whole experience.

It's for site owners who want to consider a variety of options when planning the future of their sites.

It's for everyone who is interested in the future, and the pioneers of this revolutionary new medium.

Bruce Lawson
April 2002

Summary of Contents

Introduction

beyond the buzz:
the true meaning of usability

molly e. holzschlag

This book exists to help web professionals gain perspective, not from the usability pundits that have popped up like so many mushrooms after rain, but from real practitioners. These are web developers, designers, and strategists who have spent years learning how to create great sites for audiences in daily life rather than using a one-size-fits-all methodology and possibly failing to properly address the needs of their visitors.

Usability as a term carries no absolute, agreed upon meaning whatsoever – it is a highly subjective matter. Usability, when not prefaced by the term "web" has a long history. However, in the context of the Web - which is a young entity itself – we're still learning what usability is and whether it should be our first concern when trying to provide a great experience for our site visitors. It seems extraordinarily arrogant to create an entire branch of study based on passing terminology, rather than the important issues with which the practice is really concerned.

So when the punditry surrounding web usability is over, the real-world lessons will remain. Already we see a trend away from the term "web usability," and other terms, such as "user experience" coming to the forefront. Terms such as this more accurately describe what exactly we as web professionals are trying to address in trying to make our sites a great experience for visitors. Designing a web site then becomes an audience-centric act, letting the people using the site determine the way that the site evolves. As such, we need to understand the ideas behind information design and usability, and learn the practical scope of applying them to improve our web sites, and our audience experience, for years to come.

> *"The idea of usability, sometimes known as 'human factors', existed long before the web. It involves observing users engaging in tasks and mediating between design and the end users' needs - ensuring that customers can achieve the original aims of the product, whatever that product may be."* - Martyn Perks, *"Excuse-ability"*, http://www.spiked-online.com/Articles/00000006D869.htm.

How Web Usability Came to Be

There are several disciplines that have led to the emergence of web usability. These disciplines have a long position in the world of technology design – longer than the Web has been around.

These disciplines include:

- User Interface Design. This is the design of any user interface, be it computer or product. For example, the way an ATM machine or other kiosk is designed is as important in the broader field of User Interface Design as the way a web page is designed. UI is considered a branch of engineering in many circles, and in that sense has less to do with design than the engineering of the structural components that make up an interface.

- Human Computer Interaction (HCI). File this one under your computer-science cap. The study of the way humans have interacted with computers focuses in on a variety of issues, but most especially on how people respond and react to various cues within a computer design or interface. A primary concept in HCI is that people form different opinions about the interactions they have with a computer or some aspect of computer technology based on their own mental models. For example, if you tend to be a creative thinker, your experience is going to be different from that of a more logical or linear thinker. Gender, class, and social concerns all play a role in these perceptions as well.

- Graphical User Interface (GUI) Design, a form of design specific to graphical user interfaces, referred to as "GUI" (and pronounced "gooey") design. The Internet did not have a GUI in its early days. The Mosaic web browser was the first graphical web browser, released for major platforms in September of 1993. Today, of course, most people use at least several levels of GUIs to access the Web, including their operating system, and of course their browser. As with UI design and HCI, the goal is to engineer interfaces complete with structure and cues that help the user navigate the graphic environment. The Primary focus of the discipline is on the use of color, space, shape, type, navigational menu structures, cognitive cues, and so forth. Ideally, GUIs are built based on common metaphors; think of the "trash can" or "recycling bin" on your desktop.

The concept of web usability as we know it today, then, is an amalgam of these disciplines and cultural perspectives. Anyone trying to understand the *why* of usability and the *how* of usability testing would do well to investigate the scientific, design, and human concerns that have had a much longer legacy than usability itself.

Obviously, the Web has demanded that we find new ways to describe things, and new ways in which to do them. Web usability is a big part of that, but already we find that the hype surrounding it is causing apprehension about usability: not only why we need usability, but also why we need to focus equally on audience, intent, and innovation.

Whether we are maintaining brand identity so as to be consistent with our audience and intent, or looking at new ways to provide for our site visitors, usability is incredibly important but ultimately a far deeper issue, and more closely integrated with design and technology than has been typically discussed in the context of the Web.

Components of Usability

While it is my contention that the term "web usability" is a buzzword, the work it is trying to address is no buzz at all. Rather, it is a necessary and often-misunderstood process that attempts to ensure that web sites are designed *for their visitors*. The audience experience is paramount; how we address that experience comes in myriad ways, but we must address content as well as UI design – is the content right for the intended audience? Is it laid out sensibly, in an easy-to-understand, logical fashion?

A poorly designed interface does not necessarily inhibit success, but we must bear in mind that content is just as important as a clear navigation mechanism for successfully serving a site visitor's needs.

Web professionals are striving for some method by which to make their site truly capable of being used by their site visitors for its intended purpose. This is a difficult thing to do, because it is my contention that we don't really know how to design for the Web. We have been relying on hacks and workarounds to get visual results that mimic things we already know about (print and multimedia design) but the Web is something else. It is a dynamic medium, one that does not conform to the practices of print design, or practices found in general multimedia design.

The problems resulting from browser differences, multiple technology platforms, and usability experts insisting on a one-shoe-fits-all approach to usability standardization have kept the web professional in a state of absolute frustration. As new versions of programming languages and browsers are released, new proprietary technologies are pitted against one another (the problems caused by the Great Browser Wars still linger on today), and new concerns are highlighted. For example, the need for Accessible web sites has been there since the beginning, but has only recently been widely recognized.

So web professionals have to be very flexible to meet all their audiences' needs. This flexibility is important because real usability, and the real service to audiences, comes from finding out and meeting their needs as they are *today*, while also looking at legacy concerns and future opportunities for innovation. So we should all be studying the field of web usability, bearing in mind that it is a constantly evolving one.

General Concepts

Most general concepts in web usability come from the core meaning of the word *usable* and the various disciplines that have contributed to its emergence.

General concepts in usability include:

- A product or product component, whether it is software or the design of a new stove, is measured by its efficacy.

- Ease of use is paramount.

- The time to learn features is short.

- Components within the product are understandable and consistent.

Here's a picture of a stove:

A traditional stove.

For most people in the developed world, this stove makes sense. It has a long-familiar structure with components where they should be. The lower drawer is either a broiler or storage section, and the main oven is a conventional oven with two visible racks. The stovetop is very consistent with most stovetops – even for those accustomed to using a gas range the burners are basically a familiar size and shape. What's more, the range interface has components which we've been used to for at least the last 50 years.

Now let's examine another, slightly more contemporary approach to a stove design:

A more contemporary stove.

For most people, this stove is familiar as well, but notice how simply changing a few features can become confusing? For example, the shorter top drawer is confusing to me. What is it? Is it a standard oven? Or is it a broiler?

The stove top is smooth. For most people in industrial countries, this will be familiar. But for many people around the world, a completely flat stove top might be confusing, and cause problems when using it, possibly even leading someone to burn themselves. Here, we also see an intriguing issue of cultural usability. In Asia, a round-bottom wok won't properly balance on a stovetop of this nature. As a result, both the stovetop and the wok become unusable.

Digging a little deeper, we find that the way to use this stove might be confusing as well. It has some traditional dials that keep it familiar, but the clock in the center is definitely more high-tech than the old standard. I have enough trouble trying to figure out how to properly set the time on my current stove; I can only imagine what this stove's clock interface is like!

The goal of making a product or feature useful is a good one indeed, particularly in cases where people can get hurt or, if we bring it back around to web sites, where people can be frustrated beyond belief at the poor structuring of a site.

Testing, Testing

Whether we realize it or not, many products go through usability tests to determine whether they are in fact useful and safe. The same is true with web usability. Entire processes for testing the usability of web sites exist, with little standardization.

Typically, though, usability testing breaks down like this:

- Research into user needs is conducted.

- User needs are identified and documented.

beyond the buzz: the true meaning of usability

- Wireframe testing occurs in some situations. This is the development of a basic prototype site including text and structural components.

- The site is built.

- A focus group of potential users is gathered.

- Using video cameras, one way screens, and other observational tools, the usability engineers watch the focus group as they use the site.

- Focus group members are encouraged to speak aloud as they move through the site.

The results from testing are then compiled, and changes made to the site as necessary.

Punditry, and the Problems with It

Now that you have an overview as to what usability is and some of the disciplines that have led to it, it's time to take a look at the things pundits are saying about web usability.

By far, the most widely known pundit in the field of web usability is Jakob Nielsen. Having come to the Web from his work as an engineer at Sun Microsystems, Nielsen has written and said more to the web development community about what he believes people want from the Web and how to properly give it to them than any known usability evangelist today. And most of the time, what Nielsen has to say makes tremendous sense, especially when it comes to the creation of information-heavy content. Examples of Nielsen's strengths include such ideas as proper titling of pages, focusing on accessibility for users with impairments, and a concern for resolution-independent design.

With a passion long on simplicity but short on the acceptance and integration of new technology, Nielsen

has upset a great many designers who are interested in making the Web a more vibrant, fun place to be (some try to marry this ideal to usability, some do not). For example, Nielsen refers to the use of Flash, and the creative use of HTML and CSS to create alternative link colors as "severe" usability problems.

Desplte the enormous sales of his first book, and the extraordinary popularity of his long-term web usability column at *http://www.useit.com/*, there is a large group of web professionals who choose to shun his teachings. Is that because so many of his ideas are fundamentally wrong? I don't think so.

I think the problem with punditry is simply this: You cannot take a one-size-fits-all approach to something so amorphous as web site design – it is by no means an exact science. Yes, a web page should be usable, but we know so precious little about the way the Web will ultimately be designed as it evolves, and even less about the evolution of human behavior and culture – that to enforce ideas so stringently upon us now is very limiting. What's more important is while creating simple pages – which is often precisely the right thing to do,

What is a User?

Just what is a user, anyway? Web usability pundits talk a *lot* about users. I find the term "user" to be extremely rude. Aside from the negative connotations the word has (such as, "He used me!"), the terminology marginalizes *people*. These are **people** using web sites, not some kind of automata. As such, I would like to see the term *user* outlawed. OK, so maybe that's unrealistic, but I do have two suggestions to replace user: **audience member** or **site visitor**.

Humanizing the language with which we discuss usability and related issues allows us to think in human rather than abstract or technical terms.

but sometimes precisely the *wrong* approach – to first analyze your audience, and match it with your site's goals. This is not really a hard thing to do, and will save you countless hours of trying to figure out just why a site is useful.

Another concern with the one-size-fits-all approach is that it assumes that web designers have the luxury of starting a site from scratch. But what happens when designers and developers are called upon to retrofit a site to accommodate users in ever-changing climates? Making rules up for such a complex process may be idealistic, but it is not realistic.

> *"Maybe I'm resisting usability guidelines because I'm stubborn. I must admit that I don't like rules. It's useful to understand the rules, but more satisfying to break them. What's great about the Web is that we don't yet know the rules. I don't want a formula. I don't want a guru thinking for you or me." – Dale Dougherty, Publisher, O'Reilly Networks, in* Invasion of the Usability Experts, Web Techniques Magazine.

Audience and Intent

My mantra is "audience and intent". I'm a stickler for these elements because they're often the most overlooked or rushed-through aspects of a site's development. Knowledge of the audience shapes everything on a site, from visual design to behind-the-scenes functionality. The intent of a web site – whether to sell, entertain, or inform – has equal influence on the way the site is designed and developed. Of course, neither of these issues can be addressed without proper planning of the company or organization's short- and long-term goals for the site.

Getting to Know You: Seven Things to Learn About Audience Members

If you're just starting out on a new project, you'll want to do some research into your audience. For projects with accommodating budgets, gathering a focus group can be invaluable. In less accommodating situations, you'll first want to gather any existing demographics from the industry or organization the site represents, do any research necessary to better understand your audience, and use surveys and feedback mechanisms once the site is up and running.

What is the General Age Group of your Audience?
This question is important in order to help guide your site's look, as well as the tone of language, size of text, and contrast for readability.

What is the Sex of the majority of your Site's Visitors?
Women and men respond to cues differently. A powerful example of this is color. From a general psychological standpoint, women tend to be more persuaded by softer colors, such as pastels. Men tend to be more trusting of neutral colors, especially blues. Physiologically speaking, there is a relatively high prevalence of color blindness in men (about 8% of all males have some form of color blindness, whereas less than 0.5 percent of women do). As a result, if your site is geared toward men, knowing this will help you choose color cues within your interface that are most appropriate for that circumstance.

A perfect example of usability problems that can come about for those with some forms of color blindness is the use of red as a cautionary color. Let's say you have required form fields that appear with a red highlight to ensure that site visitors know these are in fact required fields. The use of red isn't wrong, but when you think about the fact that a considerable portion of your site visitors don't distinguish red, it becomes apparent that alternative means, such as the use of an asterisk or other symbol, is required to communicate with those audience members effectively. (To learn more about color blindness, you can take the Ishihara test for color blindness, *http://www.toledo-bend.com/ colorblind/Ishihara.html*)

beyond the buzz: the true meaning of usability

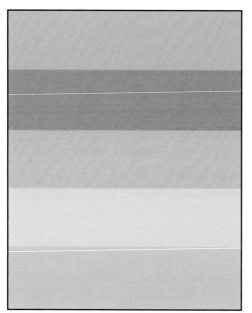

Women are generally more persuaded by softer colors and pastels.

Men tend to prefer blues and neutral colors.

What is the General Education Level of your Visitors?

While one should never talk "down" to audience members – an appropriate voice and tone in both the language and design elements of your site will help it to be more useful.

What Cultural and/or Religious Issues Might Affect your Audience?

An individual's cultural and religious background can profoundly influence perception. This is true when using color, language, and symbols. Purple, for example, is a very sensitive color to use in Western cultures, particularly Catholic Europe, where purple is religiously associated with the crucifixion and mourning. Similarly, the inappropriate use of certain non-verbal symbols such as a cross in navigational metaphor can be problematic.

Does your Audience have any Prevalence of Special Needs?

Usability includes accessibility, and all sites should follow appropriate accessibility guidelines (see the Web Accessibility Initiative, *http://www.w3.org/WAI/*, the USDOJ Section 508 homepage, *http://www.usdoj.gov/ crt/508/508home.html*, and check out *Constructing Accessible Web Sites* by Jim Thatcher et al, ISBN: 1-904151-00-0, published by glasshaus). Following these guidelines allows you to appropriately serve members of your audience with visual, auditory, or physiological impairments.

How Tech-Savvy are your Visitors?

Site visitors with greater technical skills are likely to have an easier time with unusual interfaces. However, if your site is more information-oriented, tech-savvy audience members are likely going to be frustrated by unusual interfaces that get in the way of the information. Recently, I went to a rental site for apartments in San Francisco, and the entire navigation set was based on Java applets. I was using a dialup connection, and each page had to load new applet sets in order for me to use the interface at all! Needless to say, I found another site to help me.

What Kind of Sites are your Visitors Familiar With?
If your audience members are oriented toward commerce there will be interface components with which they are already familiar: shopping carts and forms. If your audience is largely entertainment-oriented, they likely have plug-ins for Flash, audio, and video. Knowing what your visitor's habits are can really assist you in making decisions about the interface and technological elements.

Audience

Instead of regarding all web sites as being the same, and individuals as being amorphous users, there's a much more sensible approach to offering site visitors the best experience – that's simply examining your audience and allowing them to guide the design or redesign of a site.

Sounds too easy, right? It's not. Creating sites by being aware of your audience and what you wish to communicate to them is crucial to how the entire site will be dealt with. Knowing your audience intimately – as people – will help you determine all aspects of a site's design and function.

Let's say for example you are building sites for two different audiences. One site is a storefront that sells high quality teas, and another site is for a new alternative rock band. A typical audience member for the tea site might be a young woman, let's call her Marie. Marie is a young unmarried professional with a taste for quality. She is willing to spend money for higher priced items if they are good. Marie is a discriminating site visitor with a good amount of technical savvy. A typical audience member for the new, alternative rock band site is a young man still living at home. Let's call him Jake. Jake grew up with

computer games, and loves rich interfaces and multimedia. He's going to be on the lookout for "cool" factor.

Marie and Jake are two very different individuals and have to be catered for differently, from color to layout to navigation to the type of language you use. How you entice Marie to buy tea and Jake to buy a new CD is deeply rooted in how you greet them, and make them feel welcome.

While a one-night-stand might be fun for the moment, it's the long-term relationships that truly enrich our lives.

In fact, web sites should not be considered passive. Even if they are entirely academic, educational, or informational, *personality* and *quality content* is what will keep Marie making monthly purchases, and Jake revisiting time and again to check out new videos and MP3s made available on his favorite band's site. The reason for this is that the personality (and in the case of business, this relates to **brand**) expressed by your site is the foundation upon which you can build a relationship with your audience. While a one-night-stand might be fun for the moment, it's the long-term relationships that truly enrich our lives.

"The web is just too big for one paradigm to prevail. Some sites will need intensive whiz-bang branding that Nielsen's "principles" won't allow. Other sites will need moronically basic navigation and speedy download times ... " - Curt Cloninger in Usability Experts are from Mars, Graphic Designers are from Venus, A List Apart, http://www.alistapart.com/stories/marsvenus/.

beyond the buzz: the true meaning of usability

The thing about audiences – especially on the Web, where worldly and discriminating individuals abound – is that they can detect the sincerity and appropriateness of your presentations. But serving plain vanilla ice cream when your site visitor wants mango with extra whipped cream is a mistake.

Learn the flavors that entice your audience, and serve them to them packaged in a useful and usable way.

The Road to Heaven: Paved with Intent

No doubt you've heard the axiom "dress for success". People will judge you according to the way you present yourself to the world. If you appear at a corporate job interview in tattered jeans, a diamond nose ring, and pink dreadlocks, you're probably not going to be judged very positively (unless of course you're in San Francisco). Certain situations simply demand that the image match the desired expectations.

> *"Most usability issues really result from either a web site's attempt to be too many things to too many people, or the inability of its creators to free themselves from the few methods that have worked in the past."*

So it is with sites. An interface must be visually appropriate and match your business intent. Pick up just about any magazine or newspaper these days, or log on to your favorite news site, and undoubtedly you'll read about dot coms that dot bombed largely due to the fact that they didn't have a long-term plan. What's more, they didn't understand what they were trying to do, and for whom they were attempting to do it.

Speak for Yourself

Honesty is incredibly important in the design of successful interfaces. People will both consciously and unconsciously respond to the sincerity of your message. This book exists to encourage honesty and understanding in web usability, rather than to prescribe a pre-defined methodology for every site. We are, after all, professionals with vast and varied experiences, and combining our insights – along with positive relationships created with audience members – is the matrix from which useful and creative sites can grow.

This book is different from every other usability book that you have ever read, because it takes the trials and tribulations of the designers and developers involved and lets them speak for their creations, in very real and honest terms, about what usability means.

The book is organized by site type, with the idea of showing both the parallel and paradox of designing for particular audiences. The three types of sites covered are commerce sites, content sites, and community sites.

Commerce Sites

Commerce sites, by their very nature, are incredibly demanding of designers and technologists. This makes the resulting work of addressing usability particularly difficult, because trying to address the needs of visual design and interface in concert with back-end technology is notoriously challenging. This challenge is seen very clearly in the case of eBay™, where designers, technologists, and usability engineers work together to address the changing and growing needs of their site visitors. In the case of eBay™, what is particularly fascinating to me is that the problem of putting the audience first becomes crystal clear.

Jakob Nielsen and his associate, Marie Tahir, wonder in their book, *Homepage Usability: 50 Websites Deconstructed*, why eBay™ places links to categories in certain places within the eBay™ interface. Unfortunately, Nielsen and Tahir failed to dig far enough into the issue of scalability: there is no other site that has had to constantly reinvent itself without disturbing its audience members to the scale that eBay™ historically has. The reason that eBay™ categories exist as they do isn't a usability mistake – it is the result of a transitioning and growing site that cannot afford to fail its audience members by too quickly or dramatically changing interface components. Many eBay™

Getting to Know You Part II: The Power of Statistical Analysis

One of the most important things you can do over the course of a site's life is to follow server analysis.

Two primary types of statistical information that can be very useful to getting to know your audiences better are:

- Technological analysis. Tracking your audience's operating system type and version, browser type and version, color support, screen resolution, and JavaScript support will help you make better decisions regarding how your interface is ultimately designed.

- Behavioral analysis. How many repeat visitors does your site receive? How do site visitors move from place to place within you site? Where did your site visitors come from? All of this information can be tracked with server statistics.

Web service providers and systems administrators can install a range of analysis tools in order to help you learn more about myriad aspects of audience technology and behavior. You can also decide to use cookies if you want more specific information about specific site visitors. While this practice is considered by some to be ineffective because many users don't understand what they are and consider them to be a security or personal privacy risk, the use of cookies is extremely prevalent and can be a reasonable choice for assisting with your analysis.

Statistic Type	Useful For ...
Browser type and version	Creating effective cross-browser interfaces
Platform type and version	Creating stable, cross-platform designs
Screen Resolutions	Determining fixed, fluid, or combination designs for your audience's primary resolution
Color Depth	Restricting or increasing color usage
JavaScript support and version	Deciding whether JavaScript is useful for your audience
Referrals	Tracking where your audience is coming from, and learning general surfing behaviors
Visitors by time of day	Determining when to make changes and upgrades to the site while disturbing the least number of people
Search engine keywords and phrases	Knowing how people are looking for information that gets them to your site can help you make your site easier to find by including common keywords and phrases in your meta-tags
Visitor loyalty	Tracking repeat visitors can help you measure your site's success
Site types and countries	Knowing where your visitors are coming from will help you make decisions about interface components, language usage, and cultural concerns

Statistical information and how it can help with usability concerns.

beyond the buzz: the true meaning of usability

members rely on the service to *make their living*. When you hear eBay™'s side of the story, it becomes quickly evident that eBay™ is practicing usability in the real world, rather than the ideal one – no small challenge.

Our other commerce site example is one that is in many ways antithetical to eBay™. Synfonts, an "experimental" font company, uses a Flash-based interface to promote and sell typefaces. Its designer, Don Synstelien, eloquently describes why Flash, which has been considered problematic in many usability circles, was the correct way to promote his work. Synstelien's audience comprises largely designers, motion designers, and typographers – these are people that care about visual fascination, action, and typography, and Flash is truly the only currently acceptable way to get high-end visual and motion design to the Web. Many Flash designers are frustrated by usability punditry, because there is little room for experimentation in a plain view of the world. Yet a near 95% market penetration and growing usability components in Flash make it a great choice for the more experimental designer. What's particularly intriguing about including a site such as Synfonts in the book is that it lives as evidence that Flash interfaces can not only address the "cool" factor for entertainment sites, but they can be successful – when used in step with audiences – as sites that sell.

Content Sites

Content, it's been said, is king. So we looked to two kings of content to speak up about usability in the context of content: the BBC and *The Economist*.

BBC News Online is a fascinating case study because it focuses in on a broadcast medium that is redefining itself for the Web. While the Web has some broadcast features, it also comes with new challenges and opportunities. The BBC team took serious stock of these opportunities, such as effectively relating rich content to a wide range of audience types. This is especially true with their international sites, and the BBC's growth in terms of providing online news in multiple languages shows an especially strong sensitivity to the effective use of interface design in a truly international environment.

With the BBC's new design also comes a departure from usability ideals. The way links are managed goes against Nielsen's principles. In his first book, *Designing Web Usability*, Nielsen boldly states that it is "critical for web usability" to retain the standard browser defaults of link colors. As I mentioned earlier, this is a very touchy subject. The use of links with hover colors and no visited link color has been in practice for a long time among designers – especially now with more browser support for CSS, which enables designers to create multiple link colors on a page. The BBC's new main site is extremely elegant, appealing to the serious and sophisticated site visitor and demonstrating in clear terms that certain audiences do not need to be treated so simplistically.

Another area where the BBC team is doing interesting work is in their children's news (CBBC) section. You'll be able to compare the BBC News Online interface with the sports site and the CBBC design, and see how much consideration has gone into giving the sites their own personality and identity in order to best communicate with site visitors.

Economist.com is a site that is deep with rich content. The case study in this book focuses on a variety of development concerns with regards to managing large content, but a highlight of the study relates to the efficacy of brand, and how important brand can be in order to build and maintain visitor loyalty. Maintaining that brand throughout the entire site becomes paramount, especially because there are so many areas to the site. Being able to develop intelligent navigation based on strong infrastructure helped Economist.com's site designers make consistent and strong decisions about how the *Economist* brand would be best highlighted. These decisions affected typefaces used, colors and where they would or wouldn't be used, and a variety of iconographic elements necessary to assist visitors in navigating the Economist.com's content effectively.

Community Sites

Content might be king, but community is most definitely the common people, looking for common ground. Online communities have been in existence since the early days of the Internet and networked computing (BBSs, for example). But Web community has had some specific challenges associated with it, particularly finding the best technical solutions for message boards and chat sites, that have made it harder to grow and maintain communities. As a result, a lot of smaller, niche communities have come to the forefront on the Web.

Community suffers from the same naming problems as we find with usability. What online community really is can be seen as an intangible and subjective experience. You'll see this come to light when listening to what MetaFilter and evolt have to say about community and usability.

The evolt community grew out of a desire to have a Web professionals' peer community. Where evolt has been especially successful is in addressing the needs of a global audience – no easy task. *evolt.org* describes its community as only being made up of 50% US members, and although all members mostly speak English while interacting with the community, the diversity of the group is impressive.

Developing usable interfaces for such culturally diverse audiences is fraught with particular challenges. To address these challenges, evolt performed two types of testing despite a limited budget. First, co-workers, family, and friends were brought in to form informal user groups to provide feedback. Then, evolt provided a survey to its members regarding how they used the site. You'll find out how much the designers of evolt learned from this process when you read the chapter, but suffice it to say, the feedback was very precise and as a result, extremely helpful.

MetaFilter is a particularly interesting case study of a community site, because its developer, Matt Haughey, specifically decided to make several design choices outside the realm of vanilla usability ideas to reinforce appeal to his audience: very experienced technical people. In terms of interface, this meant actually making certain areas of the site more difficult to find, and making people register for the site, and so on. The idea is fairly radical: create a site for a specific audience, and then filter out anyone who can't technically fit into that audience! It's an extremely imaginative approach, but certainly one outside the realm of today's general perspectives on usability.

Summing Up

Bruce Tognazzini, a brilliant veteran of user interface design issues, spent 14 years at Apple and has written two seminal books on UI design, *Tog on Software Design* and *Tog on Interface*. Tognazzini is an unusual thinker, who says, "Effective interfaces are visually apparent and forgiving, instilling in their users a sense of control. Users quickly see the breadth of their options, grasp how to achieve their goals, and do their work."

These words are interesting. They put control in the hands of the audience, which is a great thing to do. But Tog seems to miss a very critical point in this writing, and that's that a site visitor should ideally never even realize that they are even involved in an interface. Better yet, the experience should be so useful that the goal of the site visitor is easily fulfilled.

Ultimately, what might appear to be "good" or "bad" usability in the light of punditry might actually happily appeal to your audience and merit phenomenal success, even though the so-called "rules" of usability have been broken. The idea is to be inspired by experience and learn to provide true solutions for flesh-and-blood audiences rather than apply a concept that might look good on paper, but never addresses the immediate human concerns.

BBC News Online

from broadcast to web

max gadney

BBC NEWS

http://news.bbc.co.uk

Max Gadney was born in, and is resident in London. He believes that from an explicit understanding of users' needs and attitudes, problems are made clear – and innovative design can spring forth. From this understanding, the true nature of the design problem becomes obvious and clarity of form and beauty can be achieved. This approach will work with anything from a government building to a club flyer.

Thanks to the News and Sport Design teams for their talent and conscientiousness. Thanks to the Technical team whose intelligence and wit could power a large planet. Thanks to the journalists and our bosses whose faith in the benefits of good design is an example to all in the industry.

What would you rather be doing, if you weren't doing this?

Drawing comics and making films.

Which living person do you most admire?

John Wagner – writer and inventor of Judge Dredd.

On a scale of 1 (Amish) - 10 (Star Trekkie), how geeky are you?

3.

What's your favorite building?

Bilbao Guggenheim Museum – see *http://www.guggenheim-bilbao.es/ingles/home.htm*.

What's your favorite book? Piece of music? Type of pizza?

Book: The Count of Monte Christo.
Music: La Isla Bonita by Madonna or anything by Slayer.
Pizza: Hawaiian.

If you were a superhero(ine), who would you be?

Cassidy from Preacher, but without the pain and ennui that comes from being undead.

What gadget could you not live without?

My credit card!

What is the future of the Web, in your opinion?

The functionality of products and applications that utilize information will seem invisible and better for it. Designers will need to understand users' needs, habits, and the technology to innovate as never before. Anyone not interested in this possibility should go and work in print design.

from broadcast to web

June 1997 decided to go ahead with site

November 1997 launch site

BBC News has a history of providing trusted, accurate, impartial, and in-depth news content to its audience via radio and television, not only in the UK, but also internationally through its World Service. The BBC launched News Online (*http://news.bbc.co.uk*) in 1997 with the aim of providing an online audience with an additional way to access BBC news content. News Online exists under the broader umbrella of BBC News Interactive, which is concerned with all of the BBC's digital interactive news output, including interactive television.

With over a million unique users on an average weekday, the site is now the leading provider of online news in the UK, and also has a large global audience. Creating a web site that is accessible and usable to such a diverse set of users was a major challenge for the designers and developers at the BBC.

In this chapter:

- We'll hear from Max Gadney (Head of Design at BBC News Online) about the design of the site as it is currently, and how it will change into the future.

- We'll also hear from the designers of the latest additions to the main news site: Sport Online and the new CBBC News site, designed for children.

First off, however, Mike Smartt and Richard Deverell talk about some of the motivational factors that lie behind the creation of the site, and at what it's trying to achieve and why.

A View from the Top

Mike Smartt (BBC News Online Editor-In-Chief) and Richard Deverell (Head of BBC News Interactive) talk about the unique opportunities and challenges presented by an online environment for the delivery of news content, and about some of the aims for the BBC News Online site.

Mike Smartt.   *Richard Deverell.*

The driving force behind the site is – and has been since its initial launch – its content, which has won numerous awards for online journalism.

At BBC News Online, we aim to be the world's first choice for interactive news. We strive to maintain the intelligent news agenda that characterizes BBC radio and television news in the UK, and throughout the world via the BBC's World Service. The driving force behind the site is – and has been since its initial launch

05 06 07 08 09 10 11 12 01 02 03 04 05 06 07 08 09 10 11 12

Late 1999 1st and only major redesign

Late 2002 next major redesign & move to 800 width

– its content, which has won numerous awards for online journalism.

BBC News aims to inform, enlighten, and entertain, both domestically and internationally.

While the challenges and advantages of online news and broadcast news may differ – as does the form of the content – the broad agenda remains the same. BBC News aims to inform, enlighten, and entertain, both domestically and internationally. All the work that goes on at News Online (including all the worries about layout, navigation, and usability) is geared towards achieving that goal in the most effective manner possible.

Moving to a New Medium

In moving from a broadcast world to an online one, we had to think carefully about the range of technical and editorial issues that are specific to the web. In particular:

- We have the **space** to do and include anything – in principle. Only our imagination and our resources limit us. There is room to offer far more scope and choice to the audience, so prioritization is very important.

- We have **global distribution**. Obviously, this brings its own challenges, with cultural and language issues, and the need to create content to appeal to such a diverse audience. Furthermore, all our competitors are available

globally too, though few in the UK specifically address the worldwide audience.

- Users have access to the site **24x7**, so the content – across the whole site – always needs to be up to date.

- A web site can be **interactive**, unlike traditional TV or radio. This means that not only do we have the opportunity to offer the user a voice, but also to start connecting with them in a much more meaningful way.

- The medium can make use of **connections between content** – some tangible and others lateral – to give the user potential to find out more from us than a linear broadcast allows.

No Boundaries

One of the hardest management issues for News Online is deciding what to prioritize. In television and radio we are limited by airtime, which decides how much we can do. Online, we can essentially do as much as we want. Obviously, there are plenty of limitations, the two most important being technology and resources. Often our ambitions have far outstretched our abilities to make them a reality.

We have aimed to include more in News Online than the core content of reporting the serious news. For example, there's room here for more magazine-type features, and some lighter content, as well as much more background reference information. The design needs to accommodate these differing types of content, and promote and display them as such.

from broadcast to web

No Borders

News Online reaches a global audience. Historically, the BBC has broadcast to many different countries through the BBC World Service and we are building on that work. The eventual aim is that all BBC News content will be available in 43 languages.

Designing for the world requires respect and knowledge of cultural sensibilities.

However, News Online is in a unique position in that we are the only BBC service that is simultaneously international and national. This leads to certain difficulties with how we phrase things and how we organize our content. For example, if Tony Blair is mentioned in a news item, we add "the UK prime minister" after his name, whereas if we had a purely UK audience, we would automatically assume that this was understood. The biggest difficulty, though, is the tension over the agenda on the front page. Is a major motorway accident near London a lead story? Or a new case of foot and mouth in Cumbria? In the UK, these are important stories, but not at an international level. At the moment, these kinds of stories fight for space on the front page with worldwide issues, such as violence in the Middle East, and we need to strike an appropriate balance.

Designing for the world requires respect and knowledge of cultural sensibilities regarding, for example, iconography and color. We also need to be aware of the different ways which different countries are viewing us – at bandwidth, application, and device level. Currently, we believe that about 50% of our audience is in the UK, and 50% international.

No Deadlines

The 24x7 nature of things means that at News Online, there are no deadlines. For a newspaper, if you don't get a story in before it "goes to bed" - immediately prior to being printed – then it doesn't get in the paper. Readers know this, and can be forgiving – they know that if something happens at 3 am then it's not going to be in the newspaper that lands on their doorstep the following morning. The paper is already out of date the moment it rolls off the presses. Online, you publish a story the minute it is ready to publish.

On radio and television, a news story is up-to-date at the moment it is being read out. (Often, items are being edited during the previous item.) Broadcast news is up to date until the moment it is broadcast. Even with 24-hour news, it's possible to be updating the business news, for example, while the sports results are being broadcast, but online news needs to be up to date across the board. If we get a complaint that the business news is behind on a story, there's no point us saying, "Sorry! We were busy with the sports section", because a user won't be interested in that. Every category has to be up to date all the time.

Another implication of the fact that the site is always available is that the news stories don't go away. Once published, they are available in the news archives from then on, easily accessible via the search functionality on the site. In broadcast, reports simply float out into the ether – the audience at home rarely records them, so they have precious little time to closely analyze what has been said. Even newspapers traditionally only have a real life of one day. On the web, though, news reports are immortalized for all to see. In a way, this means there is a far greater demand for accuracy.

Two-way

The fact that users also have a voice on the Web makes the relationship between news provider and audience vastly different from in the broadcast world: people can now talk back to us. You could say that a web site is interactive in the sense that people click on those parts of the site that they want to visit, and find their own way through, but in reality this is little more interactive than choosing which story in a newspaper to read, though the ability to make connections with the archive online is a big difference. Real interactivity is provided on a news web site by allowing users to voice their own concerns and opinions, and take part in interviewing and questioning experts and world leaders. In this way, the audience is no longer a passive body that receives the news, but one that takes a more active role.

> *Real interactivity is provided on a news web site by allowing users to voice their own concerns and opinions*

Integrating Media

An exciting future area is the possibility of tighter integration between the content provided via different media. We could have some kind of discussion program on the television that allowed people to vote either using interactive TV, or online, and broadcast the results in both places. Another example is the provision of an e-mail service tied to a television program. We are planning to launch this soon for BBC 2's Newsnight program (broadcast in the UK) – it will be a daily e-mail with details of what's happening in the program later that evening, what will be on, who will be on, and perhaps allowing the subscriber to ask questions on a particular topic. This kind of service allows the TV program to connect to its audience in a new way.

Hopefully, we'll see more experiments of this sort, developing closer integration of television and online content. There is a potential here for using one medium to trade on the strengths of the other. This is far more than simply cross promotion, but about offering people greater depth. Already, when there is a feature on a UK television news broadcast about school league tables, we offer further depth to the audience online by giving them the ability to search by postcode for a school in

their area to find its rating. Television or radio would never be able to offer a service like that – it's about playing to the strengths of different media. (The advent of interactive digital television can offer similar advantages, but the audience for this is still small compared to the online audience.)

Funding

Because of the unique way that the BBC is funded – from television license payers in the UK – it has a public service responsibility; it needs to be both accessible and relevant to all sections of the public, using the Internet as just another platform on which we can offer BBC news journalism. Unlike a commercial site, we can't aim our content at just one group within society, but rather we have an obligation to serve content that is useful and interesting to everybody. As part of this, we also need to make sure that the content is accessible to the widest possible audience. Not only do we make sure that the site works on all of the major browser versions, but we also offer a low graphics version of the site (soon to become a no-graphics, text-only version).

One major advantage of the publicly funded nature of the BBC is the fact that it has no advertising on its site, unlike other commercial news sites such as CNN and MSNBC. The absence of large distracting banner ads is a huge benefit for the end user, and makes using the site a much easier and more pleasant experience. From the BBC's point of view, we get to dedicate all of the screen real estate to the main purpose of the site – news. From its inception, the web site was seen purely as a content-driven site – its only aim to provide access to BBC news, and to maintain the character and quality of BBC news.

Starting Out

BBC News Online was launched in November 1997. With our history as a television and radio broadcaster, we had some work to do to make our content suitable for an online world. Even at the start, however, we were keen to experiment with the possibilities of using existing audio and visual content on the web, although technologically it seemed a way off at the time. We had a vision of a site providing the user with a true multimedia experience.

To begin with, though, it was clear that the web site would be predominantly text and images, and while we had access to plenty of pictures, we had to create the text from somewhere. Initial ideas of how to do this revolved around attempts to re-work textual material from other sources, such as Ceefax, or television and radio news scripts, but it quickly became apparent that

these neither worked online, nor were taking advantage of the new medium. In order to do that, we needed to create text from nothing, so we started hiring print journalists.

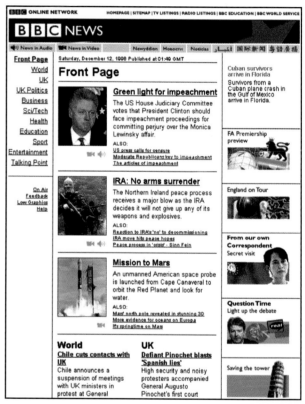

This is how the original version of the site looked back in 1998. The first redesign took place in 1999. While there have been minor modifications and updates since then, the basic design was as you see it today.

Ceefax

Ceefax is a teletext service provided by the BBC. It allows users to display text on their televisions rather than moving pictures, and consists of a set of pages, which a user can navigate to by selecting the page number on their remote control. Ceefax provides information on weather, news, listings, sports results, and background information for some television programs. Due to the limitations of the medium, only very short amounts of text can be displayed on each screen, as you can see from the screenshot.

A typical Ceefax page.

The Site Today

Here, Max Gadney talks about the design process, and some of the main design features of BBC News Online. He examines how the site is functioning at the moment, and goes on to look at how the lessons learned from the current design are influencing plans for the future.

The site has grown enormously since its launch in 1997, both in terms of content and traffic. With over 300 new stories being published per day, the archives now contain upwards of a million stories, all of which are available and fully searchable. The traffic on the site has grown from around 200 thousand page views per day at its launch in 1997, to eight to ten million page views per day on average, rising if a major news event occurs.

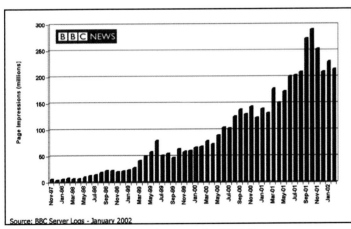

Source: BBC Server Logs - January 2002

This chart shows the page views on the BBC News and Sports sites since their launch in 1997.

Design Challenges and Processes

The sheer scale of the site, combined with the size and diversity of the audience has lead to some unique challenges that face the editorial, design, and technical teams at the BBC.

For example, with over 300 new stories being produced every day, there is always competition for promotional space on the front page. Some stories will always be obviously at the top of the headlines, but prioritizing and organizing the others is a tough editorial job. Ranking depends both on how recently an article has been published and its editorial importance – clearly, we can't have a story about a celebrity marriage break up appearing above war news. The design needs to give journalists a lot of control of the ordering, position, and relative size of the various stories. Eventually, we want to give the front page editor the same flexibility a newspaper editor has – that is, allow them to alter the appearance of the front page according to the state of the news. This will entail designing modules, which can either be linked to cover a large story or can remain different in appearance to show lots of different, lesser stories.

Labeling

For people to be able navigate in an intuitive and straightforward way, we need a sensible taxonomy for organizing content. We need to use category labels that readers will understand, abroad as well as in the UK. Choosing terms can sometimes be difficult – we need to find labels that describe things accurately in just one or two words. Internal managers are sometimes too familiar with company or industry jargon and such terms can permeate into the site labeling. Furthermore, some companies label content based on where in the company it is produced, so the site structure starts to resemble the company structure – again, users will not be able to understand this.

Communication

Naturally, for a site of this size and complexity, there are a lot of people involved in creating it, maintaining it, and developing it further. Broadly speaking, there are three main teams involved: the journalists, who create the content and have final editorial control on the site, the designers, who are responsible for the all user interface issues and production of design elements, and the technical team, who are responsible for the implementation. In order to create a well-designed and usable site with an intuitive information architecture, we all need to be pulling in the same direction. We need to understand the whole process and how everybody's roles fit in, and respect those roles. We need to ensure that there's good communication between the teams, and good communication needs people who can agree and disagree sensibly. When there are disagreements, or different ideas on how to implement things, then the discussion is always in the context of "What is the best solution for the end user?"

Whenever we're changing the site or developing a new feature of the site, representatives from all three teams are involved from the start. The journalists will explain what it is they want to achieve, what they want to offer the audiences, the designers sketch some possible options, and the technical team might advise on what is technically viable, or what the implications are of a particular design. In this way, nothing is sprung on anyone by surprise, and bad design decisions are never forced through; everyone's opinion is heard. When opinions differ, we look to research, statistics, and user tests to gain a better understanding.

The Grammar of a Site

One way to keep people comfortable and feeling at home when using a large site is to maintain a consistent "grammar" throughout the site. By grammar, I am referring to the ergonomic and visual language in the site – that allows people to use it – rather than the appearance and style of the site. All links should look and behave a consistent way. They should all be the same color, and if one is underlined, they all should be. Stick to color rules – if red text isn't clickable on one page, it shouldn't be clickable on any page. None of your users should actively notice your grammar – it is just one of those subtle things that allows them to use the site smoothly without thinking, working at quite a subconscious level. In The Design of Everyday Things (Currency/Doubleday, ISBN: 0-3852-6774-6), Donald Norman explains how a well-designed object is inherently intuitive and easy to use. You should be able to tell whether you have to push or a pull a door from the way that it appears and what sort of a handle or push-pad it has – you shouldn't need a sign to tell you, and you shouldn't need to stop and think about it. You just use it, and if it's designed well, you'll never even notice it. A well-designed web site is the same thing, and the grammar helps you out here: the user shouldn't need a big sign screaming usable.

The stronger a site's logic is, the more possible it is to bend this logic a little. For example, on the front page, we have seen users trying to click some headings in the central column that are not clickable, such as Americas, South Asia, and so on. These are not clickable and are a non-clickable color. We have to decide how their appearance would change (or not) if these headings were to be made clickable. If clickable, should they remain red? If not, do they still look like section headings? And more to the point, will people try to click on other headings that may not even have a page to go to? These arguments can bend minds – any solution we use should be based on user behavior, not on who can stay sane in a design meeting the longest.

The Design Lifecycle

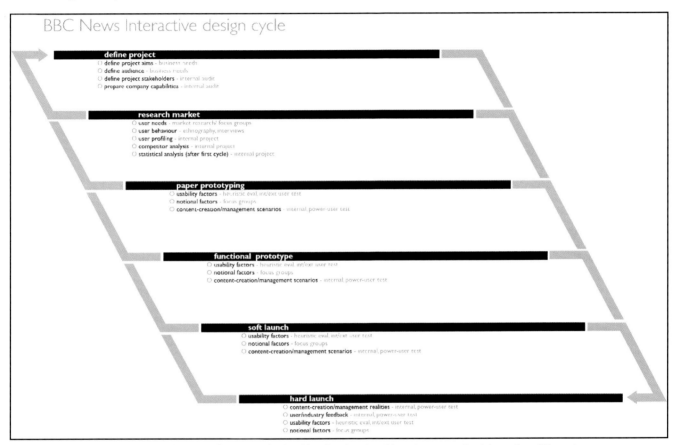

BBC News Interactive design cycle

define project
- define project aims - business needs
- define audience - business needs
- define project stakeholders - internal audit
- prepare company capabilities - internal audit

research market
- user needs - market research/ focus groups
- user behaviour - ethnography, interviews
- user profiling - internal project
- competitor analysis - internal project
- statistical analysis (after first cycle) - internal project

paper prototyping
- usability factors - heuristic eval, int/ext user test
- notional factors - focus groups
- content-creation/management scenarios - internal, power-user test

functional prototype
- usability factors - heuristic eval, int/ext user test
- notional factors - focus groups
- content-creation/management scenarios - internal, power-user test

soft launch
- usability factors - heuristic eval, int/ext user test
- notional factors - focus groups
- content-creation/management scenarios - internal, power-user test

hard launch
- content-creation/management realities - internal, power-user test
- user/industry feedback - internal, power-user test
- usability factors - heuristic eval, int/ext user test
- notional factors - focus groups

The design lifecycle of the BBC News Online web site. Varying levels of input are required from the different teams at each stage of the design lifecycle, but it is still vital that all of the teams are involved to some level at every stage. Good communication and collaboration are vital to the development of a usable web site.

In an ideal world, we would start at the top of the project lifecycle outlined in the figure above, and iteratively develop our site from there. In truth, when the BBC News Online site was started in 1997, it was actually part way through this lifecycle, somewhere around the functional prototype stage. The main aim then was to get a working site up and running, to see if it flew. Now, the challenge for us as designers is to work our way through this whole development lifecycle properly, and to truly understand our audience, who they are and what they need, and how we can best serve their needs. Research and testing are required every step of the way.

You can see from the diagram that usability testing is but one of the processes in a larger cycle. Ideally all the processes will be ongoing – web sites should be continually improved – and we can go back through the cycle and see where we could do more in different areas. For example, at the moment we are doing a lot of user testing on different parts of the site as it is today. It might seem odd to implement user testing on features that have been up and used for a long time already, but we feel that we really need to understand where we are now in terms of usability to enable us to move into the future with new developments with confidence.

A downside of process diagrams is that they can blot out sparks of creativity if allowed to dominate.

One of the advantages of working with a formal design lifecycle is that it enables everyone involved to solve tricky issues based on fact rather than opinion. For instance, suppose someone in a meeting says, "That color is no good for our younger users." The facilitator in the meeting should say, "Are younger people part of our audience anyway?" If so, then they should look at the business drivers and user profiling on this audience, and then test paper prototypes on them. This will provide more credible and useful data to feed into the discussion.

A downside of process diagrams is that they can blot out sparks of creativity if allowed to dominate the culture. Brainstorming and other exercises should be fun and open, yet focused. Honest people talking creatively for an hour in an office is better than guarded people talking when prompted. There are many books on how to propagate creative thought and practice and they should be taken as seriously as those about usability or other parts of the process.

The Audience

As part of the design lifecycle outlined above, we're starting to look at user profiling as well as doing more research into our existing audience. This will determine better who our current users are and help us to understand more about the users we want to attract to the site. The user profile will include information on when and how they use the site, and from this we can determine the changes we will make as well as the people we need to test against. Ideally we would have done all this at the beginning but, as the site is an evolving thing, we can start now. We'll incorporate all of these ideas into the next major redesign of the site, which should take place in late 2002.

On new projects under development, we've had the opportunity to put some of these ideas into practice. There's more discussion about user profiling and how it works in a later section on the proposed Sports Academy web site.

Although this work is just starting out, from existing studies, we believe that about 50% of our audience is in the UK and 50% in other countries (the largest share being the USA). Also, research suggests that the audience tends to be young, with around 50% between 15 and 34 years old, and only 10% over 55. Furthermore, it appears that a lot more men visit the site than women, making up around two thirds of the audience.

Another important way to help us understand the audience better is to track their use of the site through cookies. Initial results indicate that people tend to be regular visitors to the site, with a quarter of all people visiting once a week, and more than half visiting at least four times a week. The average number of pages visited is 4.6, but the variance is large. By looking at the traffic to the site on an hour-by-hour basis, we would guess that a lot of people use the site from their office (where they would not have access to a radio or television) and that lunchtime is a popular time to browse.

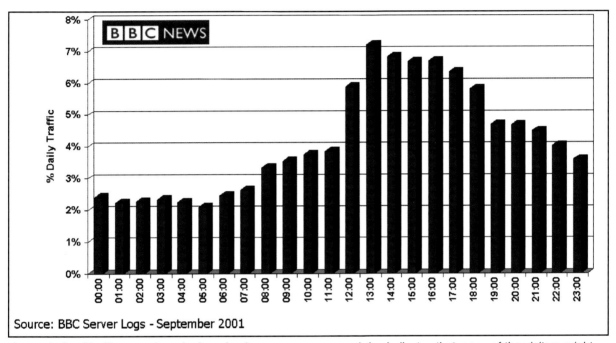

Source: BBC Server Logs - September 2001

An analysis of traffic on an hour-by-hour basis on an average weekday indicates that many of the visitors might be office-based, with lunchtime being a popular time to visit the site. A smaller fraction of people visit in the evenings. Note that all times are UK times, with an estimated 50% of the audience being based in the UK.

Clearly, there is a lot of work to be done in terms of market research and user profiling – we need to understand our audience much better. There is only so much information we can gain from cookies and we need to be careful about asking too many questions of our users. The whole point of the site is to make content as accessible as possible to the widest possible audience, and we can't add anything to the site that gets in the way of that, such as a registration form or an audience questionnaire.

One potential solution to dealing with the broad range of requirements of such a large and diverse audience is to introduce personalization. However, evidence from other large news sites indicates that personalization has not yet been made to work well. Where it is offered, uptake is around 10% of total audience, but even then, people that choose it tend not to use it. Again, this is an area where we need more research, but we feel that since a lot of the audience come to the site to see what the BBC's take on the news is – they don't want some kind of pre-selection based on their own interests. They want to see what the BBC thinks are the top five stories of the day. Where personalization can work well is on things like local news or local weather, and this might be something we consider in the future.

from broadcast to web

The front page of the current version of BBC News Online. Note that the red line indicates where the "fold" would be on an 800x600 pixels screen resolution.

Brief Tour of the Site

The site hasn't changed to any great degree since the last update in 1999, but now the architecture and page layouts are struggling a little to cope with all the new innovations and features that we've introduced over the last few years. It's being stretched at the seams. At the moment, one of our biggest challenges is in understanding how the site is functioning at the moment: how people are using it and why, what they find easy to use and what they don't, what they like about the site, how they move around it and more. Any deeper understanding we gain here will feed into the planned redesign of the site later this year.

Index Pages

The front page shows the basic layout for all of the news index pages. A simple three-column design, with permanent navigation in the left hand column, news stories in the center, and more news stories, promotions, and extra features on the right.

The gray band at the top of the page integrates the News Online site with the rest of the BBC site (which contains a wealth or background and supporting material for its many radio and television programs). The band is kept as small as possible (rather than trying to use it to promote lots of other BBC material) in order to keep as much screen space possible for the main purpose of the sites it umbrellas. The BBC

News brand bar underneath is more prominent, and contains the search box, which remains there wherever a user goes within the site.

While the front page (and other index pages) seems to be doing its job, focus groups have noted that it's too busy, too crowded. This will be an aspect of the site that puts some people off visiting. When a user loads up the front page, their eyes should be allowed to take in the site, and let the brain make a decision. Too many sites make the mistake of trying to force a user's eyes to a particular feature or area, particularly in the case of advertising. One aspect of good design is making a page pleasant and easy on the eye. We want to make the front page elegant and usable at the same time. At the moment, I don't think we've got that balance quite right. While there is a need to have a lot of news stories on the front page, to allow people to browse, it seems as though the different promotional areas (and items within these promotional areas) are competing for attention. The sheer density of information makes the page hard on the eye and this makes it difficult for the brain to decide what link it wants to access. I'd like to see a clearer, cleaner design on this page, with more use of white space.

The Central Column

The central column contains the news ticker followed by the three top stories. These are the most important stories that day and they all have a picture associated with them. This can often be an interesting challenge for the design team – not all news stories will have a picture to go with them, in which case we need to come up with a graphic instead. In case of a breaking news event, we have a breaking news graphic that can go there, or perhaps a map can be used, which is more informative. The map doesn't have to show exactly what is going on, but gives a clue as to the location.

The stories in the central column have other links underneath them that might be of interest to users. Initially, we felt that this would be a good way to promote other stories, but from analysis of user paths

The News Ticker

The news ticker is the only dynamic feature on the page, revealing, ticker-style, the latest headlines:

| LATEST: Channel Tunnel closed after immigrants found on_ |

The news ticker is featured at the top of the front page.

Strictly speaking, this doesn't add anything to the page in terms of usability; indeed, it breaks a lot of rules on dynamic content, but it is not a feature so important that denying a user access to it would severely impair their use of the site.

However, it is an enormously popular feature – users generally like the feeling of immediacy that it brings to the news. The fact that while the letters on the headlines are revealed one by one but stay in the same place means that perhaps it is less distracting on the eye than something scrolling across the screen.

Some news sites have a permanent section for "breaking news" – I find this odd because most of the time there is no *breaking* news. Breaking news is the first report of an important event or sequence of events. Some sites and broadcasters term any development (and sometimes old stories) as breaking – I feel this devalues an important promotional device and misleads our audience.

through the site, it appears that these are not as popular. Also, these links can be difficult to maintain from an editorial point of view.

As you can see from the image of the front page above, for a user with a monitor set to 800x600 screen resolution, only the two leading stories are visible above the fold (and only one on a resolution of 640x480); they would need to scroll down for the rest. Given that the main (and often only) reason that users come to the site is to browse the headlines, we're not doing so well in usability terms here. To make the site more useful, we'd like to see more news stories given prominence higher up on the front page.

> *Having said that, we have statistical evidence that users do scroll (often a worry for designers). If a story on the front page is about Britney Spears, football (soccer), or sex, then it will get a large number of click-throughs whether or not it is below the fold.*

Further down (and not visible in the image above), the page reads as an index with a main headline from each of the sections. We are in a bit of a quandary with these section headings, as to whether or not to make them clickable. Currently, they are not, but we have observed that many users try to click on them (see *The Grammar of a Site* sidebar). When we tried to make them clickable in user tests, we found that some users were surprised when they went to an index, expecting instead to click on the section heading and go to the story below.

The Left Hand Side

The left hand side stays consistent wherever you journey through the news indexes. It serves a dual role: both indicating to the user their current location within the site, and allowing them to navigate elsewhere. This is a model familiar to most people who have used the Web with any degree of regularity, so most users feel at home with it. Whatever changes are made to the site, we'll make sure we keep this, as we believe it is part of

why the site functions so well at the moment. It has consistently worked well in user tests and received positive responses. To reinforce positional information, we also use a "crumb trail" across the top of the page. These navigational signposts all act together. (One user thought that all web sites have those, as though they are almost part of the browser furniture.)

The main navigation exists in the menu down the left hand side, which includes the main categories, and – shown here – the subcategories under "World". In this section, we also include some simple graphical navigation. Note the use of the crumb trail at the top of the page, which serves as an additional hint the user about their current location within the site. Also, the right hand side of the page is now promoting features relevant to the selected region, and related stories are listed under the top stories on the index page.

The left hand side also contains a map of the world, which is an extra way for people to navigate to the world sections. We wouldn't have this as the only way to navigate there; it is simply an extra feature (and not too obtrusive). While designers are often very keen on visual navigation metaphors, we should remember that not everyone thinks visually. This is why we are keen not to overuse icons on the News Online site. One of the failings of many applications is their dependence on icons instead of text – people simply don't know what some of these hieroglyphics mean. (On the other hand, the *Trash* icon on the Apple user interface is a triumph in this realm.)

There is still room for improvement, however. One slightly confusing element in the left hand navigation menu is the way the news categories "blend in" to the other features. *Entertainment* and *Education* are subject categories for news stories, and lead into index pages for stories on these areas, but *Talking Point*, *In Depth*, and *AudioVideo* refer to differently behaving areas of the site, rather than subject categories. This has come about as new features have been added to the site over the years, without a major redesign. When we redesign the site, we'll separate these two things from each other, which should be clearer for the end user.

The only time the user "loses" the LHS navigation is on some of the special *In Depth* features and guides, where we have felt that we really needed the additional space taken up by the navigation menu. (I'll talk a bit

In some of the "special features", the left hand side navigation is removed. In this case, additional navigational features are added to the top of the page, within the brand bar.

more about the *In Depth* section shortly.) User tests have shown that most people are quite happy with this, and don't usually get "lost", although they tend to rely on the browser's *Back* button to get back to where they started, rather than the additional navigation, which is added to the brand bar for this purpose.

Under the main sections we have permanent links to sport and weather sites – closely associated with news in users' minds. We try to keep any transient links out of this area, with the exception being a short-lived but important 'mini-site' (for example, for a general election in the UK), or an area of the main site that was a prime destination at that point in time (for example, our section on the *War on Terror*). We must be careful, though, as every time we put something not permanent into the area set aside for permanent links, we devalue the logic of that area, which undermines the users' perceptions of the role of that area and the behavior of the links within.

Still further down the left hand side are the links to our services, for example, PDA and e-mail news. Although these are important to the management team, who want to drive traffic there, we must resist over-promotion. We must have confidence that as soon as people see them once they will know they will always be there as they are in the area of the site that is (as much as possible) permanent.

The Right Hand Side

The right hand side contains a mixture of elements, with links to audio-video content, special features and sections of the site, and key news stories.

The audio and video content of the site is promoted strongly in the top right of the page on index and story level. From the very start of the site, we felt that multimedia was one of the great competitive advantages the BBC has over other sites, in particular newspaper sites. Audio and video is what the brand is known for, after all. Currently, we produce around 200 clips a day on the site, so there is great breadth and

from broadcast to web

depth of content. However, from a user's point of view, the Internet is still not the best medium for audio and video; a large proportion of users do not have access to the large bandwidth required to take full advantage of these features. Despite the vast selection of content available on the BBC site, many users are put off by the installation of a big plug-in (Real) and the relatively high download times. Also, watching a short video clip in a small window on your screen just isn't that great. (It's a little like skateboarding in your bedroom – you can do it and it's quite novel, but it's not really that good!) Although things are improving with the arrival of broadband, on the whole the technology simply hasn't caught up with our desire for a full multimedia-enabled site.

The audio and video content is promoted at the top of the right hand side of the site.

Most users are simply not using this feature. They would rather catch up with the television news in the evening for this type of thing, and use the web site differently. We have to ask ourselves whether we can keep it in such a prominent place on the front page, if people really aren't very interested in using it. Is the page layout there to present a certain image of the BBC to the user, or is there to serve the users needs? We need to give people what they want – which is more headline news. On the other hand, we also need to bear in mind that the usage of the multimedia content parts of the site has grown by 45% over the last 6 months, so this is clearly a rapidly changing area.

One advantage we should be able to provide soon is that the audio and video clips will soon be fully searchable. We will use an automatic transcription technology to get text versions of the clips – these are searchable.

Further down the page some special sections of the web site are promoted, for example, the *Talking Point* and *In Depth* sections. On some days there is no need for these to be flagged up at the top – in prime promotional real estate – whereas on other days they might be more important. The new design must give the journalists more flexibility in the promotional area to flag what they feel is important at that minute.

Further down again, there are links illustrated graphically, with banner shaped promotions. These have turned out to be confusing for a couple of reasons. Firstly, we use these similar-looking links to promote all manner of different types of content, such as news stories or interactive guides. Historically, this came about for a number of

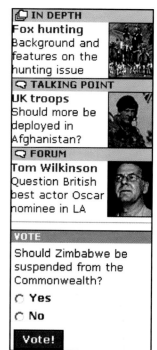

Links to the In Depth and Talking Point areas of the site.

reasons – mainly to get over the lack of room in the central column and promote more news higher up the page, but also a wish to use a different kind of space to promote light-hearted stories that might not be suitable as main headlines, but can help to lighten up the site a little. The second issue with these graphic links is that users often mistake them for banner ads! There is an adage on the web that people are looking at other sites more than yours – if your site is going to buck a common grammatical trend found elsewhere (or ape one for another purpose), it may confuse them.

Banner shaped graphics are also used down the right hand side to promote a variety of stories and special features.

A further issue with devices like these is that not all stories have good associated visual imagery that will work at 47 pixels high, and the use of just one line of text is often not enough to promote them. In addition to news stories in this area, there are also links to large *In Depth* sections, which take up the same space and add

to the clutter, without adequately demonstrating their importance.

Users are hunting for predictable links and will not mind if something is in graphics or text, as long as it explains to them what they are getting.

What these graphics do well is lend a certain character to the site, but I believe that the character can be improved with an overhaul of *all* visual elements and not just promotional items. The promotional devices below that use more text and a smaller photo are more useful for the user, as they better explain what lies beneath. The text-only links at the bottom of the right hand side are sometimes regarded as ugly ducklings by the journalists and not used as much, as they think that users will be less likely to notice the link. This is understandable but wrong. Users are hunting for predictable links and will not mind if something is in graphics or text, as long as it explains to them what they are getting.

One of the main aims of the re-launch is to rationalize the promotional spaces. We will make the special things look special,

On thin ice Antarctic ice in huge collapse

Culture shock Tough times for Andersen's well-drilled staff

Rail puzzle Trains are worse. But complaints are down. Why?

About face Oscar nominee Jim Broadbent's talent for change

Sex secret How men maintain their form

Further down the right hand side, we promote a list of further news stories.

and be found in a place for special things. Similarly, news stories will always go in a certain place. However, we will always have a module available for those funny news stories that are better presented with a picture, and enable us to lighten the mood of what is predominantly a serious site.

Information Graphics

Aside from photographs, graphics also provide key part of the background information available on the site, particularly as part of the *In Depth* section. As we try to use the Web to impart ever more detailed and complex information, using graphics as a way to illustrate it is increasingly important. Everybody knows the old adage, "A picture is worth a thousand words" and when you're short on space, this is even more crucial. There is a flip side though. Often, web designers have been guilty of using graphics just because they can, and too many graphics on a page is worse than none,

Promotion Within Stories

As well as using the right hand side of the site to cross-promote other areas, we need to look more at adding links between the *content* areas of the site – that is, cross-promote another feature from within the main body of a story, rather than expecting the user to rely on the navigation menu and index pages. This technique can be helpful as it allows users to discover and explore parts of the site that they wouldn't necessarily browse to. The difficulty here is to get the journalists to act as content managers as well as content creators. It is up to us to design systems and ways of working to help them do this as easily as possible. On this point, regular discussions with the teams of journalists and lectures by members of the design team can help foster a culture of respect for the potential of design and usability.

particularly if they are used inappropriately. Our job here at BBC news it to help our audience to better understand the world around them. We always need to keep the end user in mind.

Too many graphics on a page is worse than none, particularly if they are used inappropriately.

We're trying to use graphics in an intelligent fashion to help us to explain facts and figures, scientific information, technology, health issues, and much more. Exploring story narrative – linear and non-linear – is also a very interesting proposition. In order to do this properly, there are many aspects to consider: how to structure the various pieces of information, how to enable the user to work through it all in a logical and intuitive way, how to use color and movement, how and where to add textual explanations. This mixture of graphics and text can be very powerful, and we're only just beginning to use this medium to its full potential in the way that we structure them together.

There is a common tendency among some **infographic** sources to throw everything into Flash or – worse still – to publish massive browser-filling newspaper-like flat graphics. Different stories require different efforts and treatments.

The use of a pop-up window is useful in that it maintains the main flow of the story underneath.

Sometimes we can use a simple graphic within a text story. If it is a bit more complex, then we might opt to use an optional pop-up window to display the graphic. User tests on pop-up graphics generally show a positive response. A pop-up window doesn't upset people *per se*, as long as it's something they have asked for and it's distinguishable from the page below. The use of a pop-up window is useful in that it maintains the main flow of the story underneath. The fact that the user isn't immediately carted off to another section of the site makes it much easier for them to get back to where they were; they simply need to close the window. Getting the size and the position of the window right is therefore crucial; you need to make it small enough to retain the advantages of a pop-up – namely, that a user can see where they are underneath the window – but large enough to make the graphic inside readable, attractive, and useful.

It can be a mistake to try to fit too much information into a pop-up window. For a more in-depth type of graphical guide, we would use a structured set of pages to display the information. Our "What is global warming?" guide in the *In Depth* section on climate change is a good example of this – let's look at this in more depth (for more examples of infographics, see below too!).

This introductory page contains links in the left hand panels to the different pages of explanatory information and data, a quiz, and also links to other features in the site, such as the talking point, and another clickable guide on the politics of the environment.

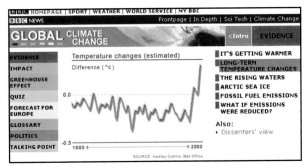

Each individual page of the guide can also contain information that the user can click through, such as charts and graphs, which means that we can use quite large amounts of information in a manageable structure – the user just accesses them in bite-sized chunks.

There are different sorts of data visualizations in the global warming graphic. There are some graphs, maps, animations, and pictograms. In this guide we have used a mixture of different data visualisation techniques, but in each instance the designer questioned the user's need for that piece of data and chose accordingly. Intricate data patterns are not always used in the right way though. It is quite a popular trend in graphic design to hijack the information graphic vernacular to satisfy the needs of patterning. Designers like patterns and repetition. Humans like to order shapes in front of them, and profligate use of icons and pictographic elements confuses, as opposed to educating. Beautifully laid out data is aesthetically pleasing without any embellishments.

Movement within a guide like this can be very helpful, but it needs to be used with caution. I like animation within a guide only when the information really includes movement, or some kind of transitional occurrence. For example, take a map of a battle situation: it might be tempting to include troops rushing in, or swooping arrows, but would this really add anything? You're more likely to want to focus on the positional information you can illustrate with a map. On the other hand, if you're trying to explain how a rail or air crash occurred, often it can help to include movement, to show sequential narrative and logistics.

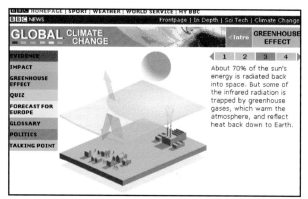

In the Global Warming guide, we included an animated element to illustrate the greenhouse effect. It shows the Sun's rays shining down, and then being reflected, and partly trapped within the Earth's atmosphere. While its arguable that animation isn't strictly necessary here, I believe that it really helps to convey the sense of the Sun beating down on Earth, and how this can heat up the Earth because of this extra layer of greenhouse gasses.

In our Global Warming guide, the dynamic effect is implemented in Flash, which has been a controversial technology as far as usability debates have run. Some will argue strongly that Flash is an inherently "bad" technology, but I think that is just daft. It is not the tool that makes for bad design – it is the designer. To paraphrase the NRA, design applications don't create bad design, bad designers do. As with any tool or technology, it's what you do with it – how you use it – that counts. Also, if you're worried about requiring a plug-in, it's worth bearing in mind that some 86% of browsers now have the Flash 5 plugin installed. Even so, we always try to offer an alternative non-Flash version.

To paraphrase the NRA, design applications don't create bad design, bad designers do. As with any tool or technology, it's what you do with it – how you use it – that counts.

On this page, a user can choose between a Flash or a standard HTML version of the guide, or they can choose to install Flash.

The Gallery

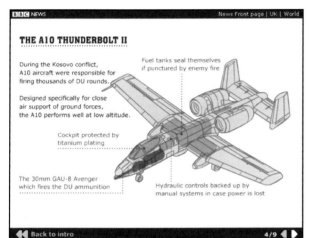

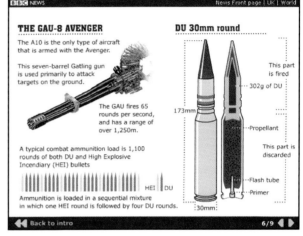

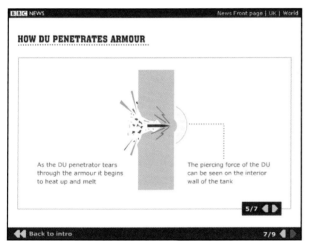

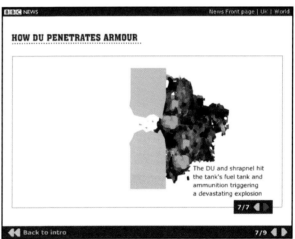

from broadcast to web

The Gallery

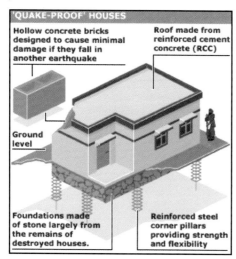

'QUAKE-PROOF' HOUSES

Hollow concrete bricks designed to cause minimal damage if they fall in another earthquake

Roof made from reinforced cement concrete (RCC)

Ground level

Foundations made of stone largely from the remains of destroyed houses.

Reinforced steel corner pillars providing strength and flexibility

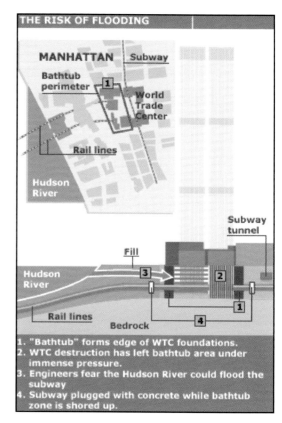

THE RISK OF FLOODING

MANHATTAN Subway

Bathtub perimeter 1

World Trade Center

Rail lines

Hudson River

Subway tunnel

Fill

3 2

Hudson River

1

Rail lines

Bedrock 4

1. "Bathtub" forms edge of WTC foundations.
2. WTC destruction has left bathtub area under immense pressure.
3. Engineers fear the Hudson River could flood the subway
4. Subway plugged with concrete while bathtub zone is shored up.

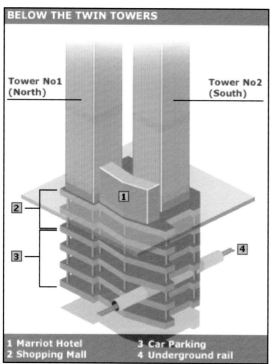

BELOW THE TWIN TOWERS

Tower No1 (North)

Tower No2 (South)

1

2

3

4

1 Marriot Hotel 3 Car Parking
2 Shopping Mall 4 Underground rail

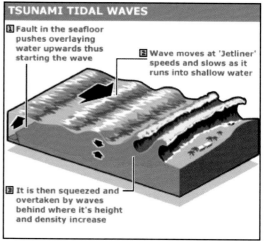

TSUNAMI TIDAL WAVES

1 Fault in the seafloor pushes overlaying water upwards thus starting the wave

2 Wave moves at 'Jetliner' speeds and slows as it runs into shallow water

3 It is then squeezed and overtaken by waves behind where it's height and density increase

The Gallery

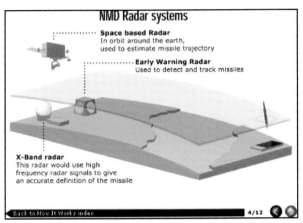

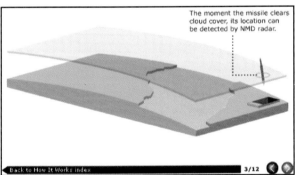

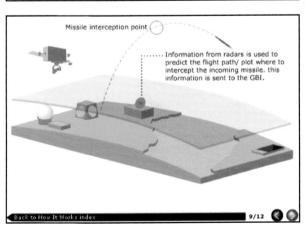

In user testing, both the HTML and Flash graphical guides have been very popular. People appreciated the way that diagrams and maps could help to clarify a story. The main problem with the Flash versions was the download time – if we can find a way to keep people's interest while the file is downloading, then we can usually work around this. Often, users stated that once they'd downloaded the dynamic guide, then they felt that it was definitely worthwhile, that it was more compelling than the static HTML counterpart.

Notions of playfulness or beauty are often missed out or even sneered at in user-centered design debates. While we will never have clown-news on the site, anything that helps (being careful not to hinder) curiosity and information uptake is a good thing.

Notions of playfulness or beauty are often missed out or even sneered at in user-centered design debates. While we will never have clown-news on the site, anything that helps (being careful not to hinder) curiosity and information uptake is a good thing.

Designers should also be thinking about the data within their Flash movies – it is often trapped in there. How can we manifest information from a central database in a variety of compelling ways that will work on many platforms and be reusable for a future where the Flash plug-in is obsolete?

The future of information graphics is an exciting one as technologies develop that allow us to do more. One area we are exploring at the moment is the use of dynamic, user-visualized maps – that is, maps with

from broadcast to web

lots of predefined data stored behind them in some form. The user then chooses what data they wish to view, in relation to what other data. Such maps could present the user with a much richer interactive experience by giving them some genuine power to exploit their understanding of the data-sets they need to know about. For example, rather than clicking through a series of images of a map illustrating a battle campaign, a user might look at just one image of a map and select the information they want to see, such as the location of all bomb strikes in the previous week. The difficulty in doing this in a daily updateable situation is finding reliable data to feed in and finding a resource-light way of maintaining it.

In Depth

The *In Depth* section of the web site was developed to allow users access to a collection of news stories and background information on particular subject areas – generally something that is in the news at the moment. We expected this part of the site to appeal to the kind of people who enjoy watching in-depth news analysis programs and documentaries, and have a lively interested in current affairs. Some examples of topics that we have covered in our *In Depth* section are the Euro, Yugoslavia and Milosevic, the War on Terror, Enron, Lockerbie, and Israel and Palestine. Obviously, the range of topics is diverse, but these are all areas where users might want to drill a bit deeper than a single news story on one day, find out more about the history and background, discover the facts, or read some analysis. That is what the *In Depth* section is there to provide – it collects together in one place all the links to related stories in the archives, pictures, quotes, analysis and discussion, fact files, guides, and other special features.

When this part of the site was created, we were just trying to think about the kinds of things that would be useful for our readers, but only quite recently have we been testing this area, to see how people use it, whether they like it, how they move around, and so on. In particular, we wanted to see if there were any areas

The In Depth sections of the News Online site include links to the related news stories, background articles and analysis, special features, and discussions from the Talking Point section of the site.

that people were struggling with, such as navigation, and see what their responses were to certain features, such as the graphical guides and "picture galleries". The results of these tests can give us a good foundation for thinking about the area in the redesign, since we will have the opportunity to change and improve it. Results from user tests have been quite positive, on the whole, but as ever, have highlighted a lot of issues about the *In Depth* section that we'll need to focus on when redesigning the site. I'll just mention a few of them here.

We can't always assume that the meaning is clear, so we need to test.

We've had many heated discussions about the willingness of users to move between areas that have a different look-and-feel. Would users mind leaving a standard template and then going into a bespoke environment (and back again)? The results of our tests indicated that they don't really mind. Despite this, we will still try to make their journeys more seamless.

The name "In Depth" conveyed a different meaning to our users from that which was intended. Most people thought that it would be a longer story on one particular area, rather than a collection point for related information. The depth and range of the information surprised them, and sometimes caused confusion. This issue highlights the difficulty of getting across meaning in a short label – we can't always assume that the meaning is clear, so we need to test.

Furthermore, there seemed to be quite a balancing act in choosing the number of articles linked to from each *In Depth* section. Users appreciated a large selection, feeling perhaps there was quite a wealth of information there, and found it easy to scan over the list of headings. If the list got out of hand, though, it became more overwhelming than useful. Users simply didn't know where to start. One suggested way of dealing with this is heavier editorial involvement, with a lot more

selection of the stories that are listed, and making sure that the same area isn't covered more than once. This would present users with a more useful selection of links.

One interesting result was the way that people moved between different stories and features. They were a lot more likely to pay attention to links and other features highlighted *within the main body* of the story, than the associated links in the right hand column. Even related information in a highlighted graphical box to the right was frequently missed. This underscores the results we have seen on the relatively low numbers of click-throughs when measuring user traffic through these areas.

Often in the *In Depth* section – and elsewhere on the site – we use a series of pictures to help tell a story. While this an interesting alternative to very text-heavy stories, it presents quite a challenge to the designer to put these together in a user-friendly way.

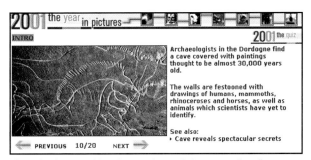

A typical way of implementing a "picture gallery" is to use Previous and Next buttons for scrolling through a series of images.

A common way of implementing a picture gallery is to place a series of images on separate pages and use "previous" and "next" buttons to scroll through them. In user tests, however, we found that many people got frustrated with this design, and often only looked at four or five pictures before losing interest and giving up. Many users preferred a design where the images were also numbered, with the full list of numbers being shown, so that if they wanted to move back to a particular image, then they didn't need to step through all of the pictures in-between. However, this can also present problems. Some users found the picture gallery from the "Day of Terror" section confusing, as they weren't sure whether the "previous" and "next" arrows referred to the next picture in sequence, or whether they would take the user to another section entirely.

Often, a series of numbers together with arrows are provided to allow users to navigate through a collection of photographs.

A more popular way of presenting images is to include them all on one page – this appeared to be the design that most users preferred. It allows them to scan through all of the photographs quite quickly, and to study just the ones that interested them most at leisure. Functionality can be added in the future to allow the favorite pictures to be enlarged too. Thumbnails were also tested, but often they are too small to realistically show what is there. Google image search has a good minimum size for these, in my opinion.

The Next Redesign

The site has now been up and running for well over four years, and over that time we've added a lot of new features to it, slowly. We've also learned a lot about the site, and about how people use it. There are lots of developments we'd like to make, to innovate and offer the users more, and there's certainly a lot we can do to streamline the design. The changes are not about the site content, but rather an overhaul of the way the pages appear and – more importantly – how the content connects, improving the user's journey around the site.

> *While there are a lot of firm ideas on how we want to handle the redesign, currently there are no final decisions. User testing is still ongoing, and will continue until we are happy with the plans for the re-launch. Unfortunately, this means that in this section I can only talk in broad terms about plans for the site, and can't show you any new designs, as it is all work-in-progress.*

Even if a change is for the better, people are still likely to be bothered by it.

The crucial thing to bear in mind before making any changes, however, is how much people love the site at the moment. There is lots of evidence for this, from the feedback we get, user surveys, and the fact that the traffic has grown so much and continues to grow. What people love about the site is the content: they love being able to get access to serious news, hard facts and impartial analysis. In fact, nearly all of the user feedback we receive is content related, which is great. It means that we're probably getting things right as far as the design is concerned.

So, the last thing we want to do now is alienate our core audience. Any changes to the site are only going to be made if they constitute a real improvement, and even then they need to be thought through carefully – and implemented even more carefully. Technical problems in addition to a new design are guaranteed to annoy your users. Even if a change is for the better, people are still likely to be bothered by it. When the site underwent its last major upgrade in 1999, we received mountains of abuse, some of it really quite vicious. A typical response was, "Why have you hijacked my home page? Why have you gone and changed everything – I was quite happy with it the way it was!" But, after two weeks, the complaints all but vanished. The feedback became really very positive; once people had adapted to the new design, they liked it. Some of the original complainants even wrote again saying, "Sorry – I actually really like this."

This fear of change can swing both ways – especially on a reasonably successful site. Sometimes, members of the management team object to changes to the site for this reason. This can happen not only when a change isn't actually an improvement, but also if it is undersold and isn't perceived as an important and beneficial change. If all the members of the management team are signed up to the idea of a product design cycle (like the one I outlined earlier) then this shouldn't be a problem, since decisions become based on facts, statistics, and measurements, rather than on opinions.

Major Changes

The biggest change that we feel is necessary at the moment is to increase the width of the site. Initially, we chose to go with a width of 600 pixels in order to make the site accessible to as wide a range of browser resolutions as possible. When the site was first launched, a lot of people were working at a resolution of 600x480, but these days we estimate that the proportion of site users with this resolution to be less than 7%. On the other hand, 53% of users have a resolution of 800x600, and 40% are at 1024x768 or higher.

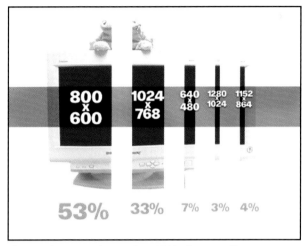

Currently, we estimate that 93% of our audience have screen resolutions of 800x600 or higher.

In order to improve overall site experience for the majority, we are going to increase the width to fit into the 800 pixel-width browser. In fact, no one will be completely excluded, as all of the content is still available on the low graphics site (soon to become a no graphics site), which should make it accessible from almost any browser. Of course, the question that immediately springs to mind is, "What are we going to do with all this extra space?" Obviously, there's a temptation to pack it full with as much information as we possibly can – but this is a temptation we'll resist.

The front page will be given a bit more room to breathe, with more white space, and a more elegant arrangement of stories. More news headlines will be brought up to the top of the page. The other headlines from the main sections will be below the main promotional area.

There will not be a right hand side, as we know it now. Instead, there will be a promotional space running across the page to flag special 'non-news story' content. This will have to degrade gracefully on the pages that don't have all this extra content. These pages will also have to be able to upgrade in the event of lots of extra special content due to a large news event relevant to their index.

The index pages will be more flexible in their appearance. If we need to devote much of the page to a specific event (we have three major states – deaths, 'events', and elections) there will need to be the flexibility to do so. It must also be noted that if all three of these things happened at once, our site would have to convey the editorial priorities. This requires tough editorial choices. Such choices are being made every day on the front page, where the editor needs to decide what out of all our content will be promoted.

Download time is also about perception. If we can design a page where the top portion loads in first and gives the user something to look at while the rest loads then the perceived download time of the page will be less.

Although we compare favorably with our competitors when it comes to page weight, we can all (and must make it our business to) do better. We aim to get our download time down by a third. This is not always a question of graphics and pictures. Often a page can be code heavy or the delivery at server level needs addressing. Download time is also about perception. If we can design a page where the top portion loads in first and gives the user something to look at while the rest loads then the perceived download time of the page will be less.

At story level, we want to give users a better idea of where they can go next. Links in the central column test positively and get good hits. We are working on a series of promotional modules to flag special content relevant to a story within that story. A few other relevant articles will be placed nearer the top and there will a button to prompt a search on that story's subject.

Designers should be involved from the beginning – helping the process along, using the product cycle, keeping beauty and elegance at the forefront of their plans.

The *In Depth* pages will also act in a more modular fashion. There are regularly elements of the 'background' *In Depth* pages that would be useful in a breaking story; if they shared more of the behavior and look of the rest of the site, then this would be possible. I can see the *In Depth* pages becoming a little more templated and the story pages becoming more modular and creative.

In addition to the main pages of the site, there are many other areas that need our attention. For example, are we doing our *Talking Point* section well enough? What else could we do with the possibilities of community? While these are editorial questions now, they will eventually become design questions. Designers should be involved from the beginning – helping the process along, using the product cycle, keeping beauty and elegance at the forefront of their plans.

Other BBC Sites

As the main BBC news site has grown, and expanded, we have looked at creating some separate sites to better address the requirements of different audiences.

A recent addition to the main news site is a site designed especially for children. While in some ways, this is part of the wider CBBC (Children's BBC) site, the design, implementation, and day-to-day maintenance are part of the remit of the News Online team.

When the news site was first launched, sport was just one of its many categories. However, it soon became apparent that reading sports stories and keeping track of the latest results was a popular use of the Web, and of the BBC's news site in particular. Sport was later separated out into a distinct web site, allowing the team to increase their sports coverage and focus on the needs of sports fans.

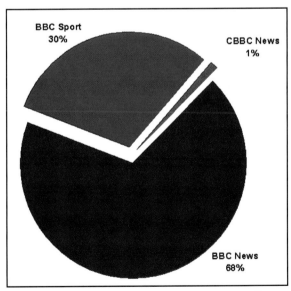

Pie chart illustrating the relative traffic to the different BBC web sites. CBBC News is the smallest at just 1%, but is also the newest addition, having being launched in November 2001.

CBBC News

Nikola Plaetz (Web Designer) talks about the design of the CBBC News site, and about some of the unique challenges involved in developing a web site for children.

Nikola Plaetz.

The Children's BBC News web site initially began as a companion web site to a television news program for children broadcast in the UK, called Newsround. Newsround was initially broadcast in 1972, and has a wealth of experience in the difficult task of making news interesting and informative for children. The CBBC news web site (*http://news.bbc.co.uk/cbbcnews*) took on a slightly broader aim, however, and was designed to be a news web site in its own right, and to be a great place for children to visit, whether or not they were fans of Newsround.

The site is aimed at the 8 to 14 age range, which presents a number of challenges in itself. Children tend to be turned off by news; it's boring, uncool, and very disconnected from their lives. Furthermore, children tend to have limited web access: in schools, often they have just a few minutes at the end of a lesson, and at home it's monitored closely, and time at the computer is shared with other members of the family. When they are online, we're competing with other children's sites, such as Popworld. There isn't really any serious competition in terms of a children's news site – CBBC is the first to try this.

Finally, there is an educational aspect to the site. There is a section designed specifically for teachers for use in schools, containing resources that can be used as part of lessons. We keep the link for this very small, however, so as not to put off the main audience, who don't tend to be very fond of teachers!

Serving a Younger Audience

Creating a news web site for children is a unique challenge. We had to consider what the particular requirements of our audience are – what they are going to find fun and interesting, how they use the Internet, how much experience they have of the Internet, how much they know and understand of the world around them.

Often, children need different information from adults, not just the same information presented in a simplified form.

The site uses several different techniques to appeal to the younger user. Stories are not taken from the main site, but instead written specifically for children. They are shorter, and information is divided up into more manageable chunks. It's important to consider alternative ways of presenting information other than the long written reports that tend to feature in newspapers and on the main news site. Here, we use more pictures and graphics; for example, we might use a slideshow to illustrate the week's news. Often, we break up the text with other features, such as fact boxes and short clickable guides. In a way, you could say that the site has more of a magazine style than the main site.

An additional consideration for the younger audience is the level of background knowledge and understanding of current affairs. Often, children need different information from adults, not just the same information

presented in a simplified form. We work hard to explain the background behind major stories in the news, be they about war, economics, or politics. The key is to make the information interesting and digestible.

There are lots of other features in addition to the news that should appeal to children, such as games, quizzes, and chat areas. The interactive parts of the site are particularly important in enabling the audience to feel that they are really a part of the site. It's great for a user to be able to see their name on the site, or better still to take part and write a report for the site.

Using Graphics

While we want to keep the look of the site graphical, colorful, and dynamic to make it more fun, we can't get too carried away with this. If the children accessing the site don't have much time, then they're not going to want to waste it waiting for a heavy download! We've been particularly cautious with our use of Flash – there's none on the front page to keep it accessible. Instead, we've introduced a few dynamic elements onto the front page using JavaScript rollovers on the menu

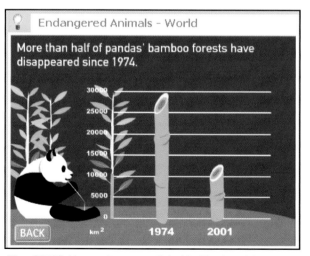

The CBBC News site uses clickable Flash guides to help get across complex information in an interesting and engaging fashion.

icons. Flash is only used on the inside pages for livening up the guides, and here (like all the other BBC sites) we make sure that there is a straightforward HTML alternative for those people who don't have (and don't want to download) the Flash plugin. Examples of places where we have used Flash include a guide on endangered animals, and a guide on bullying. By using a cartoon-style with Flash, we can make some otherwise difficult topics more engaging and approachable for children. In a way, it enables us to communicate with them in their own language

Site Design

In terms of web design, everything is simplified a lot when compared to the main news site. Obviously, with a wide range in ages, there's also varied experience online, but we certainly can't even assume the same level of web knowledge as the main site. Everything needs to be intuitive, and unthreatening. We want to make children feel that this is a safe place to explore.

> ### Nothing on the site is more than two clicks away.

The aim with the navigation was to make it even clearer than the main site. We used a few different techniques to achieve this. The menus on the left hand side of the page are quite similar, except that an icon, as well as a word, is used to represent each category. This combination of image with words helps to reinforce the idea of each category in the user's mind, and also helps to keep the look of the site fun and fresh. The icons use modern imagery, and light up as you roll over them.

The categories for news stories are a bit different from those on the main news site. The major ones such as *UK* and *World* are still there, but, in addition, there are more "light" categories, such as *Music*, *Entertainment*, and *Animals*. *Animals* is a particularly popular category, and sparks off a lot of chat in the interactive parts of the

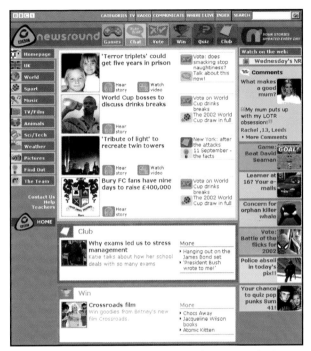

The front page of the Children's BBC News web site has a more lively and fun look than the main site, making more use of color and graphics. It includes mainstream news stories, but they are written in a style that makes them more approachable for children. Different terminology is used on the site, for example, "watch and hear" rather than "audio and video".

site. Children can get very passionate about the subject of animal welfare.

In addition, we have color-coded and tabbed navigation. The interactive "fun stuff" is clearly separated out in the navigation from the main news stories – the stories down the left, and the interactive features across the top in brighter colors. The navigation never moves and is the same on every page. We are extra careful to make sure that our users know exactly where they are, using lots of visual clues.

It is a fundamental rule of the site to keep the navigation simple – nothing on the site is more than two clicks away. (Occasionally, we may break this rule, for example, to offer Flash or non-Flash versions of content.) Similarly, we make sure that it's really easy to get back to where you were. The *Homepage* button is clear, and is present on each page.

Rather than using a breadcrumb system of navigation like the main site, CBBC News uses a color-coded tabbed system to give the users a visual clue about their location within the site.

The chat areas tend to be a lot more active than those of the main site, and – unlike the main site – they are unedited, giving the children a lot of freedom to have their say. Obviously, the comments are moderated, to ensure that there is no bad language or similar problems, and there are some basic rules to ensure (for safety reasons) that children do not use their full name or give their address. We feel that the message boards are a key feature of the site, and are integral to encourage the feeling for the users that this really is *their* site.

To encourage children to move through the site as naturally as possible, there are a lot of cross-links to different areas of the site from within stories. For example, we might include links to a clickable guide, to a picture gallery, or to a chat area, if these are relevant to the story.

There is no link back to main news from the children's site, because there is often content that isn't particularly suitable for young children, for example war images, stories of violence and so on. At the time of writing, the CBBC site has no permanent link to it from the main site, although this may be added.

On a practical note, the design for this site needed to take into account the fact that there would be far fewer resources to keep the site up and running than for the main news site. It had to be easy to add stories and graphics, and easy to maintain.

User Testing

Before any serious coding or even prototyping was done, we started out by creating many different paper mockups of possible designs. We spent a lot of time with children, talking to them not only about these designs, but also about what they thought of the Web, and whatever else they were interested in. We tried to put our preconceptions to one side, and instead asked the children their opinion on everything. We asked them about subject categories, logo designs, icons, and so on. We even showed them the site in lots of different colors – the boys did not like pink, the girls did not like green, but to everyone's relief, they all like the blue, so that was what we went with. Generally we would show them two different images of potential designs and just ask them which they preferred; that kept things simple.

Japan to import Norwegian whale meat

The site makes use of linking from within a main news story to promote other areas of the site.

We looked at the different category icons to get a handle on what worked and what didn't. All the children easily understood some icons, but others caused confusion; for example, we found that a flag worked better as an image for the UK than a map, and an electronic game controller worked better for the games category than an image of snakes and ladders.

The whole process was a relaxed one. The children who got involved initially were children of staff, or attending local schools, and we worked hard to make sure that it was a fun experience for them. If they got worried or intimidated by their surroundings (testing was carried out in the BBC Television Centre), then they could get concerned about saying the "right" answer rather than being completely open about what they thought. When they came in, we tried to relax them by showing them round the CBBC studios, stopping off for sweets and ice cream. One or two of the children spotted a celebrity, which really made their day. We worked in groups, with teachers and parents present.

This process of showing paper designs to children was an iterative one. From each stage, we learned more, and incorporated the results into the next set of designs, ready to test again. Only once we were happy with the visual look and feel of the site, and the overall structure, did we code it up to get a working version.

At this point, we got some more formal user testing done by a third-party company, who carefully selected a cross-section of our target audience. They worked in one-on-one situations with the children (although a parent was also present), setting them a few tasks, but also allowing them some time to explore freely through the site. Again, the staff conducting the tests needed to take care to reassure and relax the children. Often we would see them glancing back at their parent or guardian as if to make sure that they were doing or saying the right thing. The feedback at this stage was really positive, and only minor changes were made to the site before going live.

BBC Sport Online

James Howard (Design Manager) and Loz Gray (Senior Designer) from BBC Sport Online talk about the design of their site, and about some of the key differences between the audience requirements for sport and news.

James Howard.

The BBC Sport Online site (*http://news.bbc.co.uk/sport*) has a very similar look and feel to the News Online site, though this is largely for historical reasons. When it was separated off as a site in its own right, the design was inherited from the news site; this allowed us to use the same technical framework, and ensured familiarity from both the audience and journalists that use the site. We use the same navigation system down the left hand side, which contains a mixture of the different sporting categories. The middle column contains the top stories, and the right hand space contains a mixture of promotional features and more links to stories. For example, special features on "one off" events are listed in the right hand column, for example the Cheltenham Festival.

The whole site is simple, streamlined, and easy to use, like the news site. It avoids the use of fancy technology to ensure that's it's easily accessible to a vast audience. Again, like news, there is a low graphics version of the site.

The main front page of the BBC Sport Online web site. The design is adapted from the news online site.

Differences Between Sport and News

This wholesale reuse of the news site design for the sports site has bought with it a new range of usability issues. Since we were used to sport being a subsection of news, when we started out we didn't really consider quite how different it is in terms of what people want from the site and how they use it. The type of information that is presented on the site is different, as is the context. Some of the main issues here are:

- The way that people browse.

- The number of categories.

- The prevalence of statistics.

- The cyclical nature of sport.

In terms of organizing the structure, one of the main differences between the two sites is the taxonomy – in sport, there are a large number of very defined areas, whereas in news there are a much smaller number of broad categories.

When people come to a news site, often they just want to browse the headlines to gain an idea about what is going on in the world today by what the main stories are. They might read further if a particular story looks of interest. With sport, however, it's more likely that people are interested in specific news – what the result of a particular game was, for example, or general news at the level of a particular sport at most. The design of the site needs to address this; the navigation should allow people to get swiftly and easily to the information they are looking for.

In terms of organizing the structure, one of the main differences between the two sites is the taxonomy – in sport, there are a large number of very defined areas, whereas in news there are a much smaller number of broad categories. In a way, news can be very open with its brief when it comes to world news, or UK news, or

entertainment. Sport, on the other hand, is about tennis, golf, rugby, football, athletics – and the list goes on – and each of these then further divides into subcategories, by teams or by competition. The current navigation system does not scale easily with such a multiplicity of categories. Football alone has 22 different subcategories, and is rapidly becoming unmanageable. (We could easily have a whole site devoted to football, which already accounts for half of the traffic to the sports site.)

For US and Australian readers: the term "football" here is being used to refer to soccer.

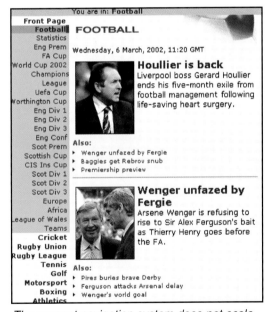

The present navigation system does not scale well with the large number of categories needed in sport; there are 22 different subcategories under football. An alternative would be to use contextual navigation, whereby on the football section of the site only football options would be visible in the left hand side navigation, which would allow us to create a more complex hierarchy of topic areas.

from broadcast to web

Similarly, the total number of different sports makes the whole left hand side list a little unmanageable. There's always competition for some of the more popular sports that are currently categorized under "other" to break out and make it onto the main list.

Another major difference between sport and news is that you really can't predict the news. OK, so you might not know which person or team will win a particular event, but you certainly know what events are happening when, years in advance.

Statistics, such as results tables, leagues, and so on, are always a big part of sports news. The advantages of sports information online are the ability to compare lots of different statistics, present different views on the information – for example, by player, by team, by competition – and also to make sure that they are always up to date. Presented well, such data can add a great deal to the user experience of the site, but it also adds a lot of complexity for the designer.

Another major difference between sport and news is that you really can't predict the news. OK, so you might not know which person or team will win a particular event, but you certainly know what events are happening when, years in advance. We can plan for sporting news. We know exactly what the big areas of interest are going to be throughout the year. Sport is very cyclical and almost entirely predictable, and this also ties into the problems with navigation outlined above. While there are many different categories, different sports will be popular at different times of the year, depending on what is going on. It would be useful, for example, to move one sport from "other" into the

main index, while a big event is going on. With the current implementation, we don't really have that level of flexibility.

Often a major event like the Olympics will attract a lot of traffic to the site for a limited period, and also generate more content than is easy to handle within the main organization. In these cases, we might have a dedicated site so that all the information is in one place, and navigation is simpler.

Finally, it is worth noting that although we feel we are stretching the news model to the limits in order to implement the sports site, users seem to appreciate the similar look-and-feel of the two sites – they understand how both sites work, and can move freely between the two, which is very good from a usability point of view.

For major events, BBC Sport Online creates a separate site, like this one for the Winter Olympics 2002. This allows us to go more in depth for the whole event, while maintaining a simple navigation system down the left hand side. Note that this page also contains a clear link back to the main sports site.

User testing

User testing has really only just begun on the Sport Online site. Like the news site, we are planning to move to a wider site (800 pixels) later this year, and so we want to test the current version of the site to better understand how and where we need to change. One aspect we are particularly interested in is how people move around the site – for example, do they move from the index to a story, then back to the index, then down to another story, or do they cross-navigate between stories? This kind of thing should help us to understand better how to promote content that's deeper within the site.

To help us get a feel for how a wider site might work, our next site specialized for a sports event – namely football's World Cup – will be at the new 800 width. At the time of writing, we are testing some paper mock-ups of possible designs for this site. Although these won't look like the final redesign of the main sports site, this smaller site does allow us to test out some new ideas about how to reorganize content and layout. It will be a step along the way to our redesign of the whole site. However, because this site is being built against an immovable deadline, the most important focus for both developers and designers at the moment is to make sure that it is up and running in time.

On a smaller scale, we always run informal user testing on any new feature that is added to the site. Recently we upgraded our coverage of football statistics to provide a much more detailed level of information. In order to find out how best to organize the vast amount of data involved and how to navigate between the various tables and different views, we tested various wireframes with several sports fans who worked in the office (but not necessarily specialized web users). We did this to see how they wanted to view the data, how they would navigate around it, whether they would recognize certain types of buttons in the navigation, and so on. We wanted to make sure that that someone who had gone from a

How User Testing Helps

For us, user testing has been most useful in taking arguments away from personal viewpoints and opinions, and basing them instead on facts about what users want. This makes it much easier to resolve problem issues in a practical way, and makes it far more likely that we'll hit upon the best solution.

On another note, it can also very healthy for us as designers. Initially, it might be a bit frightening to have what you thought of as a perfect design getting torn apart by users, but it certainly stops you being precious about your designs. You need to remember that it is the user who is the most important person ... even as you smash your head against the 2-way mirror shouting, "No, you fool! The link is on the left!"

It is always fascinating to see how people react to your designs; something that seems obvious to the designer may not to one user, or even to ten users in a row. However, you need to remember that you can't always use testing to prove that something is right or wrong – a lot of it is in the interpretation. There is a risk that user testing can be a bit anecdotal – people can take away from it what they want, so you need to be careful about how you use it and how you analyze the results. While it is likely to highlight something that is dramatically wrong, it won't always say that something is right.

Do user testing often, and keep examining the results. Don't think of user testing as a box you can tick off. Use it for what it's good at: answering concrete questions, such as whether people understand what a particular icon means, or how they use the navigation.

from broadcast to web

team's home page could also find their way to live text commentary on a particular game, and on to a results table and back again.

Redesigning the Sport Site

We plan to re-launch the sport site at the same time as the news site. The biggest change in both cases is from a 600 to 800 pixel width, and since both sites often share stories, from a practical point of view, it helps to use stories with the same format and layout, with the same picture size and so on.

The design will be a vastly significant change for the whole site. We will keep certain elements of the site the same, for example, the main navigation menu on the left hand side. Like the news site, however, the right hand side promotion column will change, as this really isn't working at the moment. We'll drop the audio-video section lower down the page, and bring more football stories up above the fold.

Currently we have a lot of content navigated to from the home page that would be better moved to a lower level in the site hierarchy. Examples of this include *BBC Pundits* (opinion section), *A Question of Sport* (quiz area), and *Funny Old Game* (football commentary). We feel we might do better to promote these from secondary sports pages, rather than from the front page.

By design, there is little flexibility in the way the left hand side navigation works. An important usability rule we have clung to in the past is, "Keep the navigation consistent, so people can find their way around the site." However, we are beginning to discover that this doesn't necessarily make sense for sport. Often, our navigation can be a little counter-intuitive because it is so static. For example, when the Wimbledon tennis tournament takes place, a user needs to navigate to coverage from *In Depth* or *Special Events*, rather than looking for it under *Tennis*, which would be a more sensible option, albeit for only part of the year. At other times, we would include the US Open or the Australian

Open instead. In Sport Online, we need more flexibility in the way the navigation works than makes sense for the main news site. We also need to make sure that we have a sensible place for "one off" events, that don't fit so well into our overall categorization, such as the Oxford-Cambridge annual Boat Race.

Finally, we need to pick our time for re-launching the new design quite carefully. We'll try to aim for a fairly quiet period when there isn't a major sports event bringing a lot of new people to the site. Also, whatever changes we make, it's important that the site maintains the look-and-feel of the news site, and of the BBC branding, so that users still feel at home when they visit.

Sports Academy Web Site

The idea for the Sports Academy came from the Education department at the BBC, who wanted a site to help and encourage children to take an active part in sporting activities. While this is a slight diversion from the main sports web site, we include mention of it here, because the work on the site so far has been such a positive learning experience for both designers and journalists involved in the project. It gave us chance to work closely together, and gain a better understanding of each other's roles and needs, as well as of the overall process of web site creation.

Since this was such a change in direction from what we were used to with sporting news, we wanted to spend time understanding exactly what the aims of the site were, and who the target audience were – what their needs were. We felt that we needed a new approach to do the job.

One of the first challenges getting started on the project was the communication and understanding between the different teams involved. The journalists who had overall editorial control on the new site had little or no experience with web site development, and came into the project with some slightly unrealistic expectations. (Often, modern marketing is guilty of giving people false perceptions about what the Web is like – for example, only a year ago, Intel was advertising its new chip using images of full screen video on a computer.) We (the design team) felt we needed to communicate to the journalists the importance of qualities such as usability, adaptability, and extensibility.

As a starting point, we had to first establish what exactly the journalists wanted to *achieve*, and then say what was possible in terms of the design. We knew the aim was to encourage children to get into sports, but in order to develop a web site to achieve that end, we needed to take a step back. Rather than jumping in at the deep end and trying to figure out what the site was going to look like, we thought instead about how we were going to plan the site, how we were going to look at the audience, and what steps we needed to achieve when. When this was 80% figured out, we started looking at the audience profiling.

We wanted to get everyone to think in terms of the audience, rather than their own viewpoints, to avoid the "religious argument". Audience profiling turned out to be a great way of achieving this. We thought about the cross section of our target audience, how they might vary in terms of web experience and sporting skills, and what reasons they would have for using the site. With this as a springboard, we came up with eight or ten "stereotypes" of the target audience, and gave them names and personalities. For example, Brian is 15 and likes computer games. He has just moved to a new area and doesn't have many friends. He wants to get into sport to get more street credibility, although he doesn't play many sports at the moment. We started thinking of this group as real people, and as a team, we "adopted" these personalities.

We picked a scenario for each personality, and studied in detail at how each person would use the site. This proved to be a very effective way of working through different use cases for the site. Instead of getting involved in arguments about the rights or wrongs of a particular design, it allowed us to focus on the user, and de-personalized arguments. It allowed people an easy

way to move from a fixed position. Discussions became focused around what Brian would really do in such-and-such situation. The process was actually great fun; it immediately became more constructive.

Once all the user scenarios were complete, we saw lots of patterns emerging, and different user flows. Three different ways of structuring the site emerged, with two possible ways of navigating: fixed or contextual. Fixed navigation is what we use on News Online – the menu on the left hand side stays the same and is available anywhere on the site. Contextual navigation means that you only get the menu options that are relevant to the part of the site that you're in, so that you only get links related to football when you're in the football part of the site, although a home page link is always available from every page. In many ways, contextual navigation makes everything simpler and more scalable, although there were many concerns that it would cause problems with usability.

> This is interesting for us for other reasons too – the possibility of using contextual navigation is also a relevant discussion for the Sport Online site.

We created a series of brief wireframes, which we could test to figure out the information architecture and how the navigation would work. Initially the testing was in-house, and on adults rather than children, since we felt that children might find the wireframes confusing. In the space of about two weeks, we did three rounds of tests – asking people to do specific tasks with the mocked up pages – and in between we revised the wireframes.

One of the key results that came out of the tests was about navigation; people didn't care at all whether it was cascading or contextual navigation. This was actually one of our biggest disagreements from the start – but now we could make a decision based on testing.

from broadcast to web

Next, we turned the wireframes into designs and did testing with children using many different designs. It took a while to start closing in on a design, and seemed almost impossible to start with; the comments we received from the children could be very diverse and random, and we had to think about what to take seriously and what to ignore, what to prioritize. We also relied on some basic principles, and a lot of the experience gained from development of the CBBC news site, such as using lots of pictures, less text, and keeping the structure simple. Like the CBBC news site, blue seemed to be the only color that kept everyone happy!

We have only just reached the stage where this is ready to prototype properly, and so can't comment on the success or failure of the project as a whole yet, but from the experiences we have had with it so far, we can say that the whole process has been educational for the design team, for editorial, and for management. Already we have learned a lot that we will apply to other projects. A lot of the ideas about audience profiling, for example, will be beneficial in the process of redesigning the main news site.

Future Challenges for BBC Interactive

Finally, Max picks up the mic again to talk about future plans for BBC News Online.

It's hard to talk about challenges for anything other than the next six to twelve months. Things just move too fast in this industry to make meaningful predictions looking further ahead. Broadly speaking, there are two main priorities for BBC News Interactive:

● To extend the audience for BBC News Online.

● To create and manage content for a diversity of platforms.

A lot of the issues raised in this chapter should address the first point – after all, that is the driving force behind them. The changes discussed for the redesign should be made as easy as possible for existing users, as well as making the site more attractive for new users. The aim from now on is to drive the reach of our site with evolutionary rather than revolutionary changes. In an effort to get more people to use the site there are a number of handles we can use, which we will be addressing in our redesign and re-launch later this year:

● Make it faster.

● Make it visually more attractive.

● Tailor the agenda for the audience.

● Add some lighter, fun-focused sections.

A bigger change for the team is the development the other services off the online content, such as email and PDA services. Currently, there are over 150 thousand subscribers using our Avant Go content (see *http://www.avantgo.com/*), which has been growing steadily at around 8% per month since January 2001. The integration of services over multiple platforms provides an exciting way for us to extend our services to new users.

A further challenge of this new multiplatform world is to develop the ability to create content once and use it across multiple platforms; that is, to automatically re-purpose content for television, phones, PDAs, and the Web. The technologies that allow us to do this are on the horizon, but it's unclear at present whether they will allow us to do it in a way that is editorially acceptable. This is crucial work that we have just started, but will be ongoing for the foreseeable future.

Finally, all the time while we are thinking about and working on these new developments, we need to maintain a live 24x7 service, and maintain quality on that service. While we have a remit of experimentation and innovation, we can't afford to forget about the day job!

Conclusions

The fact that basically one team has been involved with the development of all of the sites discussed here has been immensely useful for us. All of the designers involved in these new projects have learned from them, and have bought that knowledge back into the wider team, so that the experience then feeds into all of the new work that we do. By branching out into these new areas, we have had think more carefully about the audience, and have subsequently re-examined a lot of our assumptions.

On a similar note, we have found there to be many advantages to working as an in-house team to create these sites. The sheer size of the maintenance job on a site like News Online means that the BBC needs to have these skills in-house, but we have all benefited from that. Because of the ongoing work and the day-to-day involvement of each member of the design team with the site, they understand the iterative nature of its development and the fact that it is a living, growing, always changing project. This daily involvement with the running of the site means that even the junior designers have a good understanding of the users' requirements and the journalists' requirements. When it's time to add a feature or re-design a page, they don't need to spend days doing research – the knowledge is there, and the values of the site are internalized.

Another result of working with a long-term in-house team is the ability to develop good relationships with the technical team with whom we work, and the journalists, who are essentially our clients. A major factor in the success of *News Online* as a user-centric site is, in my opinion, the great relationships between these teams. The respect that each team has for the roles and responsibilities of the others means that we can solve any disagreements easily and without antagonism.

To create a usable web site, you really do need to have the whole team fully aware and supportive of usability as an issue – not just the team implementing the site, but the clients too. If everybody believes in it from the start, then you have a good chance of success. As graphic designers, we need to go further than just thinking about image and page layout. To create a usable web site, we need to get inside the heads of our audience and find out what they need. At the same time, every designer should endeavor to create the most beautiful and elegant site possible. You don't need to throw all your aesthetic sense out of the window to create a usable site.

To finish off then, here are my top tips for designers who want to create a more usable web site:

- Go to user tests as much as possible, and take the younger members of your team. Get your bosses to go too – the minute they see someone struggling to buy their product, they'll be begging you to help (and the 'sorry-there's-no-budget' remarks will vanish). But ...

- Remember that user testing is but one of the processes of your product cycle; there are many more and it is not the sole end (although an important factor).

- Try to engage the people responsible for corporate identity (if it is not you) to create logos and visual properties that are workable across different platforms (the faxable copy if you will).

- Only hire bright designers – intelligent people can cross disciplines, while the others bring preconceptions and wrong motives.

- Competitor analysis is often overlooked and is a good project for younger members of the team.

- Make judgments based on facts – statistics, user tests, and focus groups – but also remember that you are trained designers whose **opinions need** to be respected.

Max Gadney's Usable Design Objects

Pool ball – The numbers have passed utility staged into the iconic.

Matches – Great for striking anywhere – on walls, stubble, or even on glass.

Fountain pen – Makes writing pleasurable, not just easy.

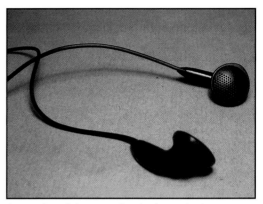

In-ear headphones – Logical conclusion to the need for portability and exclusion of unwanted sounds.

Segway Human Transporter – Let preconceptions carry on at walking pace.

See-through Disposable Lighter – Cheap, cheerful, and easily measured.

Also:

Harrier Jump Jet – This is just the beginning from the defence researchers.

Range rover car – Feeling safe and being safe on the road.

Funicular railways – A little quaint but perfect for their singular use.

Economist.com

design serving content

david wertheimer

Economist.com

http://www.economist.com

David Wertheimer is design director of Economist.com, the online division of *The Economist*. His work covers user interfaces, web page design, and site organization – everything from content delivery and page flow to branding and commercial issues. He crafted the current site layout and has designed items ranging from the Economist.com logo to the office Post-it™ notes.

David arrived at *The Economist* in January 2000. An online veteran dating back to the 1980s, he has been bringing print publications to the web for seven years. Before Economist.com, he spent four years at BPI Electronic Media, where he helped orchestrate Billboard Online's evolution into a world-class music news destination and oversaw development of the web sites for *Adweek* and *The Hollywood Reporter*. He also taught web design courses for several years at Open-i Media in New York City.

David also designs and writes a personal web site called netwert (*http://www.netwert.com*).

If you weren't doing this, what would you be doing?

Ideally, I'd like to own a record store and sit behind the counter all day listening to music. I also enjoy writing.

On a scale of 1 (Amish) - 10 (Star Trekkie), how geeky are you?

A Nerdity Test on the Web ranked me at a skimpy 30% geek, although my very knowledge and admittance of such a thing must ratchet me up a few notches.

What's your favourite building?

As a New Yorker, I love the Chrylser Building. I am also infatuated with public works, and I admire large community projects like bridges and mass transit systems. I often excitedly discuss the minutiae of the latest construction projects in the New York City subways, and I try to explore other cities' rail systems whenever I visit.

What's your favourite book? Piece of music? Type of pizza?

My favorite read is The New York Times, seven days a week. I am a fan of all catchy melodies with a minor chord in the chorus. Thin-crust New York pizza, please, heavy on the sauce.

If you were a superhero(ine), who would you be?

When I was five years old and the tree in front of my house fell down my neighbors and I played Kiss in the tree (Kiss, like the band) – I was Gene Simmons. God of thunder and rock 'n roll!

What gadget could you not live without?

My stereo!

Future of the web in a sentence

Someday we'll all have wireless broadband.

design serving content

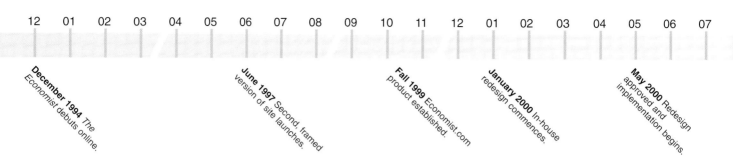

12 01 02 03 04 05 06 07 08 09 10 11 12 01 02 03 04 05 06 07

December 1994 The Economist debuts online.

June 1997 Second, framed version of site launches.

Fall 1999 Economist.com product established.

January 2000 In-house redesign commences.

May 2000 Redesign approved and implementation begins.

Designing Economist.com was an incredible balancing act. Doing it right meant getting editorial (the content and purpose of the site), commerce (the need for ad space, sponsorships, and fees), and technology (the databases, scripting, and other mechanics used to create and update the site) to run in harmony and balance, without compromising usability or visual flair.

When a design succeeds, the diverse interests manifest themselves in a world-class, content-driven web site.

When a design succeeds, the diverse interests manifest themselves in a world-class, content-driven web site. This is true of most site designs, but it is especially true in the world of *The Economist*, a global publication with a strong editorial voice and identity. The goals of designing the web site (the current edition of which was launched in October 2000) ranged far beyond simply redoing the design. We had to install new technology and recruit a complete Economist.com staff, as *The Economist* established a standalone interactive product. We created a new content management system (CMS), increased the site's editorial offerings, established several content and commerce partnerships, and transformed a four-year-old online offering into an up-to-date online destination.

Also, as Economist.com already existed for its readers, we had to keep content as the focus.

Our main goal was to deliver clean, readable articles, but a long list of commercial and technical requirements continually forced us to take a broad view of what belongs where on our pages. In the world of *The Economist*, the independent editorial voice is king, and the separation of business and journalistic interests meant that readability could not be compromised: text had to be prominent, clear, and easy to read. We took our time investigating numerous approaches as we worked on a coherent, forward-thinking design, and through open discussion and sharing of ideas, we crafted a unified site, not one created by compromise or committee. We aimed to build a site that grew forth from its content, leaving the articles as the focus, as opposed to one that made reading a secondary concern. Our work led to a redesign that won accolades upon its release and delivers a prime user experience as it continues to grow.

Concept: Good Site Content

A fundamental issue behind the redesign effort was a deceptively straightforward question: what constitutes a good content-based web site? My job as design director for Economist.com was to define quality content delivery, and to both embrace and expand that definition for our site.

Our redesign would ultimately share numerous organizational cues with other successful content-driven web sites. We were not interested in cribbing others' designs, but we did want to reflect upon the successes of other sites and integrate good ideas that had been established elsewhere. What, then, are the

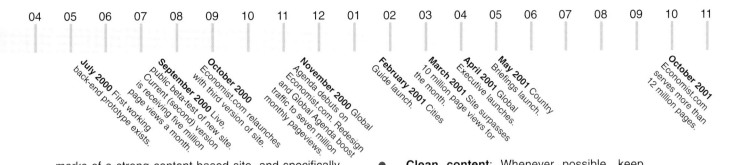

04 05 06 07 08 09 10 11 12 01 02 03 04 05 06 07 08 09 10 11

July 2000 First working back-end prototype exists.

September 2000 Public beta-test of new site. Current (second) version is receiving five million page views a month.

October 2000 Economist.com relaunches with third version of site.

November 2000 Global Agenda debuts on Economist.com. Redesign and Global Agenda boost traffic to seven million monthly pageviews.

February 2001 Guide launch.

March 2001 10 million page views for the month.

April 2001 Site surpasses Cities.

May 2001 Executive launches.

Country Briefings launch.

October 2001 Economist.com serves more than 12 million pages.

marks of a strong content-based site, and specifically, what aspects of content design had to be stressed and maximized by Economist.com?

- **Identity**: The overall design has to reflect the voice and style of the offline component. The site's logo is prominent and in the same place on every page. Our site in particular represents the brand in a unique design without imitating the print edition.

A fundamental issue behind the redesign effort was a deceptively straightforward question: what constitutes a good content-based web site?

- **Navigation**: The site should be easy to use regardless of what page the user is on. Pages within the site are often linked to from external sources, meaning that users do not necessarily enter through the homepage. The same basic navigational elements should be in set locations at all times.

- **Page length**: While long pages can reduce navigation, and articles on content sites are often cut into multiple pages to increase ad impressions, most pieces are best read in one sitting, and displayed on a single screen when possible.

- **Clean content**: Whenever possible, keep navigation and advertisements from getting in the way of reading an article. Ads should be labeled as such to help readers identify page components. Content sources should be labeled so users can easily identify items originating from the print edition.

- **Strong header**: In a site with multiple content areas, the top of the page should signal where the reader has landed, giving context to the article and/or links on the page. This sense of place helps with orientation and navigation.

- **Consistency**: As noted in the items above, the site should use the same elements repeatedly – similar locations for many items, and the same functions on each page, minimizing the user's need to learn to use the site more than once.

- **Frequency**: Establish a publishing schedule and convey it to the readership with date stamps and prominent placement of new content.

- **Balance**: When a site has paid content, provide enough free material to give users a complete unpaid experience, and enough value past a pay barrier (separating unregistered visitors from subscriber-only content) to entice users to join.

In addition to this list, the development team had to consider editorial needs, such as a browser-based content management system, and publishing flexibility, like exporting text to both web pages and wireless PDA files. Balancing all these requirements would prove to be a far more challenging and exciting project than I had anticipated when I was hired. I was a veteran at delivering content, having worked on text-heavy web sites since 1995, and I was brought on board because of the experience I had presenting print publications online. But *The Economist's* values, from its content to its rules regarding commercial interests, were unlike any I had worked with previously.

Early Designs

The Economist found its way onto the Internet in late 1994, as the World Wide Web was first coming into public focus. A few resourceful *Economist* editors registered *The Economist's* Web domain and self-published *The Economist* online.

Background

A short history lesson is essential to understanding the goals Economist.com had as it put together the site that launched in 2000.

Edited in London since 1843, *The Economist* is one of the world's most respected independent journals of political, business, and scientific analysis. Its circulation is more than 830,000 with a readership three times as large. A full 38% of its audience is located throughout continental Europe, Asia, Latin America, the Middle East and Africa. A substantial proportion of *The Economist's* readership consist of men and women of considerable influence: ninety-three percent have a college degree; more than half are between the ages of 35 and 54; nearly half the subscriber base earns more than $100,000. These people rely on *The Economist* to be their weekly digest of world events. Articles, presented without bylines, summarize an issue in several descriptive paragraphs, and then weigh in with a viewpoint and forward-thinking resolution. With this concise intellectualism and its worldwide coverage, *The Economist* creates a fierce loyalty from its readership – many readers, upon meeting an *Economist* employee, immediately gush, "*The Economist* is my absolute favorite publication. I can't wait to read it each week."

The first Economist.com, circa December 1996.

They began with a few special reports, and then slowly added more content, until *The Economist* finally made its web operations official.

A second, more complete site was launched in 1997, developed by Online Magic (now Agency.com), who designed and built the site in London. It was a high-quality, well-assembled site for its time. Framed across the top and left side in a black and gray pinstripe, content was presented in a main white frame with plenty of white space. Graphical navigation cascaded down the left-hand side of the page, mostly set as white-on-black GIFs beneath a prominently positioned *The Economist* logo; a horizontal ad banner filled the top frame. Select articles were made available to all visitors each week, while the full contents of the print edition were accessible to print subscribers or paid users of Economist.com.

The second Economist *site, circa 1999.*

While handsome and effective in its basic presentation, the format had become too inflexible for the site's needs.

By late 1999, this design had begun to show its age. While handsome and effective in its basic presentation, the format had become too inflexible for the site's

needs. The framed layout made scrolling and printing difficult and placed space at a premium. As with many sites' technologies in the mid-1990s, Economist.com lacked persistent URLs; linking to or bookmarking an article, already difficult thanks to the frames, was made impossible as addresses changed when articles were archived. With the rigidity of the framed layout, no space existed for new advertising, and expansion was nearly impossible. Search, registration, and subscription opportunities were all either hard to find or not displayed to maximum effect. The site was also limited to publishing articles from *The Economist*, as there was no way to distinguish or include original content. In order to grow, the site needed to address these shortcomings, and it needed to rethink its setup in order to do so.

As with many sites' technologies in the mid-1990s, Economist.com lacked persistent URLs; linking to or bookmarking an article, already difficult thanks to the frames, was made impossible as addresses changed when articles were archived.

The Economist.com team, organized in late 1999 and early 2000, was put to work fast. The new Economist.com was to enter a live beta-testing mode that summer and launch in the fall. In addition to a visual overhaul, the new site would include:

- A content management system, built in-house and based in Java, that would allow editors to file and edit stories from any location; it had been determined that we had the expertise to build a system ourselves that would be customized for our needs and cost less overall than an off-the-shelf implementation.

- New page presentation through XML and ColdFusion, which would allow us to parse a single set of data to both the main web site and secondary channels, like AvantGo wireless browsers.

- New content, from specific city and country guides to continuously updated articles, a first for *The Economist*.

Redesign goals

The goals of the redesign were ambitious. Economist.com would rethink every aspect:

- The logo, fonts, colors, page presentation, utility, and layout would all be rethought.

- The new site had to be more inviting, user-friendly, and widely accessible.

- Navigation and page identification had to be prominent, simple, and straightforward.

- It had to be flexible for expansion into additional content and commercial opportunities.

Also, it needed to preserve the editorial integrity of *The Economist*, which has long had strict rules regarding the placement of advertising, and which was not going to forego its usual church-and-state separation of editorial and commercial interests.

- Better sales and marketing opportunities.

Economist.com also wanted to establish partnerships with third parties, from book resellers to stock-market data services to wine merchants, alongside its usual content and ads.

Foundation

We started the redesign process by analyzing sites whose ambitions mirrored our own. The short list of competition and inspiration included *The New York Times* on the Web (*http://www.nytimes.com*), *Salon* (*http://www.salon.com*), *The Washington Post* (*http://www.washingtonpost.com*), *Slate* (*http://www.slate.com*), *Financial Times* (*ft.com*), *International Herald Tribune* (*iht.com*), Cnet/News.com (*http://www.cnet.com*), and even ESPN.com (*http://www.espn.com*). *The Economist* considers itself a newspaper, and we intently studied news-driven sites. The print edition publishes weekly, but articles were to be added to the site more frequently, leading us to review many newspapers' online sites as well as web-only magazines and other content- and information-heavy designs.

Like any news-oriented web site, the central display of the home page had to have a lead story, and we gave the editors control of updating content at their discretion, without the involvement of the production or development staff. Editorial navigation found a natural resting place on the left-hand side of the page, near the top of the screen; many content-based web sites, including the old Economist.com, do the same.

The remainder of the left side would be used for additional site drill-down into such areas as the archives and subscription services.

Access was a prominent concern. The site would be designed for a screen resolution of 800x600, with a center column of 350-450 pixels, which is a comfortable width for reading lengthy articles. The design would also break at an appropriate width so users viewing Economist.com on old 640x480 monitors could navigate the site and read the content down the center column without scrolling to the right. Level 4 web browser users (Netscape 4.7 and Internet Explorer 4 in particular) comprised a considerable percentage of the site's readership, so pages needed to be optimized for 4.x viewing. *The Economist* has long been used as a research tool, so the search functionality had to be displayed prominently near the top of the page.

Commercial guidelines came into play as well. The site had to support several ad sizes upon launch: 468x60 "banners," 125x125 "buttons," 120x240 "towers" and 120x800 "skyscrapers". The main screen, above the "fold" – as the first 600 or so vertical pixels had come to be called by print staff – needed at the very least an ad banner, if not more. Prominent links were needed for registration, subscription, user-login and account management. Paid *Economist* articles needed to be marked as such, providing an upsell opportunity for new or unsubscribed users who could not see all the content available on the site. One thing we did not follow was the trend toward an all-free web site. While the site was planned in the giddy heights of 1999, it needed to have a clear profitability plan, and our business goals outweighed the conventional wisdom of the time of letting *Economist* content run free online. Extensive internal debate ensued over "mindshare" (the process of ingraining *The Economist's* name and product into consumers' consciousness), mixed-

Navigation schemes

We briefly explored navigation schemes atop the content, and to the right-hand side of the page, but discarded them both: the horizontal top-of-page navigation was too restrictive for our lengthy offerings, and the right-hand nav was counter to most sites' designs at the time, and risked being hidden from viewers with low-resolution monitor settings.

revenue models, and selling to our audience. The resulting design stressed that *Economist* content was worth paying for, and the majority of the site would remain paid.

> *Ultimately, Economist.com could not just be a copycat; it had to be one of the best-executed examples of its genre.*

Much of this sounds rather straightforward, which should not come as a surprise. The Economist.com redesign came in 2000, several years after the Web came into its own as a medium, and many of the possibilities of web page design had already been explored. Economist.com chose to assume the same basic principles noted elsewhere and proceeded accordingly, its dedication to paid content notwithstanding. Think of print design: most magazines start with a glossy cover, follow almost immediately with a table of contents, progress to a series of shorter, topical pieces, sprinkle in some commentary and behind-the-scenes reports, proceed to feature-length articles, and conclude with a fun and diverting last page. The composition of a web site is not the same, but the philosophy that drove Economist.com's redesign was. We were to find what worked and improve on it. Ultimately, Economist.com could not just be a copycat; it had to be one of the best-executed examples of its genre.

Structure

To accomplish this, we had to determine the direction we were heading with the voice of the site – *The Economist* has a strong, memorable editorial tone, and we wanted the site to reflect that – and its features. A week after my arrival, I was presented with a draft editorial plan for the Economist.com redesign. The document, prepared by Anthony Gottlieb, the site's editor, was a wonderful summation of *The Economist's* opinion of Economist.com as well as of the web site's goals and ambitions. The summary said it all:

> Boldly stated, the aim is to be to the web what the paper is to print. Just as the paper is many things at once – a source of reference on international affairs and business, a source of entertaining information, a clear explainer, a respected tool of economic and financial analysis, a crisp and measured encapsulation of the news with a distinctive tone of voice, an organ of provocative opinion and debate – so too Economist.com should not limit itself to a single function (such as business news or country information). Our task is to build outwards from the paper and exploit web technologies to extend what we do in print.
>
> To do this, we'll draw not only on relevant editorial material from elsewhere in the Group (always clearly branded as such) but also external content: newswires, market data, an external archive, links to related sites, etc. We shall, in other words, become a mini-portal. The distinctiveness of Economist.com will lie in its personality, which is that of the paper, and in the fact that it combines global political news, business news, business research, reference, entertainment, education and more.

The document also called for daily site updates and a country database, site additions that launched not long after the redesign went live. To a large extent, these guidelines are still in place on the live site as this is written; users can access *Economist* articles, background summaries attached to new pieces on evolving issues, content from other Economist Group products, external news and financial information, and written-for-the-Web supplemental links. The expression "mini-portal" may sound a bit dated, but the philosophy still stands, and the Economist.com that exists now is a direct growth from this vision.

Executives at *The Economist* gave the dotcom team the freedom to redesign the site as we saw fit, which enabled us to embrace usability and web-centric design theory. We set out to create a web site that enriched the user experience. The team did not often discuss the site in terms of "usability" and "the Economist.com experience," but the philosophy was there, culled from several years of growth in what had become a restrictive web site. The redesign aimed to make the site as user-friendly as possible, opening up sensible and intuitive methods for readers to navigate and use the site. As such, certain basic tenets were determined before the visual process started.

Editorial and design were ultimately joined at the hip.

Economist.com's producer, Mark Drasutis, worked with Anthony for months preparing an organizational structure for the site redesign. The two drafted an article flow then went to work dividing, merging, and deleting categories, trying to find the right balance between *The Economist's* standard sections and an intuitive structure for the web site. Our first step in the design would be to integrate this structure. Editorial and design were ultimately joined at the hip as Mark noted in an e-mail two weeks after I arrived:

> I have started the ball rolling on the site architecture process. I am compiling a document, which will detail the content elements for each section within the site and also have asked Anthony to add the generic elements. ...
>
> As this is tied implicitly to the design process, I have attached the first draft so that you can

add your comments on the best way to approach this.

Along with that message came the first draft of the Economist.com site structure, which broke down the site's sections into the following:

- Opinion
- World
- Business
- Science and Technology
- People
- Culture
- Books
- Databank
- Reference Toolbox
- Fun
- User services
- Help

Each of those sections in turn had sub-sections, and each sub-section presented its own content. The document included most specific pages, for example:

```
Business
    └─Business surveys from The Economist
            ──Article content
                ├─Paragraphs
                └─Cross-heads
            └─Graphics
                    ├─Photographs (transformed into JPEG or GIF format)
                    ├─Charts/Tables (transformed into JPEG or GIF format)
                    └─Maps (transformed into JPEG or GIF format)
```

Item drill-down within an Economist.com category.

This provided the basis for both the user interface and back-end development system that would be created for Economist.com. With a team developing an in-house CMS we were able to define the site structure with precision. The organization was revised extensively, over several rounds of e-mails and discussions between producer and editor; the sections eventually metamorphosed into two areas, content and function, and a new breakdown, as follows:

CONTENT
Homepage
Opinion
World
Business
Finance & Economics
Science & Technology
People
Culture
Books
Markets & Data
Video (Evision)
Reference
Fun
FUNCTION
Mobile Edition
My Account
Help
Advertise
About

This second structure largely held firm through the redesign, with only minor additions and deletions. Most of the content options were placed in the main left-hand-column navigational scheme, while the functional items were placed around the home page and inside pages where they made sense.

I took the second site architecture document and married potential layouts to each possible page on the site. This enabled us to see how the sections and subsections would relate to one another, and provided us with real numbers showing how many different designs we'd need to get the site up and running. As I explained in an e-mail to our producer:

> There will be variations on the themes, of course, but as far as I can tell there are five basic page layouts to be created: the home page; a section index page; a content page; a country page; and a finance page, with a portfolio/market report display area.

> There are also a batch of pages that don't fit in any one layout that we should probably play by ear, as well as several areas of the site that need to be fleshed out separately but won't need a 'template' per se for updates (advertising area, reference materials).

As we worked on the site architecture, we were also designing the visuals, based initially on our general concept of what the site would require, then on the architecture as it solidified. The fine-tuning included everything from editorial categorization to discussing simpler section names to replace our lengthy section titles.

Defining Identity

Economist.com was designed with a distinct purpose in mind. The site was to reflect the print edition without mirroring it, as the previous design tried to accomplish. Economist.com meant to exist on its own as a stand-alone product within *The Economist* brand.

Economist.com would develop its own content, design, and revenue streams while bringing articles from the print edition online each week. The online team was therefore free to devise a unique style for the site, so long as it preserved the authoritative, intelligent, and independent nature of *The Economist* itself, and allowed readers of *The Economist* to use it as an online version of the magazine if they wished. From a design standpoint, the restrictions posed an exciting challenge: how does Economist.com showcase its strengths, such as *Economist* articles, and still stand as an independent entity? From the outset, the redesign hinged on our ability to capture the straightforward, powerful, and exclusive nature of *The Economist*. We did not dissect the print edition's typeface or the then-black-and-white layout of the print edition. By focusing on the goals, rather than the precedent, the site was able to take on a look of its own without undue constraints.

The same tenets applied to the site's identity. Economist.com had to develop a unique product, and needed a logo separate and distinct from *The Economist* itself. This presented a unique challenge: what do we call the site, and how do we best represent that? Management quickly decided to use the standard name-plus-dotcom usage, figuring that such a name was logical and descriptive, and a nice extension of the main *Economist* brand.

The logo of The Economist.

The basic idea for the logo came about quickly, as we decided to play off the strength of our parent logo. The obvious move would be to keep the defining red color, but what from there? We experimented with numerous prototypes, utilizing alternate typefaces, less red, and outside imagery (a newsroom-cliché globe was an early favorite) – they were interesting, but not particularly successful.

Some of the discarded logo prototypes.

> ## Ultimately, simplest was best.

During the logo design, we had an extensive internal debate about the leading *e* in Economist.com; Graham Barron, our new-economy-savvy business development director, lobbied for small-e "economist.com," in keeping with Internet industry style and the visual convention of presenting all-lowercase URLs.

Ultimately, simplest was best. I shrunk *The Economist's* usual rectangular logo into a longer, thinner box, and used a slight variant on *The Economist* typeface to type in a simple Economist.com. The first letter remained capitalized to retain brand identity.

The new Economist.com logo.

The logo, now a straightforward interpretation of *The Economist's*, found widespread if unsurprised approval.

The Economist and the Economist.com logo use a custom-designed font called, appropriately, Ecotype. At the time of the redesign, *The Economist* font family encompassed a wide range of styles; the one we used in our logo and related materials, EcoDisplay601, had firmer downstrokes and narrower spacing than the traditional body text font. It anti-aliased better than Ecotype, which makes for better presentation when reduced to a GIF. Several months of mild experimentation ensued before the logo settled into its final form, with definite proportions (3.75:1 with set red-space restrictions) and a decision on its color, which we left at bright red (RGB 255/0/0) to minimize alterations in browser displays.

How We Worked

Just before the redesign commenced, Economist.com was established as a separate entity within the Economist Group, the parent company of *The Economist*. Economist.com became its own product under the main *Economist* brand, and a management team was established comprising both Economist Group employees who knew the publication well and outsiders who knew the Internet well. The department was staffed and operated as one department by a 50-person team located in both the United States and United Kingdom. The concept was to take advantage of *The Economist's* roots and editorial headquarters in

London as well as the new media marketplace, talent pool, and wide readership in the US.

Overcoming the Geographic Divide

We went to great lengths to overcome the hurdles faced by a trans-Atlantic team, installing webcams in both offices and making weekly videoconference calls to unite our members. I installed Yahoo Messenger on my computers shortly after my arrival and got the developers in London to join me, opening fast, direct communication routes beyond telephones and e-mail. We embraced intercontinental travel, and I spent considerable amounts of time in London over the summer.

The dual location setup was not ultimately as great a hurdle as aligning our departmental interests. The different sectors of Economist.com – design, editorial, business development, sales, production, development (our technical team), marketing – were each essential to the success of the site as a whole, and we worked hard to coordinate our efforts. Fortunately, the heads of the Economist Group were happy to leave Economist.com to find its own voice, a level of understanding that was striking in its foresight and welcoming for our team. Anthony, the editor, knew exactly what he wanted from an editorial perspective, but he was willing to let us determine how the design would manifest itself.

Equipment and Testing

The Economist is almost entirely a Windows company, but I was a Mac user at my previous employer, and getting an Apple enabled me to work comfortably from the start without learning the intricacies of, say, Photoshop for the PC. I also considered the Mac environment superior and more comfortable for heavy design work.

Despite the ease and comfort of designing on a Macintosh, nearly 95 percent of Economist.com visitors were in the Windows environment, making testing on Internet Explorer for Windows a necessity. To this day, however, three percent of its audience is on Macintosh, and 10 percent are Netscape users, which forces Economist.com to develop its site for a wide array of visitors. Thus all pages on the site were tested for optimal performance on many browsers, including IE 4 and 5 for Windows, Netscape 4.7 for Windows, IE 4.x and 5 for Mac and Netscape 4.x for Mac. The site also takes flat-panel display users into consideration, as most Economist.com staff worked on LCD screens, which have brighter, more washed-out color tones and less contrast than CRTs. Our color decisions reflect a desire to balance our viewing experience between both types of monitors.

Designs were crafted with an editorial-first-and-last mindset. We would begin with an edict from the editorial staff, and pages were created to maximize content presentation, with advertising and aesthetic considerations as embellishment. The commercial, technical, and business development teams would then weigh in with their requirements. Designs were reworked to include all interests, and then handed to the editors, often with explanations and the occasional presentation of ideas to ensure everyone approached the designs from the same angle. Editorial assessed where we had succeeded and failed, and what needed to be changed to meet our goals. We discovered that the editorial viewpoint was the most unwavering, and showing them last worked to everyone's advantage. Not only did this give us approval across all levels, it also placed the final designs in the hands of knowledgeable, veteran readers of *The Economist*. As a relative newcomer to the publication – and not a reader when I was hired – I was grateful for the checks and balances.

As a result of this setup, the creative process was extraordinarily collaborative. The editorial department was strong in its desires but receptive to lessons in wise Web-design tactics. While I devised each design, and editorial had the final say, suggestions and feedback came from every department and employee. Add to the mix freelancers and an outside agency that started the design process, and we had dozens of eyes, hands, and voices affecting the redesign. I encouraged feedback at every step, and the resulting flow of ideas and information led to a far better conceived site.

Home Page Design: Baby Steps

In the months before Economist.com had grown into a stand-alone business, *The Economist* had retained an outside design agency, a startup company in New York City called Methodfive, to conceptualize the redesign. Methodfive put an excellent staff to work on the redesign and came up with numerous possible design directions for the new site. Methodfive continually devised new solutions. Each time a design was presented, *The Economist* would make a set of requests, and Methodfive would return with a completely new interpretation. By the time I joined Economist.com, Methodfive was on its seventh visual run-through, and three designs were in active discussion.

Methodfive's better pages were only partly successful, and none had been seen through to a final, workable level. In particular, Methodfive liked to explore alternate usability tactics: at one point they tried placing our site's navigation on the right-hand side of the page, past 600 pixels in width, where a portion of our audience would never be able to see it. As I got acclimatized into my new job, we slowly dropped Methodfive's involvement so we could bring the design work in-house, to achieve better responsiveness and quicker turnaround. We ultimately worked from the Methodfive concepts as a convenient starting point.

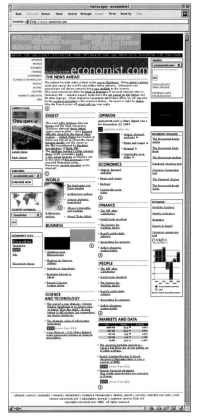

Methodfive designs.

design serving content

Before coming to Economist.com, I spent years working as an in-house designer with a small staff, and I felt I could do a fast, efficient job with my own hands – so I decided to take over the design work myself for a while. However, tackling this project on my own, as a single employee redesigning a large and intricate web site, was perhaps the single greatest mistake I made in the redesign process. I failed to realize the importance of outside analysis and creative thought, and of working with others whose strengths complement my own. While I thrive on feedback and collaboration, I did not recognize the significant contribution that third-party designs and thought can make to our progress. I also had not realized how close Methodfive had come to a workable, handsome design, and as they finished their work I chose to deconstruct their theories and craft my own solutions.

So, instead of picking up where Methodfive left off, I printed out their last designs, taped them to the cabinets next to my desk, and began redesigning Economist.com myself. In HTML. From scratch.

Redoing the web site was a good exercise in understanding the organizational scheme and basic design requests put forth by the department before my arrival. It was also a great way to make a mess. My first complete design was, to say the least, less than spectacular.

The first internal design (called home01).

72

I knew what I wanted to accomplish by making an initial design on my own, but I failed to convey that to anyone else, and the result was a step backward. I used HTML to get a better grasp on spatial layouts – what fitted and what didn't in an authentic browser environment. But my design was a wreck, full of disjointed elements, flat-looking images, text where GIFs belonged and GIFs where text belonged; it made sense but it looked terrible. The initial reaction around the team was, passively but noticeably, one of horror, and the emotion was nearly palpable: *This is the guy who's supposed to make our site pretty?*

> *I like to feel a page out by its organization first and visual presentation later, to maximize the usability of the site, but usability sells much better when married to strong visuals.*

Visuals aside, however, I was on my way, and some good would come out of the mess I made. It enabled me to view our goals from a practical aspect rather than a graphical one, which greatly aided my working style. I had dissected the organizational elements and was staring down the usability issues that Economist.com was facing, along with some pet concepts that were being kicked around. We wanted navigation to be prominent, simple, and useful. We wanted a date-stamp and a tagline – "News, Views & Analysis," a term that made it into our promotional materials but never got implemented on the site. We wanted a full column of utility that held links to all our assorted reference, data, and subscription pages. And we wanted a fourth column that held advertising and supplemental information. By identifying these components, and by literally putting each one in place, I was able to keep moving forward.

The office got bogged down for a while with the ugly details of my mockup. I had made the mistake of designing an HTML file without bothering to design strong visuals or a wireframe for it. This worked well for me; I could tell what would work and what wouldn't, and I didn't spend hours fine-tuning Photoshop mockups that would later need converting into difficult web pages. But I would have benefited tremendously from presenting an attractive if unworkable visual design to the rest of the office. I like to feel a page out by its organization first and visual presentation later, to maximize the usability of the site, but usability sells much better when married to strong visuals. Without a pretty page to look at, those not working directly on the design had a hard time sensing the direction in which I was headed, and many people were disappointed with what they saw. In addition, my function-first perspective at the time, which was based on the page I had crafted, manifested itself in ways that slowed development considerably. For example, I would look at a Photoshopped design and deconstruct it in my head as an HTML construction, looking at where it would and would not work smoothly, and note, "We can't draw X like that; it won't convert to clean HTML." Such moves were rooted in practicality but tended to drain productivity.

Not long after the first home page debuted, an e-mail from Anthony tore apart the designs, pointing out many of its visual and structural flaws. My designs kept excluding items that others were expecting to see; I knew they could be added later, but the designs didn't make sense on the outside without all the elements, including areas that wouldn't be included for months after the initial launch. Office discussions ran the gamut on decisions we were making about the design, from the color and style of dividing rules to the placement of the search box, including the items listed in the form's drop-down box.

design serving content

After a week of talking and tinkering, that first train wreck of a design had led us to this:

Progress on the home-page design.
This one was called home08.

A separate left-hand column held our site navigation and all our supplemental content materials: search, research tools, database and archive exploration, our cities' and countries' web features, and subscription information. Content streamed down the center, from a conceptual news feature entitled The News Ahead taking the main article slot, down to two columns displaying the various content areas of the site. The right-hand side had evolved to a clearinghouse for advertising, and an external news feed. Subscriber links were prominently placed above the content. The elements we identified in the first design, both editorially and spatially, were starting to fall into place. Many of these details now made sense and were carried through positionally to the finished design.

Visually, the site was still off. I received several comments critical of the horizontal gray pinstripes I had drawn in the left-hand column; depending on the point of view, it was either too bold, too distracting, too subtle, too much like the old site, or too confusing. The graphics were starting to look a little better, although the widespread use of *The Economist's* serif font was growing stale. Ecotype looks good in print, but it doesn't translate well as a presentation font: witness *The Economist's* own use of a sans-serif font for its printed covers and page notation. In addition, the page head was too messy when compared to the structured page beneath, an inconsistency that needed work.

I continued to evolve the design as we fine-tuned the layout. As we continued, we toyed with alternate layout concepts.

What if (we wondered) we stuck our leading ad banner in the middle of our content display, rather than atop the page, to free up the header and keep the logo in the top left corner?

74

Another iteration: home14.

This layout worked well – as expected; similar designs existed on *The Washington Post* (*http://www.washingtonpost.com*) and MSNBC (*http://www.msnbc.com*) – and the overall design was warmly received. But it also split the top section of content from the lower areas too strongly, which removed the power of the overall page and the logo. We were also worried about usability – a busy, animated advertisement might interfere with the reading of the page, so we eventually gave up on it. This page, however, shows our first real success designing a clean, intuitive search box, even with graphics missing. And it exposed the site's need for photo captions and credits.

What if we slimmed down the HTML to make a light, white-space-friendly, low-intensity home page? With this brief in mind, we developed the page codenamed Hernandez.

Why the Page Design Codenames?

After a while, numbering pages became too much to bear and a trifle embarrassing – one forgets whether one prefers style 72 or 63. Quantifying the number of times we redid the designs wasn't much fun, and as distinct designs took shape they deserved their own personality. The designs took form during the heart of spring training for baseball season in the United States, and I spent numerous hours talking sports with my colleagues. And since I'm a fan of the New York Yankees, the names came easy: Hernandez, Posada, and Rivera played for the Yanks. The London office, which was busy following Formula One racing rather than American ballclubs, got a good laugh out of this.

design serving content

A home page design, code-name Hernandez.

This actually flew as an accepted design concept for a while. Most people liked the open display of the content and how quickly the page loaded, which could have been a boon to our users. But the simplicity of the page was ultimately too far removed from a useful design. There weren't enough elements on the page to identify the brand or the product, and it did not give the content any weight. It did give us a new appreciation for display simplicity, though, and reminded us of the importance of white space.

During this process, the News Ahead content feature that anchored the home page got an official name, the Global Agenda, and some editorial direction. We also continued to wrestle with the organization and layout of the navigation, which seemed cumbersome at times and limiting at others, as we tried to determine which items belonged where. As we hacked through our conflicts and experiments, a layout emerged that we carried forward for several weeks. Code-named Rivera, it retained many of the touches of the ad-in-the-center layout earlier (although the ad itself soon retreated to the conventional top of the page).

A home page design, code-name Rivera.

> *One of the lessons I learned during this process, significantly and reluctantly, was that no large-scale redesign can find successful resolution completion at the hands of a single person. I had to let go of my one-does-all motivation and solicit some help.*

Rivera was clean, handsome, and eminently usable. Unfortunately, it was also rather boring. The site worked, but it didn't compel; there was a sense of authority behind the design, but no warmth. The components had fallen into place but what good were they if they didn't draw the readers in and compel them to read? A new direction was needed, something to kick-start the visuals.

One of the lessons I learned during this process, significantly and reluctantly, was that no large-scale redesign can find successful resolution completion at the hands of a single person. I had to let go of my one-does-all motivation and solicit some help.

Home Page Design: Going Outside, Reeling It In

While we had ended our relationship with Methodfive early in the redesign process, we continued to look to the outside for assistance in establishing the design. This did not come without a modicum of stubbornness – I often assumed I could do a great job on the design, period – but getting an outside designer's opinion and input often helped craft successful pages and designs. Several freelancers were used throughout 2000 to conceptualize the design and, later, to flesh out content areas and presentations. We kept the design process in-house, as planned, but objective work from an outside eye always gave us a fresh perspective.

> *I often assumed I could do a great job on the design, period – but getting an outside designer's opinion and input often helped craft successful pages and designs.*

Most significant by far was the contribution we received from a single outsider, a former creative director at Methodfive, who had left the agency shortly after we stopped working with them. Kenneth Goldsmith was familiar with the Economist.com redesign project, and had seen the Methodfive designs before I had started my design work. Our business development director noticed that our creative process had begun to stall and recommended getting some feedback from Ken, so I contacted Ken and brought him into the office. He reviewed our progress and I asked him for help: the designs were progressing nicely, but lacked the visual impact needed to define and shape the new site.

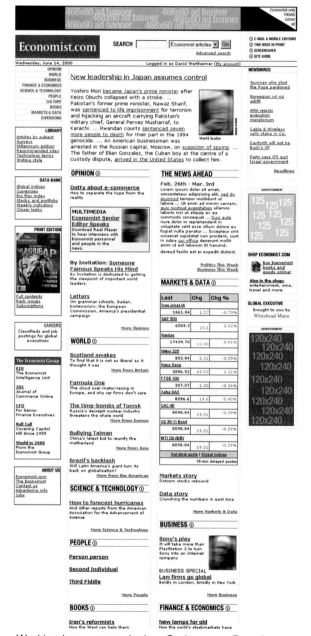

Working home page design. Code name: Posada.

Ken's independent eye combined our ideas in ways no one at either Methodfive or Economist.com could have. Instead of giving raw feedback, he brainstormed solutions and joined me for an afternoon of hands-on design exploration. His main inspiration came from an area we had basically disregarded: why not take the most compelling Methodfive design and marry it to the structural successes of our internal work?

We spent an afternoon toying with the assorted page designs. Wisely, after we had dug into them for a while, Ken departed for a few days, essentially turning me loose to see where the designs would go. I began deconstructing our preferred Methodfive design, the one they referred to as i2, and merging it with my own pages. The result, which took the codename Posada, was a handsome, usable design, one that became the final style leading up to the relaunch.

During the restructuring that created Posada, I altered the following:

- **The page header** was retained almost entirely from internal designs, with the Economist.com logo flush left, a search box prominent in the middle, and character lines carrying up from below. The strong page header anchored the page, giving the eye somewhere to begin. The horizontal ad space atop the page was cleared of everything but a single ad, and remained dark – a useful idea from Methodfive's earlier designs, which gave the top of the page greater weight. Instead of imposing black or bland gray, a dark blue became the lead color, providing a nice offset to the bright red of the logo. The header still retained a comfortable amount of white space to give the logo proper emphasis. The date/member services bar carried over from the internal designs, as it was a useful tool and an easy area to place membership options.

- **The left-hand navigation bar** was inspired by Methodfive designs, while the organization flowed from our internal site structure documents and experimentation. The sections remained in stylish red type and boxes, anchoring the top of the left-hand side, with the red asserting the navigation's relational importance. The design was a direct nod to Methodfive but presented with even more force. Supplemental content areas appeared boxed below, along with print edition navigation and the week's cover.

- **The search box** stayed front and center atop the page, to the right of the logo, to maximize its exposure. It was flanked by lots of white space and a handy advanced search link. The drop-down menu increased in importance as we expanded our search offerings, and the box's prominence reinforces the site's dedication to giving the reader flexible usability.

- **The main content columns**, as with the left-hand navigation, yanked their entire visual layout from the Methodfive design. We replicated the earlier design's section titles and circle-arrow bullet-style icons, or "dingbats". We extended the utility of the bullets by placing them next to clickable graphics in a subtle but useful navigational cue, letting the arrow signify more text within (and subtracting it where an image was not linked).

- **The right-hand column** became a home for external content and advertising; the limited use allowed us to place restrictions on left-hand advertising and keep a pristine editorial zone that largely persists today. The same philosophy was then applied site-wide, a devotion to delivering easy-to-read editorial content that defines the site overall.

- **The overall page structure** grew from our internal designs. I established the use of one-pixel light-gray and black dividing lines running vertically down the columns, which defined the layout and comfortably boxed-in our content. I also placed a standard spacer width (17 pixels wide or tall) between each vertical and horizontal element. This gave the new page a balance that none of our previous designs, in-house or out, had achieved.

- **The fonts** basically found themselves. Ken suggested a few handsome sans-serif fonts to replace the ones Methodfive had used, and I settled on a dense Helvetica Neue as the font for text GIF images. Verdana had long been the preferred text font around the Economist.com office, and it was used on most text items around the new design and, eventually, the whole site.

The finished page, Posada, debuted April 26 2000, following several weeks of fine-tuning.

What amazed me was how smoothly and sensibly a discarded design was revived. For months, the Methodfive designs hung around the office, providing inspiration and lessons learned, a starting point for our work. More than once we looked toward version i2 as an example of what worked well but not well enough. What we had failed to do was integrate the existing successes. I had chosen to reinvent the wheel – rather deliberately, if ignorantly – yet the combination of factors really made the page succeed. After four months of working solo, a few hours of fresh thinking from the outside put a smart new spin on our work. Ken's eye had given me a perspective I was unable to find on my own, and that new-found inspiration, coupled with the work we had put into finding the right spatial and organizational balance, brought the design to a new high.

Once the page was established, we had to integrate the upcoming Global Agenda into the design formally.

Launched a month after the Economist.com redesign, the Global Agenda was *The Economist's* foray into publishing continuously updated content, with topical articles posted directly to the web site. The design requirement for Global Agenda articles was quite simple: find room for it on the home page. Everything else was already prepared, from the standard article layout to the related items boxes. As it stood separately from *Economist* print content, it was not included in the site navigation; until a decent number of articles were in the archive, it was not included in our search options. We decided to place Global Agenda front and center, anchoring our home page with our most up-to-date and frequently changing content. This had the odd effect of making the home page the sole navigational tool for using Global Agenda, and it also enlivened the home page overall, which worked greatly to our advantage, giving a dynamic element to an otherwise weekly publication.

With the Global Agenda integrated, the design was shared around the department. Internal display of Posada brought widespread praise and encouragement. Comments around the department focused on design cues rather than the over-arching effect, such as our font choices, underlining, and use of red; I knew we had created the right design. On May 11, 2000 I received a green light from the editor to build out Posada into a full range of pages, and 11 days later, the editor-in-chief of the Economist Group signed off on it as well.

Content Pages

While the home page was being developed, parallel work was being done on the other page templates needed for the site. Section indexes were designed mainly to mimic the home page layout, but articles needed a display of their own. The delivery of the content was arguably the most important component, for while we fretted over the design and impact of the home page, the articles were always the destination.

Economist.com · WORLD · **NORTH AMERICA** · SEARCH (Advanced) · Go · ⊙ E-MAIL & MOBILE EDITIONS · ⊙ PRINT SUBSCRIPTIONS

A content page header.

To create smart, usable content pages, we rethought the design from the top down, starting with the basic page layout. In order to display more content faster, and to keep the home page identity stronger than the inside pages (a decision I regret, because any page on a web site can feasibly be the entryway), the header row was reduced in height from 60 pixels to around 40. For best visual effect, I had in early designs made the Economist.com logo the same width as the column directly beneath it, a good style cue that I ignored on the home page but preserved on content displays. The final logo came to 125x34; I threw some white space around it, providing some much-needed height for the GIFs that would appear in the center of the header. The Economist.com branding at this size was just barely clean enough for presentation, and it became our minimum size for logo usage.

I brought to Economist.com the concept of category titles rendered as page-header images. They were the source of some confusion for a while, as we hammered out the specifics. We had to display both sections (World) and subsections (World: North America) in the same space, without confusion; and that space had to also squeeze in our search bar. We made everything fit by using a two-deck header, made up of a smaller, red-text category title and a subcategory beneath it. On main category pages we dropped the small red text.

The search box for internal pages got stripped down and condensed. The text box was shrunk to fit next to the page header GIF, and the drop-down menu was eliminated; the contextual search functionality remained, but not the ability to select a sub-section for localized searches. We preserved the Advanced search link to provide users with full functionality. I toyed at length with the size of the search box because of browser settings, ultimately making the box small

enough so the "Go" button would not break the layout with even the largest custom font settings.

Several user options exist on Economist.com content pages. All have a printable-page option and e-mailing functionality, and some also have e-mail newsletter signups and discussion boards. We had to lay these options into the content area sensibly and without cluttering the text, and ended up "attaching" the options as a hanging box beneath the search form, a solution made possible because of *The Economist's* short headlines. This served two purposes: it got the box out of the way of the content, and it tied in visually to the search box, providing a catch-all spot for the user-activated functionality of the page. I drew simple black and white graphics – 12x12 pixels apiece – for each of our supplemental navigation components:

E-mail this page · Printable page · Get e-mail alerts · Discuss

Icons (or dingbats), various.

The Search Box

The ideal visual size chosen for the width of the search box, 12 characters, only worked when Internet Explorer users had "medium" font settings selected. When the user chose *Larger* or *Largest* fonts, the *Submit* button (labeled "Go") widened, and the tight space of the page head caused the form elements to text-wrap, breaking the layout. The box's size was reduced twice (from 12 to 11 and again to 10) before enough "wiggle room" was created.

design serving content

With layout and functionality determined, we had to find ways to present diverse content with relative consistency. Besides words, articles could contain headlines, rubrics, fly titles, date and location stamps, photographs, caricatures, charts, graphs, maps, and data tables. Our requirement was to make each content item render cleanly.

In the content header, we experimented with color for various items of text, as we needed variants for the numerous elements near the top of the content area. The fly title that appears on some pages (which gives an over-arching category definition to an article) became bold red, while the supplemental article info, such as date, location, and article origin, switched to a light gray complementing the gray separator lines around the page. We decided to use red text for links intended to grab the user's attention, such as "Get article background", a feature installed post-launch that provided a pop-up window with background information on a subject.

Economist.com had decided earlier to use black as the default color for links, with a red hover as a visual cue. Using black, while not an expected link color, minimized the intrusion when a link was presented in the middle of an article or other content. By the same token, we chose to leave underlines in place, eschewing a popular trend of turning off underlines; we determined the underlining would be our functional focus rather than the color, with the hover as an additional aid. Our color and size differentiation for prominent links therefore made the content leading into the page welcoming and easy to decipher.

An Economist.com article display.

Images

Image requirements were among the tougher aspects of the content page. We wanted to present images in the best possible visual format, as *The Economist* is known for its charts, graphs, and maps. The emphasis suggested large graphics that would not lie in a page particularly well. For a time we explored Details boxes, which would display a thumbnail image and a graphic of a magnifying glass; with a click, a pop-up window would show a large, detailed version of the image, giving proper focus to a chart. I was adamant for a time about right-justifying images, especially photographs, and letting text flow. We discovered, however, that most of our charts and maps could be cleaned up to render smoothly in the designated space, so the Details boxes fell out of use, except where images or charts are particularly large.

> *While we had a standard template, editorial and business needs led us to devise multiple variations on the theme to maximize our flexibility.*

The Economist also makes frequent use of cartoons and caricatures, especially as an anchor image at the beginning of an article. The print edition's caricatures are popular, and making good use of them online was essential. I had hoped to reduce and right-align them like our other images, but shrinking the artwork down did not do the caricatures justice. It also changed the nature of the piece from an editorial standpoint. Instead of leading with the graphic, the art became a supplement, which was not considered appropriate. I did not understand this nuance and disagreed mightily, fearing for the visual integrity of the page, but the editorial sensibility rang wise and true. Articles with leading artwork now have 443-pixel-wide graphics (the content area is 447) between their headlines and beginning paragraphs, and the result is a white-space-filled article lead that gives proper weight and consideration to the image.

For photo credits, we tried embedding the text in the image source's `alt` text, which kept the page clean. Our clever solution fell apart, however, when the credits, designed to appear as a ToolTip when the cursor was pointed at the image, didn't work automatically on Macintosh browsers. The credits had to be brought to the visible layout instead, and they now reside atop the image, in small, light gray text.

The Economist.com "related-items" box was an essential inclusion for the new layout. The old site had lengthy paragraphs containing explanatory text and links that directed readers to supplements of interest, from other areas on Economist.com to resources elsewhere online, and the sites of companies and individuals named in an article. We knew this box would carry into the new design, but where? Early sentiment had the items remaining at the bottom of the page for continuity between the old site and the new. For space and design purposes, the box found a home at the top of the right-hand column, in place of the news feed on most article pages. This decision slightly altered the editorial use of the box; what were once lengthy paragraphs have shifted toward delivering bits of information and links. But it also brought the utility to a centralized location – the right-hand column was now a launching point for additional content on almost every page, and it advantageously pulled more content toward the top of the page. We also made a usability decision to pop off-site links into new windows, a maneuver that goes against standard link protocol but, we believe, gives the user added utility. (Links within Economist.com always stay in the main window.)

With the elements covered, we set about building the pages. Mostly, the editor gave rules to the production manager that were implemented during and after test runs of the weekly site update. I spent a few weeks fine-tuning layout requests, approving and tweaking editorial's needs and production's output to ensure our pages matched the visual goals. I also jumped in for the occasional major change, such as our business development director's discovery that certain markets and data tables wouldn't fit in our main layout; he and I wound up designing a "wide layout" page that eliminated the right-hand column in order to allow content to flow to 600 pixels rather than the standard column's 447. While we had a standard template, editorial and business needs led us to devise multiple variations on the theme to maximize our flexibility. Ultimately, the divergent needs between departments came together in a set of clean, readable content pages.

Economist.com added several content-based feature areas after its relaunch. Some were add-ons to the main site, while others were completely new content areas and products that extended the reach of Economist.com. These areas were the reason the web site exists as its own product with its own logo, as it has become more than just *The Economist* reposted online. Each feature had its own design and functional requirements, and several received fresh designs that created additional methods of delivering our content.

Global Executive

Our executive-focus area grew out a partnership struck with the executive search firm Whitehead Mann in late 2000. A new Economist.com careers area was to debut, containing *Economist* articles packaged for convenient topical reading by business executives. It included Economist.com's classifieds section, which moved there from the main site. The Economist Global Executive (GE) would thus receive a different design than the rest of the site. We wanted a style that recalled the look and feel of Economist.com without being the same site, so I recruited an outside designer, someone with a fresh eye – since working with Ken had been such a success – to craft a similar, but different, design. The results were terrific. The freelancer crafted a unique design that paid homage to the basic values of Economist.com, from the placement of the logo and

structural items to the use of a wide variant of the Helvetica Neue font used on the main site.

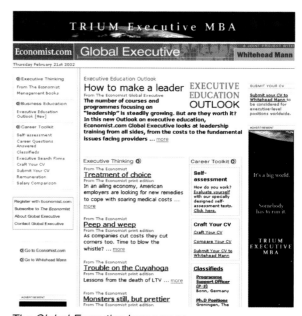

The Global Executive home page.

The design build-out was performed in-house, where we added the necessary sponsor and advertisement areas and I designed a header integrating Whitehead Mann's and our logos with the new GE brand. We did encounter a problem in our implementation when we discovered that the layout was not developed with a wide-enough content column to accommodate our 443-pixel-wide editorial graphics. The right-hand side of the page had to be reconstructed and the designed gutters altered so the center column would be the right width. Once that was altered, GE launched rather smoothly. It has held up well, and proved very adaptable for the features and promotions we have added to it since.

Articles by Subject/Innovations

Similar in concept to Global Executive, Innovations was developed as an opportunity to highlight focused areas of content found in our archives. Articles by Subject, already live, consisted of straightforward lists of articles at that time; we aimed to feature pieces and promote topical interests. The new areas became microsites, which then became a lucrative sponsorship opportunity for advertisers. We took some topics and brought them into their own design, loosely based on the Global Executive pages. We added "sponsored links" text boxes to enhance the value to the advertiser, who, by sponsoring a subject, would make paid articles in the area free to all users. The sponsorships were a way for us to glean revenue from batches of content without corrupting *The Economist's* essential church-and-state separation. The Innovations concept worked well but was too limited, so we altered our plan and integrated Innovations with Articles by Subject. For this, we devised another separate layout for Articles by Subject as a whole.

The Articles by Subject design built upon the Innovations design but with a looser, more text-based layout. We tried to save space and enhance functionality by integrating the drill-down menus into the page header, which worked as promised but resulted in a somewhat less than compelling visual design. However, the usability of this area was far better than Innovations, and allowed us to expand more easily.

Top-of-page design screenshots of Articles by Subject and its predecessor, Innovations.

design serving content

Backgrounders

As planned in the initial design, get the background links were to preface select *Economist* articles and give useful historical information, complementing the coverage of a current subject. To display "Backgrounders" without confusion, the editor requested they be displayed in pop-up windows that kept the relevant article (print edition article, Global Agenda piece, etc.) readily available. We designed a pop-up that looked very much like our clutter-free administrative pages, only narrower.

A Backgrounder pop-up.

Within the pop-up window, we struggled to identify free and paid links; I wanted to lay our E+ images (used to denote pay content; see below for details) into the text, but the editor hated the interruption in reading. We wound up using an old-fashioned footnote: gray text appears in the pop-up window explaining the paid links and providing direction on taking out a web subscription. The pop-up has lead to few reader complaints, thanks to its editorial and functional nature.

Links to the Backgrounders themselves were inserted in bold red text just ahead of the first paragraph of an article, as a sign that we could prepare an under-informed reader for the article that lay ahead. Once we built up a sufficient number of Backgrounders, we added them to the Library area of our site and to our search capabilities.

Cities Guide

Economist.com launched a Cities Guide a few months after the debut of the redesign, and in honesty, these layouts gave us a lot more trouble than they should have. We could not decide whether the area should strike out on its own into a new design, a sub site like Global Executive, with its own stylistic cues, or whether it should adhere more closely to Economist.com site style and follow our traditional guidelines. I tried to accomplish both and for several months wound up with neither. We found the guides' niche in a layout that broke the Economist.com mold without straying too far; the right-hand column loosened up significantly, and a horizontal navigation bar topped each content column.

Cities Guide home page.

The guides' overall home page combined an image-mapped global map, with clickable cities links, and highlights boxes that pulled out content features from select cities. A year after its launch, the editors consider the Cities Guide home page a particular design success. Interestingly, we designed a print version of two cities' material for an offline Cities Guide, and the layout was an unqualified success, which should provide new design cues the next time we work on the area.

Country Briefings

Installing Economist.com's Country Briefings was notable not for its overall design, which kept the main site template, but for the components we needed to add to each page.

Significant pieces of content were being supplied by *The Economist's* research arm, The Economist Intelligence Unit (EIU), and we needed to co-brand the pages with their logo, which we had done with Global Executive but never in our standard design. We wound up placing their logo alongside the page header graphic that announced the country name.

Country Briefings. This is the Australia index page.

For the first time, we had commercial promotions within the content columns, as the EIU sells full-length reports for the countries we covered. We designed light gray boxes, rather than the white or light-blue ones used elsewhere on the site, to designate commercial activity, and laid in simple checkboxes and submit buttons for functionality. We also branded the EIU Store wherever possible, which was both useful for our readers and pleasing to the EIU.

We had to figure out a way for the user to navigate to 60 countries off one page. At least half a dozen schemes were tried before we settled on the rather straightforward system we have now: three columns of 20 countries each, set in a table with a world map behind it. In a subtle nod to consistency, the map behind the list is the same one used to navigate the cities area, in a similar blue hue. Navigation into City Guides and Country Briefings is presented in a single box in our left-hand site navigation with the same map as their brand.

Country Briefings remains an interesting project thanks to its dense array of data and the unique partnership between Economist.com and the EIU.

Components

Once the basic page design was complete, we dived into the mechanics and organization of Economist.com. The many details we assessed helped define the site both editorially and functionally. Some changes occurred quickly and painlessly. We killed the "News, Views & Analysis" strapline, for example, and streamlined the sections to eliminate a tentative Reference section; other decisions, however, took more time and contemplation.

Subject Navigation

We spent a considerable amount of time determining how to organize the different components of the site navigation. We began with all the components listed in a single graphic, which simplified design but made organization difficult. We tried multiple colors for the fonts, and underlining, in attempts to group the components. As early as February 7 2000, editorial pushed for a subsidiary nav bar for useful regular features/functions, which was too complicated to be useful. The idea of two navigation bars on one site was deemed cumbersome and unnecessary, and not until we happened upon the multiple box solution were we able to simplify the main navigation and focus on the essential content areas. Fortunately, the editorial section list remained virtually identical from concept to launch. Items got moved around and renamed, but the editorial strategy stayed the same, giving our designs a consistent theme as we developed the nav.

One of the more difficult items to solve was our subsection navigation. Some sections of the site had subsections within them, like World, which was split into North America, Latin America, Europe, Asia, and Africa and the Middle East. They were all available as index pages, and displaying them was crucial both to present information and show the user our departments. The concept was the easy part: we knew we wanted to insert the subsections into the navigation. Making it work, however, proved troublesome. We tried graphics and text, static menus and JavaScripted open-on-click designs, left- and right-aligned lists, but nothing felt quite right.

Our ultimate solution was fairly straightforward: small black text, right-aligned to match the rest of the main navigation, set into a table with a matching hairline and white space to keep the nav whole. The nav would "open up" beneath a selected category and display the sub-nav whenever the user was on a relevant page.

Supplemental Navigation

It seemed like a great idea at the time: let's give each item or group of items that doesn't fit anywhere else its own box in the nav. So, by the time we launched, there were boxes down the left for:

- Library (containing Articles by Subject, our Internet guide, and Surveys, which are *The Economist's* in-depth special reports).

- Data Bank (with stock market information, currencies, *The Economist's* weekly indicators and the Big Mac Index).

- Cities and Countries, which have differing purposes (one is a travel guide, the other a research tool) in a joint box with a map serving as a logo.

OPINION	OPINION	OPINION	OPINION	OPINION
WORLD	WORLD	WORLD	WORLD	WORLD
NEWS	News	News	News	News
EUROPE	Europe	Europe	Europe	Europe
THE AMERICAS	The Americas	The Americas	The Americas	The Americas
ASIA	Asia	Asia	Asia	Asia
AFRICA & MIDDLE EAST	Africa & Middle East	Africa & Middle East	Africa & Middle East	Africa & Middle East
BUSINESS	BUSINESS	BUSINESS	BUSINESS	BUSINESS
FINANCE & ECONOMICS	FINANCE & ECONOMICS	FINANCE & ECONOMICS	FINANCE & ECONOMICS	FINANCE & ECONOMICS
SCIENCE & TECHNOLOGY	SCIENCE & TECHNOLOGY	SCIENCE & TECHNOLOGY	SCIENCE & TECHNOLOGY	SCIENCE & TECHNOLOGY
PEOPLE	PEOPLE	PEOPLE	PEOPLE	PEOPLE
CULTURE	CULTURE	CULTURE	CULTURE	CULTURE
BOOKS	BOOKS	BOOKS	BOOKS	BOOKS
MARKETS & DATA	MARKETS & DATA	MARKETS & DATA	MARKETS & DATA	MARKETS & DATA
DIVERSIONS	DIVERSIONS	DIVERSIONS	DIVERSIONS	DIVERSIONS
CAREERS	CAREERS	CAREERS	CAREERS	CAREERS
SHOP	SHOP	SHOP	SHOP	SHOP

Some of the cutting-room-floor left-nav options along with the final design (far right).

Print Edition Information, with the weekly cover and subscription and contents links.

- The Economist Shop.

- Careers, for classifieds and, later, the Global Executive microsite.

- The Economist Group site list.

- About Us, a catch-all for help pages, FAQs, and contact information.

We had been overrun with boxes, and we still are. The visual effect is nice but the continuity is lacking, and it is one of the site's worst flaws. It did, however, solve a lot of problems for us as we worked through the details, and made site expansion easy.

Also difficult was determining the merits of "more" links in the content areas of the home page.

We noted that the GIF that headed each section would link to the stated area, and the circle-arrow dingbat was meant to signify that a GIF was an active link. But we also all felt that users look for text links faster than they look to images, or even to a navigation bar, and that the "more" links would be user-friendly. We kept them, and we even made them red so they would stand out when a user glanced down the page. We also discovered that they had navigational importance: Economist.com eliminated some sections that appear in print, such as Britain and United States, and we were able to include these missing sections in our *More* links. "More from Europe (including Britain)" became an important pointer when the site was first launched.

WORLD ⊙

America and the Middle East conflict
America's policy looks like muddled support for Israel. A fair judgment?
Apr 4th 2002

How powerful is America's Jewish lobby? E+
However entwined the sentiments, the national interest comes first
Apr 4th 2002

Sex offenders in America
The Catholic church is not the only institution that needs to confront, and deal with, sexual crimes against children
Apr 4th 2002

More from North America

Costa Rica's resistance to change
How much longer can Costa Rica afford to be different?
Apr 4th 2002

More from Latin America

Signs of hope in Afghanistan
Is the country at last on the mend?
Apr 4th 2002

More from Asia

Ukraine's messy election
The result of the general election spells both hope and danger for Ukraine—and more worries for its neighbours
Apr 4th 2002

Unrest in Moldova
The future of Europe's most dismal country looks ever bleaker
Apr 4th 2002

Corruption in Germany E+
Scandals continue to embroil both of Germany's two main parties
Apr 4th 2002

Social mobility in Britain
Meritocracy in Britain? It would be a good idea
Apr 4th 2002

More from Europe (including Britain)

Peace in Angola?
A ceasefire could herald the end of one of Africa's oldest and nastiest wars
Apr 4th 2002

More from Africa & the Middle East

A close-up of a section of the home page, featuring "more" links.

"Others" Navigation

A handful of links exist in the top right-hand corner of the page. They are meant to draw attention to special features or handy areas of the site that would otherwise be hard to find. They have, over time, highlighted all of the following: *E-Mail Services*, *Mobile Edition*, *Site Map*, *Help*, *Screensaver*, *This Week In Print*, and *Print Subscriptions*. This space, lovingly referred to as the "others nav," is either a great success or great flaw of the site; I personally suspect the latter. In truth, it exists because the space it fills, next to the search box, was empty, and we needed something other than advertising to place there. Strikingly, the four links presented on the home page reduce to two when the user clicks beyond the home page.

⊙ **E-MAIL SERVICES**
⊙ **MOBILE EDITION**
⊙ **SITE MAP / CONTENTS**
⊙ **HELP**

An example of the "others" nav.

Status Bar

Displaying the date and login info for each user, this space has been fairly static since early designs. The user information area has expanded over time, to include links for registration, login, account services and help, but little else has changed. We sometimes worry that it is too subtle to push users to subscribe, but it is also in a convenient and smart location for registered users. It also serves as a useful guide, calling out an explanation for "E+" articles (see below).

The status bar.

Page Layout

Firm rules regarding each area of the home page (as well as internal pages) were established as the design became final. The left-hand column would be home to all internal site navigation and, ideally, little else. The right-hand column, on the other hand, was the home for all supplemental items, from advertising to promotions to our external news feed. The center of the page was to remain clean and easy to read at all times; the home page and section indexes developed strong rules about what items went where, and what components of each got displayed.

Boxes

We had to figure out how to feature content on the home page and index pages, and we opted for simple and useful: light blue boxes, a complementary shade to the dark blue atop the page, with dark borders and similar text formatting to the rest of the page. For our markets and data box, which provided up-to-the-minute stock market information, we designed a table with alternating shades of blue. The boxes were straightforward and handsome, and got their point across with a minimum of fuss.

Worth noting here is the level of complexity involved in our navigational-column tables. Every box had a black border, a header image (black text in a GIF with a white background and light red underline), and content that required `cellpadding`. Nested tables were used in early designs but discarded after they dragged the load time in Netscape browsers to unreasonable levels. Instead, the boxes have intricate spacing and spanning, and spacer GIFs in almost every cell to preserve the layout:

```
<table width="125" border="0"
cellspacing="0" cellpadding="0">
  <tr>
    <td width="1" bgcolor="#000000">
      <img alt=""
src="images/blocks/spacer.gif" width="1"
height="1">
    </td>
    <td width="123" bgcolor="#000000"
colspan="3">
      <img alt=""
src="images/blocks/spacer.gif" width="123"
height="1">
    </td>
    <td width="1" bgcolor="#000000">
      <img alt=""
src="images/blocks/spacer.gif" width="1"
height="1">
    </td>
  </tr>
  <tr>
    <td width="1" bgcolor="#000000">
      <img alt=""
src="images/blocks/spacer.gif" width="1"
height="1">
    </td>
    <td width="123" bgcolor="ffffff"
colspan="3">
      <img alt=""
src="images/blocks/spacer.gif" width="123"
height="1">
      <br>
      <img alt=" "
src="images/nav/title.gif" width="123"
height="14">
      <br>
      <img alt=""
src="images/blocks/spacer.gif" width="123"
height="3">
      <br>
    </td>
```

(Continues on next page)

```
      <td width="1" bgcolor="#000000">
         <img alt=""
src="images/blocks/spacer.gif" width="1"
height="1">
      </td>
   </tr>
   <tr>
      <td width="1" bgcolor="#000000">
         <img alt=""
src="images/blocks/spacer.gif" width="1"
height="1">
      </td>
      <td width="3">
         <img alt=""
src="images/blocks/spacer.gif" width="3"
height="1"></td>
      <td width="117" bgcolor="ffffff">
         <font face="verdana, arial,
helvetica, sans-serif" size="-2">
            <a href="#">Link</a><br>
            <a href="#">Link</a><br>
            <a href="#">Link</a><br>
            <br>
         </font>
      </td>
      <td width="3">
         <img alt=""
src="images/blocks/spacer.gif" width="3"
height="1">
      </td>
      <td width="1" bgcolor="#000000">
         <img alt=""
src="images/blocks/spacer.gif" width="1"
height="1">
      </td>
   </tr>
   <tr>
      <td width="1" bgcolor="#000000">
         <img alt=""
src="images/blocks/spacer.gif" width="1"
height="1">
      </td>
      <td width="123" bgcolor="#000000"
colspan="3">
```

```
         <img alt=""
src="images/blocks/spacer.gif" width="123"
height="1">
      </td>
      <td width="1" bgcolor="#000000">
         <img alt=""
src="images/blocks/spacer.gif" width="1"
height="1">
      </td>
   </tr>
</table>
```

This table layout looks like the following:

This has its drawbacks – the number of images requested from the server is too high, even with the widespread use of a common `spacer.gif` – but the visuals are perfect. Additionally, we only launched with five or six distinct areas down the left-hand side of the page, and three on the right; as the site has grown, so has our quantity of boxes, which has slowed down the page.

Marking Premium Content

A good idea is often a combination of hard work, thoughtfulness, and embracing the obvious. Take, for example, the red "E+" logo that appears on Economist.com, denoting premium content.

The live E+ logo.

The team struggled for months to find the right way to convey the difference between free and pay articles. As the site has a tiered access system, we needed to display that distinction for readers new and old. But how to do that gently and sensibly? I had initially wanted to alternate link colors – red for pay, black for free – along with a note of explanation. I then tried using a key image, and I drew some rudimentary security icons, which failed. I also considered using a square "E" image as sort of a slug, and over the course of a few days threw a bunch of them – black E, white E, red E, hollow E, E in brackets – onto a page for sampling. But nothing we tried had any elegance or meaning.

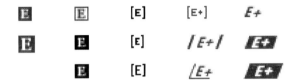

Many flawed E+ designs.

I then cut the situation down to its essence. What were we trying to show with this dingbat? We were saying, "This is *Economist* content, but it's extra". Premium. More. A step beyond what any random user can see. Addition, more, extra: plus. Bingo. I drew an E with a plus sign next to it and tried it out. The image didn't work at all; my E+ was hand-drawn red pixels with an awkward bracket around it. But the concept caught on, so I kept toying. My fifth try used an italicized E+ in alternating colors, the E in red on white, the plus in white on a red parallelogram raked to the same angle. We hit it: I asked around the office for feedback, and no

one had anything to add. The E+ looked nice and was a fitting description. This icon got installed into the final design, appearing next to the link of any article that resided behind our pay barrier. We never found an adequate way to denote pay pages from within, a feature that gets requested by users from time to time.

> *"Let the reader determine how the text should be displayed", I commanded. This met with heavy resistance in our London office, where our chief technical officer and developers rallied hard for the opposite. New font faces like Verdana, they argued, were designed for maximum screen readability.*

Fonts

We spent months debating the merits of defining fonts for our users. When I first came to Economist.com, I was a full proponent of minimal site intrusion, preferring to leave most font sizes variable and faces undefined. I believed that if usability and readability were our prime concern, it was best to leave font selection alone. "Let the reader determine how the text should be displayed", I commanded. This met with heavy resistance in our London office, where our chief technical officer and developers rallied hard for the opposite. New font faces like Verdana, they argued, were designed for maximum screen readability and they should be used whenever possible. Users cannot be trusted to set their computers to an optimal setting, the argument went, and we should provide them with

Dingbat

Main Entry: ding•bat
Pronunciation: 'di[ng]-"bat
Function: noun
Etymology: origin unknown
Date: 1904
1 : a typographical symbol or ornament

Excerpt taken from http://www.m-w.com/ – thanks to Merriam-Webster.

the best possible experience we can. We thought about using the following:

Verdana.

Headline (bold +1)

Dateline (gray -2)

Content display text. The quick brown fox jumped over the lazy dog. (normal -1)

Times New Roman.

Headline (bold +1)

Dateline (gray -2)

Content display text. The quick brown fox jumped over the lazy dog. (normal -1)

Ecotype.

Headline (bold +1)

Dateline (gray -2)

Content display text. The quick brown fox jumped over the lazy dog. (normal -1)

Font samples of Verdana, Times, and Ecotype.

I was also leaning toward default fonts because most users' browsers stay set to Times New Roman, which is a serif font, and one not dissimilar to Ecotype, the proprietary font of *The Economist*. As someone who doesn't alter default settings often – I like to try to simulate the generic user's viewing environment – I had become accustomed to doing most of my web reading in Times New Roman. In the end, however, I capitulated, and we went with a sans-serif font set with Verdana as the lead option. Economist.com is better for it – the site is much more readable, especially in our small-font sidebars, where Verdana reigns supreme. We use the font in virtually every occurrence of text on the site, and we are context-sensitive with sizing. We still use relative font sizes rather than stylesheet-dictated pixels to preserve some user flexibility. The only slight problem is that Verdana is a particularly wide font, which makes some text-based designs tough to fit into tight spaces. Chalk up a victory for usability in this

case, one that took extensive internal debate but led to a well-researched and wise decision.

As noted earlier, we also stuck with underlined links to maximize usability, rather than using scripts to turn off underlines. We did select black for our link color, which, while not the most usable for finding links, was the most reader-friendly in the context of content passages. Readability trumped usability in this case, and the decision has not only made pages easier to read but kept the designs handsome as well.

The administrative and functional aspects of the site were the last to be designed, as they relied most on technical and user-interface decisions rather than editorial and commercial necessities. Basically, anything with a form, such as registration, search, and e-mail, was left for a later stage.

> *As registration is fairly labor-intensive and often discouraging, I considered it essential to not give the user any encouragement to abort the process.*

Forms

Most forms on the site were set in basic two-column formats, with instructions on the left and form elements (text inputs, checkboxes, submit buttons) on the right. To add a touch of style without a heavy hand, light gray horizontal lines were placed in between items of the form:

A sample registration form.

Economist.com's registration and user administration pages were set in a different style. Analyzing the purpose and requirements of a registration page, I decided registration and subscription signups needed to minimize the distractions on the page. I wanted to keep the focus on the signup process, which is often perceived by users as burdensome. That led me to kill most of the all-supplemental content and navigation, and also meant we could not place advertising on these pages, a move I still find myself defending on occasion. As registration is fairly labor-intensive and often discouraging, I considered it essential to not give the user any encouragement to abort the process.

Stripping out all these elements meant we needed a different page layout to emphasize the content and compensate for the minimal available options. I designed a page identical to the rest of the site but without the entire right-hand column; we also deleted the status bar and search form, leaving the page at its bare essentials:

A two-col layout, live-site style.

This design was placed in all administrative pages and also became our template for pop-up content windows.

Search

Our search pages posed a complex problem, as the search engine was considered an important tool for research-hungry Economist.com users. We licensed Northern Light to be our search engine so they could manage our pay-per-view article searches and offer EIU content along with *Economist* archives. Their data included *Economist* article archives with context-sensitive search results (keywords found in both headlines and content, sortable by date or relevance) as well as data from the EIU, our sister division and research arm. Therefore, our search page needed to toggle between options without confusing the users. We settled on a drop-down menu listing the available selections, a style that would come in handy listing in-category options on other pages.

The columnar layout of the site lent itself well to including Northern Light's options down the right-hand side of the page, leaving the center section clear for the search results. The results themselves were initially placed in a multi-celled table, to capitalize on the amount of data the search form produced, but we soon pared down the display to a more standard title-summary-date setup. The advanced search page was left as a simple form design.

The search results page.

URLs

We also had intense discussions over the way we should establish the site's addresses. Economist.com had plans for marketing its mobile editions, executive site, and other projects. Up for grabs were the addresses: which of these made more sense to the average user?

http://globalexecutive.economist.com or
http://www.economist.com/globalexecutive

Each one had its benefits: the former is shorter and more of a distinct departure from the main site, while the latter is more self-explanatory and may be less confusing to non-Web-savvy readers who see an offline ad campaign. While business development lobbied hard for sub domains, arguing that short URLs worked best, the technical team had a steadfast preference for subdirectories, and the intuitiveness of the /area style became the Economist.com naming convention. This eventually carried through to all our sections, including the cities and countries areas when they launched.

Advertising

Economist.com was designed for maximum flexibility with the Internet Advertising Bureau's standard ad sizes of the time. We had comfortable space laid out for 468x60 ads, top and bottom; buttons in either sidebar at 120x60, 120x90, 120x240, 125x125, along with a customized 120x800 skyscraper; room for a spare 120x60 in the top advertising bar; and places to drop in an 88x31 ad button. One of the great benefits of the layout was our ability to add and subtract advertisements, as we needed. The site launched with a handful of the IAB-standard ads, and placement has moved around over time. We have run into trouble more recently, in attempting to integrate large messaging unit ads into our layouts without corrupting our design, which calls for content areas free of commercial interests. Clever solutions have kept the design intact, such as floating right-hand columns and

bottom-of-page placements, but the challenges continue.

All advertisements and sponsorships are clearly marked. The 486 banners were well separated from the rest of the page, the top ad in its dark blue box, the bottom outlined with gray lines. The ads down the right got placed in boxes of their own, with light red borders rather than the black and gray that signified content. Each ad had "ADVERTISEMENT" written above it, in small capital-letter text, and in areas where we had insufficient room for a box around the ad we placed the "ADVERTISEMENT" GIF free-floating above the ad. This separation between content and advertising set the standard for preserving editorial integrity on the site. Later, when sponsorship came into play, we devised similar layouts that included "about sponsorship" links.

A sample "ADVERTISEMENT" box.

design serving content

Page consistency

Independent of content pages, the section indexes – essentially compilations of articles on a single subject – followed the home page's lead; the basic aesthetics would remain the same. The left-hand navigation carried into the article displays, for two reasons:

1. A common scheme made the site easier to follow from page to page.

2. Equally importantly, the nature of the Web made any page a potential entry to the site, and all essential options had to be visible from the first page to the last.

Thus the presence of our main red section navigation and the Library and print edition boxes on all pages. The same went for the status bar, as date-stamping and login status are useful on nearly every page.

Footer

We always assumed we'd have a footer that displayed our copyright and mimicked the main sections of the left-hand nav, and sure enough, that's what we have. Along with it came our legalese in the form of links to our privacy policy and terms and conditions. A link back to the Economist.com home page rounded out the area. We spent some time tinkering with layouts and determining how many links to display, and once the

Fixed width font e-mail

```
PACIFIC VIOLENCE
After the coup in Fiji, an ethnic MILITIA IN THE Solomon Islands seized
control of the capital, Honiara. It captured and then released the
prime minister, Bartholomew Ulufa'alu, saying that parliament should
decide his fate. Fighting between different militias intensified.
- - - - - See article: The storm in the South Pacific -
http://www.economist.com/editorial/justforyou/current/index_st2112.html


- - - - - - - - - - - - - - - - - - - - - - - - - - - - ADVERTISEMENT -

Looking to dolor your lorem ipsum? Look no further? Super Lorem ipsum
is the answer to all your dolor needs! Visit Lorem ipsum and new Lorem
Diluxe at http://www.economist.com/referralID=ecomail
```

Variable width font e-mail

PACIFIC VIOLENCE
After the coup in Fiji, an ethnic MILITIA IN THE Solomon Islands seized
control of the capital, Honiara. It captured and then released the
prime minister, Bartholomew Ulufa'alu, saying that parliament should
decide his fate. Fighting between different militias intensified.
- - - - - See article: The storm in the South Pacific -
http://www.economist.com/editorial/justforyou/current/index_st2112.html

- ADVERTISEMENT -

Looking to dolor your lorem ipsum? Look no further? Super Lorem ipsum
is the answer to all your dolor needs! Visit Lorem ipsum and new Lorem
Diluxe at http://www.economist.com/referralID=ecomail

editorial staff determined its contents, the footer was finished.

In any large-scale site design, the myriad minor details truly give the site its sensible design. Minor details can make or break a design: get enough of them right, and the site will feel vastly improved. Miss too many, and no amount of pretty design can make up for the site's flaws.

> *In any large-scale site design, the myriad minor details truly give the site its sensible design.*

E-mails

Economist.com provides newsletters to approximately one million users via e-mail. Each e-mail arrives with a consistent subject line listing the type of content ("*The World This Week*") and the publishing date. At the time of our launch, we had two standardized, non-customized weekly e-mails, which we put into both HTML and text-based designs. We made an HTML design 600 pixels wide with no right-hand column, in a similar format to our administrative pages, with advertising, and a text newsletter set for 72 characters hard-wrapped.

The dashline style of the text e-mail looked unique, appropriate and clean as long as the reader was viewing it in a 72-character, fixed-width-font e-mail client. In a proportional-width font, the result was quite different.

The design worked fine but the effect was lost. The usability is good, but a less clever design – which we did not consider until after launch, and which is no longer a primary concern, as we migrate toward HTML e-mails that reflect our site style – would have worked even better.

Going Live

With the bulk of the layouts designed and approved, we proceeded to put the site together, and we started aiming for a fall 2000 relaunch. The technical team compiled ColdFusion (CF) modules from the designs' HTML and commenced testing the CMS. A pair of freelancers worked on supplementary pages and areas that needed some attention to detail. I spent much of the summer tracking the CF modules' implementation, fixing HTML errors and guiding developers when we encountered bits that had not been addressed in the initial designs.

The development team did a fantastic job marrying our visuals to their new system, requiring only minimal redesign work to align form and function. I was able to concentrate almost entirely on front-end concerns while our developers got the site up and running. I busied myself with the creation of a style guide for use by the technical and production teams to streamline the development of new pages and features.

As the supplemental elements fell into place, the creation of the back end and ColdFusion modules was nearing beta-test phase. We set a beta-launch deadline for late July and, with a few glitches on the technical side, we got our new site into beta on time. I spent considerable time in the London office in July and August, helping launch the beta designs with a minimum of visual gaffes. By the end of the summer, we had a full development process established, with a posting system that included a multiple-server testing system that eventually relegated page design to a pre-production process. Five designers and thirteen developers had pitched into the site's creation by this point, along with invaluable input from our production and editorial teams. The development team began integrating outside content, such as our news feed (from *http://w.moreover.com/*) and financial market data (from Reuters), along with the Economist.com's CMS. By late August, I had essentially been relegated to a proofreading role, as the front-end development was almost complete.

design serving content

In early September, with the beta site nearly complete and articles being entered into the new CMS, we entered a soft launch phase and opened the new site to our users. We added a pop-up window to the home page of the existing Economist.com inviting our readers to see our new design. We walked the user through several pages and requested feedback in both ranked categories (much better-much worse) and with written notes. We also opened the beta site to the public and allowed users to explore it as though it were live. The resulting feedback was solidly in our favor, and the written responses were largely encouraging. We also learned a lot about our audience and our early mistakes based on the negative response. Among the comments:

> "The navigation is much easier. It's good also to see dates underneath each title."

> "As a long subscriber of The Economist and a regular visitor of the web site, I'd like to [applaud] the new design, and most of all, the constant improvement of quality of the site. Keep up the good work!"

> "The screen really looks cluttered! It's an information orgy. One word: simplify."

> "I love The Economist and I am happy to see that I can now start to use your online edition too."

> "It looks great; many thanks. I am a subscriber to print edition, but this is a great addition."

> "Now The Economist looks just like everyone else: busy graphics, links to newswires, pages needing but not designed for scrolling, and worst of all in an age of branding, no similarity in layout or style to the magazine."

> "Congratulations on your 'New Look'. The site is much easier to use. I will be a more frequent visitor in the future."

> "When did The Economist take an interest in looking like every other American business online magazine? I like change, but the older site is distinct from other online business mags."

> "What have you done to The Economist Web site? Your earlier pin-stripe design was one of the best designed Websites on the Internet. The user interface and the elegant design of your earlier layout was, in my opinion, perfectly suited to a sober, business-minded, and well informed global audience. It had class and credibility. The new Economist Web site is just the opposite."

> "The new Website is a thousand times improved!"

> "I just wanted to write about your new site design. It is superb. I am seriously considering subscribing to the web edition now that is actually easy to use and there are no frames."

Assuming each positive comment carries as much weight as 8 to 10 negative ones – on the theory that people are much faster to send a complaint than a compliment – the notes in our in-box, which had more good remarks than bad, were rewarding and encouraging. The re-launch was go!

The last few weeks went by without much intervention on my part, and over the weekend of October 1, 2000, after eight months of discussion, design and development, the new design was launched. In the New York office, we left on Friday afternoon and came to work the following Monday to a sparkling new site and customer feedback that ran a full 85% in favor of the changes. Site traffic increased 40 percent in the months after the relaunch, from five million to seven million monthly page views, proving we had hit the right notes with our redesign.

Conclusions: Successes and Failures

On the whole, the Economist.com redesign was a rousing success. We brought the site into the present day in terms of design, layout, organization, and interfaces. We greatly increased the visibility of our content and made the site easier to use, from the straightforward navigation and search to the readable Verdana font. Site traffic has continued to increase from the roughly five million page views the month before launch, September 2000, to more than 12 million page views in February 2002. Revenues have increased and feedback from users was, and remains, overwhelmingly positive. The new web-only features, such as the cities guides and Global Executive, were smoothly added to the site and fast became popular additions to the base content. In the time since the relaunch, our design has proved to be strong and flexible; we have added, subtracted, and reorganized our information without breaking the overall scheme and, in the best compliment of all, we managed to reflect the voice and identity of *The Economist* while carving a distinct style for the web site.

Some of the steps we took were less outstanding than others. The table-heavy design of our left- and right-hand boxes looks nice but slows down the page load time, as does the reliance on spacer GIFs. Page weight has peaked and is now, wisely, in decline, but our site has gotten weighted down with our continued expansion. Our use of blue to accent the red/white/black color scheme looked nice at launch, but as austerity has become more popular, we are receiving more negative feedback from our users about the color. Our need to accommodate level 4.x browsers, while important, has slowed our integration of style sheets and JavaScript. And, of course, there are a million little things that one notices when one looks long enough – "that's too much white space!" "Where'd the border on that go?" – but they manage not to detract from the site as a whole.

> *In the end, the reaction of the user base is all that matters, and in our case, reaction skewed about 85% to positive response based on the site traffic of and e-mail sent to Economist.com. No other support is necessary for showcasing our level of achievement.*

Economist.com continues to grow in multiple directions. Recent additions to the site, through winter 2002, include education specials within Global Executive and a bulletin board providing forums for technology and executive features; still more projects are in the works. The overall design of the site continues to evolve, and we are actively working on lessening our reliance on placeholder graphics and nested tables. I have numerous ideas of directions in which I would like to see the site grow, and as a team we continue to search for ways to improve the user experience, from improving load times to simplifying site organization. Our content continues to excel, and it is growing, as all of our Web initiatives – Global Agenda, Global Executive, Cities Guide, and Country Briefings – are producing online-only material. Eighteen months have passed since the debut of our first beta site for the redesign, and the challenge we face is to continue our work so the Economist.com that exists 18 months from now is as much of an improvement as the current site is over its predecessor.

In the end, the reaction of the user base is all that matters, and in our case, reaction skewed about 85% to positive response based on the site traffic of and e-mail sent to Economist.com. No other support is necessary for showcasing our level of achievement.

Ten Lessons Learned

1. **Don't do it alone.**

While I was the creative lead for the project, my role as design director should have more readily embraced the resources that I had at my disposal. I listened to others' opinions (see below) but it took a long time for me to look beyond my own hands and collaborate. Similarly, don't be afraid to work with someone better than you: spending time with a senior-level creative director gave me the fresh perspective and inspiration needed to craft a great site.

2. **Make the most of outside information.**

Absorb the items contributing to the work, from editorial constraints to the subtleties of the print component's design to the atmosphere in the corporate office. Monitor competitors' sites and redesigns. Get demographic user data. Track site usage statistics. Find new tricks in Photoshop. Learn some of the back-end programming language. The more you can understand about the aspects of a site beyond the designer's realm, the more you can successfully channel that energy into the design.

3. **Listen to feedback.**

Everyone in your company, and every one of your users, will have an opinion. Almost all are valid in some way. If a user says, "I think your graphics are ugly," a silent response of "Well, what does that guy know!" is shortsighted. That perspective matters as much as your own, for that person is using the site. Projects get done faster and new ideas come more often when the question posed is "How can this work?" instead of "Why won't this work?" Try to understand the theory and decisions behind other designs, and implement the lessons learned into your own processes. Listen especially to the opinions within the company; these are the people who know the product best and can tell whether the design feels right in context.

4. **Take charge.**

I took a long time to warm to the tasks before me as design director, and I would have been far better off grabbing too many responsibilities at once than trying slowly to get comfortable. When the redesign gets underway, lead meetings. Solicit opinions (as noted above). Look beyond your work before others peer in. Had I done all of this, I might have saved several steps in the design process.

5. **Remember the audience.**

You, the savvy Internet veteran, may not need links underlined to know they're links, but your user base certainly might. Load times, insignificant on a 1.4 ghz Linux machine on a T1, matter to users on dialup AOL accounts. Too much minute text is good for some and terrible for others. I learned quickly at *The Economist* that while I was the site designer I was not its target demographic, and I designed the site to be comfortable for the less web-centric user who would be visiting it most often.

> *Projects get done faster and new ideas come more often when the question posed is "How can this work?" instead of "Why won't this work?"*

6. Don't be afraid to delegate.

I got myself into a lot of trouble when, early in the redesign process, I convinced myself I could do the bulk of the redesign work on my own. The same rule about trusting someone more experienced for guidance applies to your own ability to guide others to execute your vision.

7. Meet your team.

A few days spent in person with coworkers outweigh a year of telecommuting and conference calls. You and your teammates will learn about one other in ways a virtual office cannot express. You need not rely solely on face-to-face interaction; once you've gotten to know someone, their styles and work habits make far more sense from far afield than they did before you met. Take the time early in the project to make the acquaintance of your peers, and maintain those relationships after you're back working from afar.

8. Keep the lines of communication open.

Early in the redesign process I implored the development staff in London to install instant messaging applications on their office PCs. The resulting interaction helped me get to know the other office better and saved us from countless phone calls and lengthy e-mails. One flaw I have unearthed more recently is an over reliance on IM - some questions are far better answered with a simple, short phone call. Vocal interaction still trumps typed responses and emoticons.

9. Give developers exactly what they need.

People work literally when they are implementing something conceived by someone other than themselves. For better or worse, they will do exactly what they are told, particularly when you don't work in the same office. Be sure the designs handed over to a programmer don't include something extraneous or contain any assumptions whatsoever - these things will occur as they appear on a page, right down to the smallest mistake. By the same token, keep an eye on the final output to be sure the goals were met.

10. Maintain a clear version control and approval process.

So many times, before and after launch, an item will get implemented that shouldn't go live, or a decision will be handed down on an incorrect page. Track version numbers of all proposed works and save e-mails that opine or approve. You'll need them to convey instructions to the development staff and to coordinate implementation.

Most of all, don't forget your goals. There is a task to be achieved, and the final product will reflect both your input and the office's final output. Stay intrigued with your work and strive to create a web site that betters anything you've done before.

David Wertheimer's Usable Objects

Pop-top aluminum cans – Remember when opening a can required tearing a sharp-edged metal tab off the top? The pop-top has been such a success that we no longer know any other way.

) site accessible to people with disabilities

Post-It™ Notes – One of the greatest inventions of the last quarter-century is the note pad that sticks without tape and doesn't leave a residue.

Zippers – More secure and insulating than buttons or laces, and the zipper's slow public adoption is a classic case of usability taking a while to take root.

Credit cards – A portable wad of cash, no visits to the bank necessary. Ingenious.

The iPod – It is, in essence, a trendy gadget, but the iPod is so intuitive that after one or two tries, the owner can navigate the entire device without looking.

Courtesy of Apple.

Also:

Car door handles that can be grabbed and pulled from either above or below – So many automobiles have doors with grab-from-underneath handles, but the open-both-ways style is easier and often more visually intriguing.

All cordless and wireless electric/electronic devices – Obvious. Taking a product that needs to be plugged into something else – a phone, a razor, a drill, a computer – and making it work just as well without the wires is as user-friendly as product design can get.

Touch screens – As technology becomes more prevalent in society, tapping directly on a monitor eliminates the need for arrows and "use the buttons at the left" explanations.

eBay™
the world's online marketplace™

kelly braun and tom walter

®

http://www.ebay.com/

Tom Walter has been working with (or for) eBay™ since 1997 when he redesigned the eBay™ home page. As Executive Creative Director, Tom manages a team of a dozen graphic designers who are responsible for all of the visual elements of the eBay™ web site. Tom joined eBay™ from CKS Interactive where he was a Senior Art Director doing online creative design for key clients including Apple, Prudential, Mazda, Silicon Graphics, Hewlett-Packard, and United Airlines.

Tom received his BFA in Illustration/Graphic Design from California College of Arts and Crafts long before computers were used in design. He's also received an advanced degree from the School of Hard Knocks.

Tom has many other interests including creative writing (as proof, his lousy first novel is hidden in his desk drawer), old movies, action figures, his three darling kids, and his wonderful wife Beau.

Kelly Braun has been working for eBay™ since 1999, where she currently manages the Usability Engineering team. Before eBay™, Kelly was a Senior Usability Engineer with Oracle Corporation. She started her career as a software developer with BNR, the research and development arm of Northern Telecom (now known as Nortel Networks). She was awarded a scholarship from BNR that allowed her to pursue her graduate degree on a full-time basis.

Kelly received her Ph.D. in Experimental Psychology from Duke University. Her BS is in Computer Science from Georgia Tech.

Kelly enjoys needlepoint and has won several competitions where her work has been shown. Her most exciting and important design, entitled "Josie", arrived in 2001.

If you weren't doing this, what would you be doing?

Tom: Writing films and/or comic books.
Kelly: I would be teaching – although I do have fantasies about spending entire days doing needlepoint or becoming a pastry chef.

Which living person/people do you most admire?

Tom: My wife – 3 kids under the age of 2 (and a husband who, on occasion, isn't much better). She has the patience of a saint and the strength of Superman.
Kelly: My parents – they've been together 45 years and raised 4 kids in a loving environment. By the time they were my age, they had 2 kids in college. I don't know how they did it all – they are my heroes.

On a scale of 1 (Amish) - 10 (Star Trekkie), how geeky are you?

Tom: I can quote from many *Star Trek* episodes, so you make the call.
Kelly: I'm probably a 7 – My favorite TV show is *Buffy the Vampire Slayer* – does that count as geeky?

What's your favorite building?

Tom: The John Deere Building off Route 83 north of Baltimore, MD. It has this weird undulating roof held together by cables sunk into the ground. As a kid, I always wanted to cut those cables just to see what would happen. Either that, or the Chrysler Building in Manhattan. They just don't build them like that anymore.

What's your favorite book? Piece of music? Type of pizza?

Tom: My favorite book is "A Prayer for Owen Meany" by John Irving, an American writing in the tradition of Dickens. My favorite piece of music is a toss-up between Beethoven's Ninth, Fourth Movement with the "*Ode to Joy*", The Beatles' "*You've Got to Hide Your Love Away*", and Elvis Costello's "*What's So Funny 'Bout Peace Love and Understanding*". My favorite pizza is pepperoni with mushrooms and onions.
Kelly: My favorite pizza is plain cheese pizza from New Jersey like I used to have when I was growing up. I can't watch *The Sopranos* without craving a slice of "real pizza", Jersey style.

If you were a superhero(ine), who would you be?

Tom: The Batman – because he kicks ass and is smart besides.
Kelly: Sarah Connor from T2 (Terminator 2). She's strong, determined, and changes the course of the future.

What gadget could you not live without?

Tom: DirecTV – I love my dish.
Kelly: Tivo – I love Tivo's capabilities, and they did a great job on their UI.

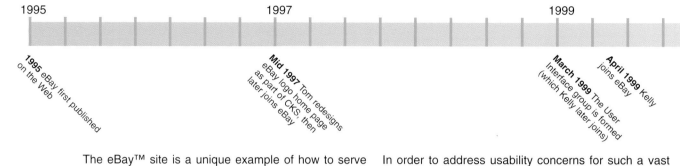

1995   1997   1999

1995 eBay first published on the Web

Mid 1997 Tom redesigns eBay logo home page as part of CKS, then later joins eBay.

March 1999 The User Interface group is formed (which Kelly later joins)

April 1999 Kelly joins eBay

The eBay™ site is a unique example of how to serve an audience appropriately. What makes a case study of eBay™ so important is that, not only is the site almost as old as the Web itself (it was created in 1995), but its user base is enormous – 46 million at the time of writing – and is, demographically, extremely varied.

In order to address usability concerns for such a vast site, eBay™ has developed and integrated two teams, Usability and Design. This model works very well now, but it has taken time to emerge and to be refined. Kelly Braun heads the Usability team and Tom Walter runs the Creative Design team.

eBay™ Home Page, 1995.

2001   2002

1999 Second major site redesign – usability and design begin to merge

2001 eBay site design significantly matured

2002 more new components added to site

History of Design

Tom Walter leads the Creative Design group at eBay™. He offers his perspective in this section.

Since I have been with eBay™ for a while longer than the Usability team, I'll write a bit about the historical and design issues that we've had to deal with, and let Kelly write more about our usability ideology.

I originally worked for an integrated marketing agency called CKS (now defunct). eBay™ came to us about mid-1997 with a project to redesign its logo, which we completed – it's the same logo you see on eBay™ today. eBay™ also wanted us to update its home page to give it a new look that would go with the new logo, and I was one of the art directors given the task.

The eBay™ logo.

I had a whopping two weeks to do the job, on the understanding that the full site would be visually redesigned within six months. I knew little of eBay™'s demographics, apart from a basic idea of what the site was trying to achieve and the brand personality, so I addressed the issue simply by taking the bright colors of the logo and using them to enliven the home page and make it more fun.

However, after all the planning and frantic work that went in to it, the redesign never went ahead, so I ended up with three years in which to look at that home page! I have always maintained that if I'd known I was going to look at it for that long, I would've asked for more time. Still, this was the look that, in many ways, came to symbolize eBay™.

> *Form absolutely must follow function.*

As time has gone by, I've learned some very interesting things about eBay™ and about designing such a huge site with such a huge audience in mind. A major lesson eBay™ has taught me is that form absolutely *must* follow function. My role is to make the site look good without getting in the way of the cash transaction – which is ultimately what eBay™ is about. In my view, although there are a lot of sites that are more elegantly designed than eBay™, there are a greater number of such sites that aren't around any more. The site has grown both organically and exponentially. The visual design was never thought out from first principles – we've been more or less making it up as we went along, working as fast and as furiously as possible! Actually, there are many places where eBay™ looks the same as it did when it launched way back in 1995 – and there's a good reason for that: it works!

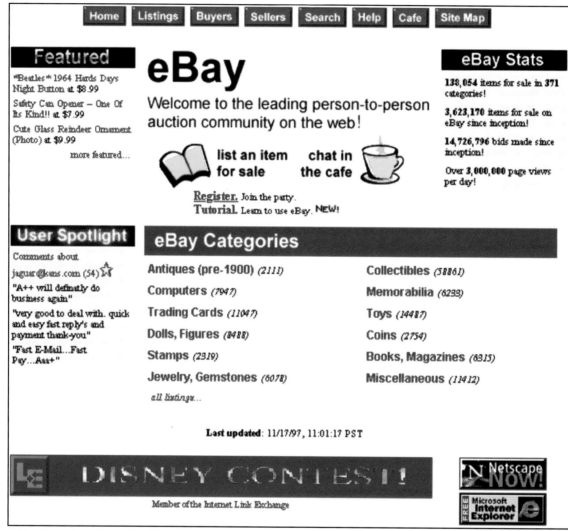

eBay™, early 1997 before Tom's redesign.

The user base of eBay™ is enormous, highly diverse, and somewhat resistant to change. This is natural but it's also very humbling. The minute you start to forget that you are designing for the user community, you will fall on your face. The work we're doing is affecting millions of people on a daily basis. People are making their living on our site – people who have quit their regular jobs, to sell on eBay™ full time. That's a tough order to design for because if you mess it up, you can seriously affect the livelihoods of scores of people – instantly. This is less likely to happen with other e-commerce sites.

One thing I try to keep in mind is the question: are you speaking "with" the person or "at" them? When you speak "with" people, they usually remember what you're saying: when you speak "at" them, it goes in one ear and out the other. We always have to speak with our user base. It's imperative.

We always have to speak with our user base. It's imperative.

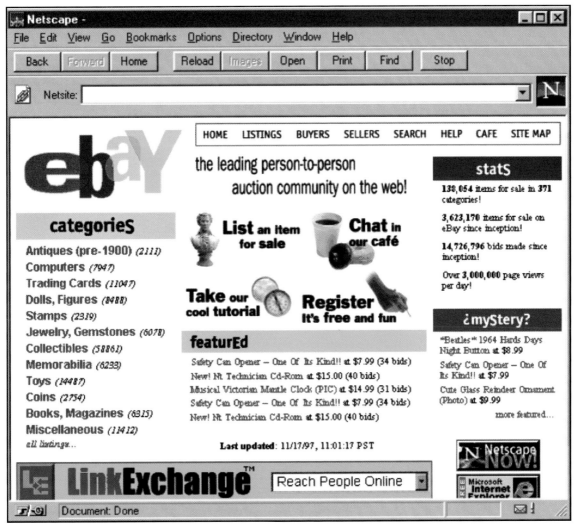

eBay™'s revised home page, 1997.

Before joining eBay™, I worked for CKS, where I did most of eBay™'s banner ads, category pages, and upper-level pages, including the home page. What I wasn't doing was working on any of the lower-level pages – the forms and more function-oriented parts of the site. This was done in-house at eBay™.

eBay™ soon realized it needed someone in house, to get a better grasp on its design. Because I had a deep understanding of what was going on with the site at that point, I was asked to come and work directly for eBay™: I never hesitated.

> *"All of us at eBay™ have to be highly respectful of the elements that have come before. I'm also very careful about any precedents I set. I wasn't that careful when we first started, however, and as a result, some things became legacy issues because of a capricious whim."*

Tom Walter,
eBay™ Executive Creative Director.

Change

I've come to see that change must come about through a genuine need, and that you have to make new introductions gently. This is what our user community is asking for and we understand this. Say you walk into your local supermarket for milk – If they move the milk around each time you visit, you start getting irritated.

Moving Toward Usability

What was interesting was the way that creative design, interaction design, and usability were separated when I first came to eBay™. Creative design was pooled with the marketing department, while anyone working on interaction design or usability issues was in the engineering group – there wasn't any real marriage between the two. However, it was then decided that overall design and usability should be combined into a single group, and it was at this point that we really integrated our goals.

> *The way I see it, usability is, in a sense, the art of keeping those of us in visual and user interface design honest – that's the way a site should be built.*

That was a defining moment for eBay™ in terms of usability. We had the chance to take a look at the entire site. There were some nicely designed pages that weren't at their functional peak, and some functional pages whose visual design had never been touched. We were able to bring everyone together and start to do the work the way it should be done – as a team. The way I see it, usability is, in a sense, the art of keeping those of us in visual and user interface design honest – that's the way a site should be built. UI says how it works, visual design says how it looks, and usability makes sure we're doing it clearly, cleanly, and simply.

eBay™, 1999 – Usability and design begin to merge.

My Creative Design team is like a small agency. We understand many of the usability issues, and know how to design around them. Things like, avoid white text reversed out of red backgrounds, stay away from certain colors, and if something's a link make it look like a link. We try to design to the commonest set of standards we can so that the largest possible number of our users will be able to use and enjoy the site. Our site can be confusing enough at times, so we don't need visual elements compounding the matter.

Something else we've had to learn is that (certainly in our case) web development and redesign is an evolution, not a revolution. A lot of people would probably come in, rip it down, and build it all up again from scratch. While you get a better control of the experience that way, we don't have that luxury. We have to take the clay we've got and craft it into something good. Some people would call that constraining, but I find it another challenge that's inherent in web design, especially in designing a site that's being used by so many people so frequently.

Another issue that makes designing a web interface difficult is screen resolution. It's a bit like doing a print on a balloon: the balloon can be under-inflated, perfectly inflated, or over-inflated, and the pattern on it has to look good in all three states. That makes it difficult to come up with something that not only works but is also visually appealing.

By 2001, the eBay™ look had significantly matured.

Again, form follows function. So many designers forget that they're designing an interface – something that someone is going to use. They get caught up in visual pyrotechnics – "how does this look?" – until this becomes their only criterion for success. If you want to make art, go paint a picture. At eBay™ we're designing software – software that people use daily for their livelihood. That's a huge responsibility.

> *If you want to make art, go paint a picture. At eBay™ we're designing software – software that people use daily for their livelihood. That's a huge responsibility.*

We still have a long way to go. We'd like to make the site a lot simpler to use. I think we've made great strides in cleaning it up from a visual perspective. A lot of the pages not only look better but they also work better. It's a slow and patient process – as far as visual design is concerned, we will probably never be able to unveil a complete redesign.

The challenge for a lot of designers is that of keeping the design simple. Always look at what you can pull off a page, as well as what you can put on it.

eBay™ 2002 – Note the integration of earlier components with new components.

Enter Usability

Kelly Braun, PhD, leads Usability efforts at eBay™. She offers her perspectives in this section. Kelly's PhD is in Experimental Psychology – her area of specialization is Cognitive Psychology.

The User Interface (UI) Group, as we were originally called, was created in March of 1999 and lived under the Product Development organization in the engineering arm of the company. The UI group started with three functional sets of people: usability engineers, interaction designers, and those software engineers who specialized in writing the code for the interface.

Tom Walter's Tips for Design

Here are a few quick tips from Tom Walter for designing a site of any kind:

- Putting on a fresh look does not make up for stale content.

- In a commerce site such as eBay™, form must follow function. This is not art in the traditional sense.

- Keep things simple.

- Ask yourself what you can take off a page as well as what you can put on it.

- If you're not improving something by changing it, don't change it.

- Don't let visual elements get in the way of the site's main goals and function.

- Introduce new things gently if you have a well-established audience.

The original development engineers, who had been working on the site and creating the user interface from the beginning, had good usability instincts but the site was growing so quickly we had challenging usability issues coming up constantly.

When I was interviewed for the job at eBay™, I thought the way the UI department was being built was really innovative. Usability, interaction design, and development were all reporting into a first line of management. A problem many usability groups have is that when they identify a usability project they then have to sell it to a development group in order to get those changes built. eBay™'s new UI group was going to have all the resources in one place – I knew I wanted to work in that type of structure. I also wanted to work at eBay™ because I thought it provided the most challenging usability issues I had seen anywhere.

So, what makes eBay™ such a challenging usability environment? One factor is the sheer scale of things. How do you scale the interface for new users while not hindering the experience for existing ones? We have over 42 million registered users. Originally our users were collectors with *lots* of incentive to find that *magical item*. However, as the site grew and became the cultural bazaar that it is today, more and more people wanted to try it out. These people may not have been as motivated to find things as the pioneers were, because they didn't know everything eBay™ had to offer them. Furthermore, as more people tried the site, more items became available for sale. We didn't want to lose users because they were overwhelmed by the sheer volume of items we had on offer; that's one of the things that makes eBay™ such a fabulous site: you can find practically anything for sale. But that abundance could make finding a specific item difficult.

Our users determine what is up for sale at any time. They also determine how to categorize those items and how to advertise them with their listings. This means that eBay™ can provide structure and suggestions, but ultimately it's the user who is filling its shop window. So unlike most e-commerce sites, we need to create an interface not just for people trying to buy something but also for people who want to sell something. This adds more complexity and another serious challenge for the usability team. How do we create tools to help users list over one million new items each day?

eBay™'s user community is very diverse. There are sellers who make their living on eBay™ as well as sellers who sell just a few items once in a while. There are buyers looking for a prized collectible as well as buyers looking for a great deal on a commodity item like a PDA. There are people who use WebTV or bought their first computer to use eBay™ as well as corporate and government entities that have found eBay™ to be a most effective product distribution channel. Each of these user groups has different needs and expectations from the eBay™ interface.

> *We've all heard the comments about "Internet time" – how fast development must be to stay up-to-date – it really is true at eBay™.*

Over time, as the UI group grew, the organization evolved into what is now called "eBay™ Design Labs". The Design Labs organization combined the usability and interface design resources with the creative design resources in Tom's group. While the development resources are no longer in our group, we still have no problem getting development resources for usability features. The corporation made the commitment that usability and design were vital aspects of our business success.

I think this new organization strengthens the bonds between all design and usability components. The commitment from the corporation to build such an organization reinforces the importance of the User and means that eBay™ has a very user-centric design.

Usability in No Time

We've all heard the comments about "Internet time" – how fast development must be to stay up-to-date – it really is true at eBay™. I've worked in packaged software and by comparison, Internet development is done in an incredibly fast pace. We needed to adapt our usability methodologies to accommodate our rapid development environment: we do not have weeks to complete studies or create reports. Sometimes we are testing concepts as they are evolving. We want to keep a history of what we've tried and why we've chosen not to go in that direction but we can't spend a lot of time creating an archive.

Some of the methodologies and test considerations we've found successful are discussed below.

Diverse Participants

As mentioned earlier, eBay™ has a very diverse user population. We try to ensure that this diversity is represented in our testing. Three broad user groups are usually included in every test: Newbies, Buyers, and Sellers.

- The "Newbies" group has no eBay™ experience whatsoever. They've never used eBay™ before. They represent people having their first time experience with eBay™, an experience that could make or break their future relationship with eBay™.

- The "Buyers" group has used eBay™ as a Buyer. They have looked around eBay™ and are familiar with the eBay™ idioms and concepts.

- The "Sellers" group is the most experienced. Most eBay™ sellers start out as eBay™ buyers. They usually have a solid understanding of eBay™ concepts. Some sellers use additional tools to manage their sales or create their eBay™ listings.

We will also test products and features that are geared towards a specialized population; for example, tools that help volume sellers manage their businesses. We would test users who already use other business management tools as well as sellers who don't. We want to make sure that our features are usable for everyone who might want to use them.

If your products are geared towards a diverse population, be sure to test a representative sample of that diversity. Different user groups may find different usability problems.

> *If your products are geared towards a diverse population, be sure to test a representative sample of that diversity. Different user groups may find different usability problems.*

Prototype Testing Methodologies

When we have a feature that requires a lot of user interaction – for instance, refining searches – we create a prototype of that functionality and employ rapid iterative testing methods to see how well it works. This gives us the opportunity to study how a user really interacts with the system and what happens if we make changes to it.

Creating highly interactive prototypes, especially ones that need to mimic database functionality, is expensive and time consuming. We only use highly interactive prototypes when the feature being tested requires this high level of interactivity to properly gauge user responses. Search is a perfect example: without a high level of interactivity it would be difficult to test tasks like refining searches. However, for activities that do not require high level of interaction, like completing a form, we use simpler HTML prototypes.

Good Old Usability Testing

We also do the standard usability test with about eight users. I think usability tests are best when you are looking to find out *why* people are having a problem. Just identifying that people are having a problem is not enough. You want to make sure you know why so that you can modify the design accordingly.

People new to usability testing often scoff at the idea that eight users would be enough to identify issues. They mistakenly think that results need to be "statistically significant". The first thing you have to accept is that usability test data is never statistically significant and there is no need for it to be. Usability tests gather data to help identify problems and possible solutions. Looking for statistical metrics instead of how to fix the problem defeats the purpose of usability testing.

We do usability testing on prototypes and on live features. We also do usability testing when we roll out a new feature. We often put new features out as a beta and during this beta period we collect live data from the site, as well as doing lab usability testing.

We use "think aloud" methodology in most usability tests. This is where we ask the users to say what they are thinking out loud as they work through the test tasks. The exception is when we do baseline testing that captures timing data for later comparison. Think aloud methods do slow down performance time because people are talking about what they are doing rather than just doing it, but I have found that detailed thoughts from the user about how they find the interface as they are actually using it are more meaningful and helpful for our needs.

Surveys

Surveys are not always thought of as usability tools, since they are normally employed more for marketing-related tasks – asking users about their likes and dislikes. However, we have found that carefully constructed surveys can provide good usability data. Surveys can be used to validate and expand upon user requirements. They are particularly useful when paired with previews of new features or design ideas. However, you need to avoid just asking the user whether they like something: you need to get at the specifics of their likes and dislikes if the answers they give are going to be helpful.

Site Performance Data

Another rich usability data source is the site itself. We can track how many times buttons or links are clicked and how many times pages are accessed. We can track (on an aggregate basis) how users get to a page and where they go from that page. So while we do not know an individual's path through the site we can tell that X users started on page Y and X minus n proceeded to page Z. If the goal of the page is to move people from Y to Z, the usability goal is to reduce the number of people (n) who do not get to that goal.

Because of eBay™'s scale we have to remember that making a feature more usable for even 1% of our population can mean we are improving our interface for nearly *half a million* people. But we need to know the starting point in order to measure the change. Collecting baseline data is necessary if you want to know the impact you have made.

A recent example is the redesign of our "Sell Your Item" form. This is the form sellers fill out to list an item for sale. We collected web log data and found out how many people accessed the form, went through the process of filling it out, and successfully listed their item for sale. We also found out how often the form was accessed but not successfully completed. Once again because of the scale of our site, if we increase the

success rate by just 1% we can potentially increase the number of items listed in one day by 10,000 items.

Reporting

My staff and I come from Experimental Psychology backgrounds. We were raised to "document the life out of" every study we ever did, but this is neither possible nor necessary for usability testing at eBay™. We need to get usability findings and design recommendations to teams within 24 hours of the last participant, and we usually test all participants over a 2 day period, so that doesn't leave much time for write-ups.

We have found a few quick ways to record data that have helped. One is to create a matrix with usability problems and which test participants had the problems – at one glance we can see where the problems lie. We start the list of issues with problems we think may occur and add to this list as new issues are observed. In this form, data can be reported immediately to teams. We also have it captured for archive purposes.

Dealing with Scalability

As eBay™ grew, we found that the original interface did not always scale, especially as the number of items available on the site increased. We need to design with an eye towards the future, knowing that the number of items and users will continue to grow.

One example I like to use relates to the number of categories of items listed on eBay™. There are currently over 18,000 categories. Obviously we didn't start with that many. One of the "old-timers" told me that the original way to choose a category when listing an item for sale was to pick from a list of radio button choices. As the number of categories grew, so did this page until there were about 350 radio buttons on this one page!

The interface was then changed to be a drop-down list for each of the eleven top-level categories. Each drop-down list contained around 30 categories – more than your standard amount, but certainly better than 350 radio buttons.

When I got here in 1999, the drop-down menu was still used to choose from over one thousand categories. The drop-downs had more than 100 categories in them. Needless to say this was becoming unwieldy. We designed another interface, this time using JavaScript. While JavaScript was fairly pervasive on the Web by this time, we needed to ensure that those who did not have JavaScript could still list an item. We provided a link to the old drop-down method of selecting a category for those who did not have JavaScript.

Another misconception about "Internet time" is that you can be more experimental with interfaces on the Web. This may be true for some sites but eBay™ is a user transaction based e-commerce site. eBay™ provides a site where individuals can transact business. When we make changes to the interface, there is the potential for those changes to affect how our users do their business. We take this into account whenever we make changes to the site.

> *At eBay™ any feature that influences the user interaction or could affect the user's ability to buy or sell an item, receives a usability review.*

A good lesson for any web designer or usability specialist is to prioritize what needs attention first based on the needs of your users and your business. For instance, at eBay™ any feature that influences the user interaction or could affect the user's ability to buy or sell an item, receives a usability review. We give top priority to

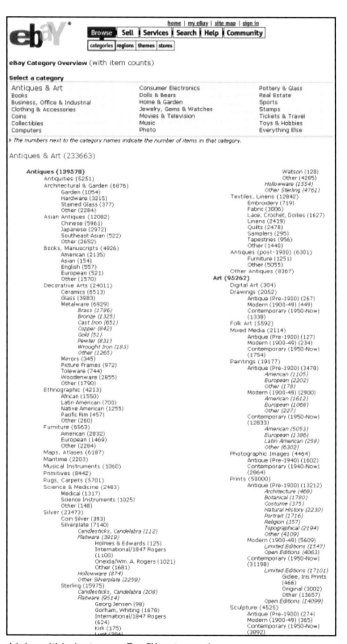

Links within just one eBay™ category!

the interface elements involved with buying, selling, and displaying items.

A good example of this is the "Sell Your Item" Form. This is the form sellers fill out to describe the item they are offering for sale. For this form we used a variety of the usability testing methods mentioned above. We prototyped the new design before it was developed. Testing on this prototype gave us very early feedback. We were able to create solutions for problems found at this early stage before they were developed into the system. We also did a beta release where we solicited user feedback as well as lab testing on the beta. This allowed us to design solutions that would be implemented before the feature was fully rolled out. We used surveys to get feedback from users trying out the beta.

Usable Discoveries, Usable Technologies

Users often use features differently from how we expect them to when we design them. This is an interesting phenomenon, and something we need to be aware of and learn from.

For instance, we were looking at redesigning our *View Item* page. This is the page you see when you look at an individual item that is for sale – the seller creates the item description part of the page and decides what category to list the item in – we do not control this. There's a portion of information at the top that eBay™ specifically asks for in the "Sell Your Item" form. We populate the top of the *View Item* page with this information.

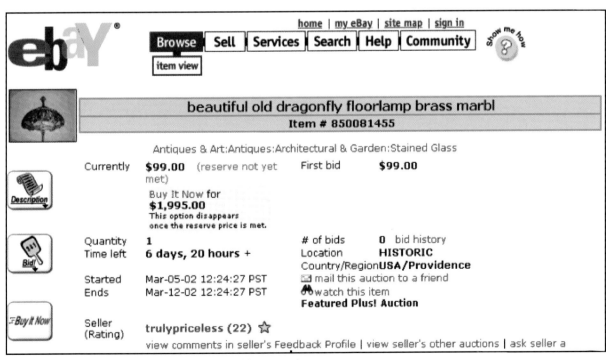

A View Item page – Note the description and item number.

We were moving information around on the page and discovered that if we moved the item number from it's current location it made it harder for seller's to cut and paste the title and number into the e-mails they sent to their buyers. We decided not to make this change because it affected the usability of the page. I think this is a great example of why you shouldn't make design changes without evaluating the usability implications. Assumptions don't work; you must know what your user population is doing in order to serve them best.

We have to be very careful about the changes we make and the technologies we use. For example, we haven't used Flash yet for anything that is a critical piece of interface. Our data indicates that about 80 percent of our users' browsers support Flash, but we wait until a technology is *really* reliable across platforms and browser types before we consider using it on eBay™ (that is, when the figure is closer to 100%). We also try to provide ways for people to use the site without needing the newest technology. Our JavaScript category selector mentioned earlier is a good example. We continue to support the drop-down box solution for those without JavaScript.

Kelly Braun's Usability Tips for Transaction-Based Sites

The following tips can help designers and developers address concerns when building, designing, redesigning, or testing transaction-based sites.

- Remember the purpose of your site. If yours is a transaction-based, revenue generating site you need to be concerned with enabling that business. Slick graphics and cool technologies are fun but they shouldn't hinder the real goal of your users. On eBay™, the goal is to allow users to buy or sell things.

- Provide simple flows for people to follow. Make tasks obvious. Direct people towards their goals.

- Make things easy to read - not just in terms of language, but font size: don't use tiny text.

- Don't make the user think about the interface or about how your site works. You want the user to concentrate on the content of your site, not the interface.

- Wherever possible, reduce the cognitive load for the user. Give users choices rather than blank slates. Pre-fill forms with the data you already know.

- Follow standard metaphors! Don't use obscure references for your shopping cart. Call it a shopping cart. Don't re-invent something that already works. It's fine to borrow ideas from the bricks and mortar world if they work.

- Get user feedback. Find out what works and what doesn't.

- Study user performance. How long does it take to perform a given task? The time it takes to do things has got to be reasonable.

- When people make a mistake try to provide plenty of ways to help them out of it. For example, use clear error messages and on-line help.

122

Managing Challenges

So what do people really feel about using eBay™? What are their complaints and praises? Tom Walter addresses design and feedback concerns in this section.

When you have a user base of 42 million, you're not going to please everyone. We don't get too many consistent complaints about the visual elements of the site, and when we do there isn't generally a common thread. A user often complains about something else on the site, and criticizes the look and feel of it, in passing. There have been some amusing complaints about the use of color on the site – as in, "Hey what's with all that yellow?", referring to the predominant use of yellow on the site. As I said earlier, we used the colors from the logo throughout the site to create a strong sense of brand. When we first introduced the dominant yellow color, someone asked if we didn't have any *more* colors in our Crayola box. At one point, we tried to put cartoon illustrations in the navigation bar, but members of our community said they found these infantile. This kind of feedback is important because you don't want to talk down to your audience.

I'm personally very proud of the form designs that we've done. It may sound trivial, but visually designing the input forms is one area where graphic design is able to improve even the functional pages, and make them look really good.

When it comes to managing design and usability challenges, sometimes the pendulum swings one way, then another. There were times when we conceived specialty sites to be very different to the main eBay™ site. We ultimately found that there was much more power being in the core eBay™ design than carving off and trying to do the "And Now For Something Completely Different" thing. We were trying to create different looks and behaviors as a strategy for business reasons, but it just didn't hold as much water as we thought it would.

eBay™ Japan – The colors are slightly more muted, but the look and feel are basically the same.

Another challenge for us is creating international versions of the site. When we first rolled out all of our country sites, we used the same home page template and allowed them to be localized. So the idea was that the look and feel would change as needed, but all the tools would be the same. We then decided that there should be a more consistent look to keep the brand consistent worldwide, so we unified them. For us, localizing a site became an issue of content and not design. We do allow cultural differences to manifest – for example, color means very different things in different markets.

For example, the Japanese tend to respond better to softer colors, as opposed to primary ones, so the Japanese eBay™ site makes more use of softer pastels than bold primaries.

Conclusion

Generally, the user feedback we get is extremely helpful and insightful. Both Kelly and I are very, very proud to be a part of the eBay™ team and to be working on what is a revolutionary site in so many ways: we are serving people – many of whom have made real life and work changes as a result of eBay™.

The Design Soul of Tom Walter

Disposable Diapers – Worth their weight in gold if you know what I mean.

Light Switch - Very easy interface, either on or off (unless you have 2 switches controlling the same light).

Also:

The Macintosh – Again, very easy interface and seems to be the computer for the rest of us.

The Etch-A-Sketch™ – Very easy to understand yet maddening to control. We've all tried the simultaneous knob turn to create a curve.

The Design Soul of Kelly Braun

Velcro – Functional and simplistic.

3.5 inch "floppy disk" – I started my career with floppies that were floppy! These are tough, can be transported without damaging them, and fit into the disk drive in only one way – they are foolproof.

Disposable diapers – as a new mom I can't imagine life without them.

Also:

Post-It Notes – Taking a failure (glue that didn't stick) and turning it into a useful product – no functional fixedness for 3M!

SynFonts

Flash is 99% OK

don synstelien

http://www.synfonts.com
http://www.synstelien.com

Don Synstelien has been an Interactive Creative Director, Design Director and a Freelance Interactive Developer since 1992. In addition, he served some time doing print design before computers became popular and teaching teachers how to best use digital media when computers were first introduced into the classroom.

His work on SynFonts has spanned his interactive career and will likely continue to progress as long as people are interested in his growing type library.

In addition to his own company – SynFonts, he has produced work for companies such as 3M, Trilogy, IBM, Lucent, AT&T, Pillsbury, Motorola and many others. He currently works and resides in Atlanta Georgia where he is busy helping to create dot-com failures and is seriously considering buying a boat and becoming a pirate for a living.

You can learn more about his work and get tips, tricks and free fonts and images from his web site located at *http://www.synstelien.com*.

If you weren't doing this, what would you be doing?

Consulting for Enron.

Which living person do you most admire?

I most admire those men and women who marched into the destruction of the World Trade Center to save people and those like them who risk their lives every day in the same venture. Fire Fighters and Police Officers place our lives before their own, and that kind of selflessness goes beyond any other. I am moved to tears every time I think of the will and self-sacrifice that it would take to march into certain death on the hopes of saving someone that you don't even know.

On a scale of 1 (Amish) - 10 (Star Trekkie), how geeky are you?

I've done a lot of demo work. Things like handheld computer-based web sites and programs that wow the audience, impossible ideas and dreams of the future, seemingly realized today. These ideas in themselves are too far ahead of the curve to be widely useful, but they often help to sell a more realistic project to a client. This kind of work also lends itself to buying the newest toys right after they come out so that I can stay on the cutting edge. Once you get started on this, it's an addiction that's hard to stop. As a result, I sleep on a pile of these discarded techno toys. So I guess that makes me a 14.

What's your favorite building?

The Stratosphere in Las Vegas – the idea of a roller coaster 1000 feet in the air is so completely original. The whole building is designed around the idea of having fun.

What's your favorite book? Piece of music? Type of pizza?

Book: Invisible Monsters by Chuck Palahniuk, but this changes with almost every book that I read, this just happens to be my current favorite. Music: I have no one favorite piece. It all depends on my mood, I have music in my collection ranging from "A Boy named Sue" by Johnny Cash to "Ziggy Stardust" by David Bowie and tons in-between. Pizza, however, is a very religious topic. There is no pizza like a good piece of Big Fred's pizza located at 120th and Pacific in Omaha, Nebraska.

If you were a superhero who would you be?

Tough question. I have the heroes that I admire, Captain America, Superman, The Tick. But I have way too much of a dark side. I'd probably be more like Frank Miller's Batman. But for utility's sake I'd probably choose Reed Richards of the Fantastic Four above all others... think of the implications! I could reach a soda from the kitchen without getting out of my seat.

127

Flash is 99% OK

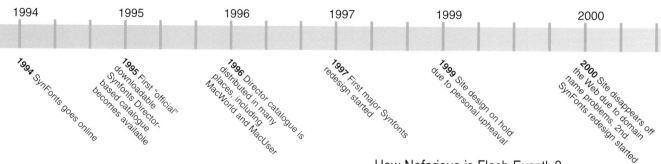

1994
1994 SynFonts goes online

1995
1995 First "official" downloadable Synfonts Director-based catalogue becomes available

1996
1996 Director catalogue is distributed in many places, including MacWorld and MacUser

1997
1997 First major Synfonts redesign started

1999
1999 Site design on hold due to personal upheaval

2000
2000 Site disappears off the Web due to domain name problems, 2nd SynFonts redesign started

A Potted History

1994

SynFonts is created, offering typefaces for sale over the Internet via AOL, eWorld, Compuserve and local user groups and bulletin boards using the shareware sales model. Later in the year a prototype web site is created to explore the idea of web sales, but it is never released. The Internet is still a playground for hobbyists and early adopters and there are no WYSIWYG programs to develop with, so building a web site is frustrating and difficult.

My focus at this time is on "cool" graphics. "Usability" as a buzzword is years away from entering the mainstream. I was publishing a 'zine called @Type.New that showcased my type designs and served as a downloadable catalog.

1995

I begin toying with Macromedia Director to make the @Type.New catalogs more robust. The first "official" SynFonts downloadable Director-based catalog (which behaved similarly to how a Flash file does today) is released and wins a silver award in the Optima Design contest held by MacWorld magazine.

How Nefarious is Flash Exactly?

I'm not into absolutes. Flash is just a tool, and tools are always at the mercy of the people who wield them. There are a lot of Flash based sites that are total garbage, but that's not the fault of Flash... heck, there are a lot of straight HTML sites that are garbage also. I'd say that Flash is as nefarious as any other tool in a web designer's arsenal. And furthermore, this doesn't necessarily make web designers the bad guys either... We're *inventing* how this stuff gets done right now, and this is merely an inherent problem with developing something so early in the timeline of a technology. Think back to the early days of television, or even printing. Was the quality as good as it is today? Hardly.

In this chapter, I will attempt to solve all the Flash usability problems you will ever have. Period.

What can I Expect from Reading this Chapter?

In this chapter, I will attempt to solve all the Flash usability problems you will ever have. Period.

Well, most of them, anyway. Furthermore, I'm going to do this at no cost to you beyond the cost of this book. How will I do this? I'm going to tell you about my mistakes. I'm going to let you in on all the things that I've found out that I didn't know. I'm going to lay myself bare.

synfonts.com has gained a reputation for being a good example of a simple, **usable** Flash-based web site. It

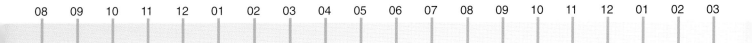

isn't perfect, but it's good. A lot of sites that have armies of experts working on them strive to be this simple and fail. This site was funded, designed, and built by a one-man army... and a lot of time learning from mistakes and listening to input from volunteers. Hopefully in this chapter you'll see how anything can be done if you're willing to make mistakes and learn from them.

When I started designing this site in the first place, I knew nothing about web sites. I hadn't written any HTML and I had no preconceptions of what it could be. None of the technology required for the final build existed when my project started and there wasn't anybody in the world that knew enough Flash to create any of the files that the site would eventually require.

This is true because the design for this site started back in 1994. I could not have created the current version without everything that I learned along the way. Each design iteration or site update would give me new insight to what worked and didn't work from a user perspective. Each misstep or award-winning accomplishment would evoke responses from a faceless audience that would voice accolades or complaints on seeing each new creation. And it's only by listening to the feedback of users and volunteers that I have made any real improvements to the site.

This sort of experimentation was common in 1994 and in many respects remains a commonly-used tool in the toolbox of almost any interactive designer to this day. However, when I started this site, professional web design didn't even exist, and it is arguably still developing as a craft today.

A Potted History (continued)

Also at this time, I make arrangements with a few publishers to distribute both the catalog and typeface samples on the CD-Rom media that is becoming a popular addition to books and magazines during this time. The look and feel of the catalog is very nice but does not translate to the Web. Later in the year I release the first public SynFonts web site. The site opens up a new world of customers. Until this time, sales have been almost exclusively North American. To make Internet ordering easier, I apply for a merchant account and take orders using a non-secure email form!

1996

By mid-year the Director catalog was being distributed in MacWorld, MacUser, The Net and Nautilus Magazines and the Adobe Type and Illustrator Magic books and had also been featured in the book *In Your Face – the Best of Interactive Interface Design (Daniel Donnelly, Rockport Publishers, ISBN: 1564962601).*

The Internet is now advancing daily in the area of technological possibilities so I begin to experiment with appropriate plug in technologies as they surfaced. I start to explore and implement "plug ins" into the web site, and finally settled on utilizing Shockwave for Director (which turned out to be far too large to use effectively), and Shockwave for Freehand (a vector image plug in much like Flash is today, but far less powerful).

Flash is 99% OK

A Potted History (continued)

Interactivity in 1996 (outside the standard underlined link) is fairly uncommon on a web site, so I also begin to experiment with different ways to entice people to explore each interface. Mostly this consists of making buttons that beg to be clicked, but occasionally leads to artwork that is too big to be effectively downloaded.

Since most visitors don't have the plug ins installed when first visiting the site and the download times for the plug ins is quite long, I develop non-plug in alternative content. The plug in content actually causes people to leave the site.

The web site moves to *www.synfonts.com* and I begin to understand the power of the web. The offline catalogue makes sales, but I never know who is looking at it or how they received it unless I ask. But the web site allows me to process the user logs and determine how many people visit and from where they are coming. This gives me the ability to start understanding my visitors better. I also start doing more research on how people feel about the designs that I'm using; I ask for harsh and honest reviews from friends and associates.

Later in the year, online ordering is implemented using a third-party sales agent that provides secure immediate downloads, but takes a hefty percentage of the profits.

Who am I and Why Should you Listen to Me?

Many of the people who I have worked with have described me as a digital "renaissance man". I write, design, create, consult, and code. Some of these things I do better than others, but I can do all of them when I need to. I've developed these widely varied talents because of my unique professional "upbringing." I've had jobs in education, advertising, and programming. I've worked for large companies and I've been self-employed. I've been both a peon and a king. But because most of the time I'm the one on the line if a project is left unfinished, I've always had to be the guy that gets things done.

I have worked on projects for Audi, 3M, Clarus, Trilogy, IBM, BMC Software, Sevista, ScoreBoard, The Ford Motor Company, Nortel Networks, Lucent, Pillsbury, and many others. I've won awards both for work that I have contributed to and for work that I have completed alone. I have been published in books on the subjects of interface design and type design.

But with all my experience in creating digital media, I don't really have any formal training in usability. And since most usability experts that I know tend to come from an academic background, that pretty much means that I'm not really qualified to tell you anything about usability. So take everything I say with a pinch of salt.

If you have ever sat with me in a meeting you will remember me as the guy who never said anything was impossible, but instead approached each problem trying to figure out if there was a way to make it possible. By approaching everything with an open mind and a lot of the right questions, you can often drill down and find out a new way of tackling a problem that makes things possible even when nobody else can see a way to do them. This is as true for solving usability issues as it is for anything else.

Many professionals that I have encountered in the interactive industry, however, are afraid to take this kind of approach. People generally prefer to stick with what they know rather than accepting the idea that they may not really know the answer. Since this approach generally tends to question the very fiber of what we think we know, it tends to open up a lot of opportunities to appear ignorant about your profession.

Enjoy reading about my site. I hope that you walk away with something useful.

What is SynFonts?

SynFonts is an experimental font company, created by and selling the designs of Don Synstelien... me. Get it? **Syn**stelien+**Font** Foundry = **SynFonts**!

I started designing type in 1994 on a shareware basis, providing designs by trust to the world at large, with no guarantee that any of them would actually give me any money. Back in 1994, this was a fairly rare thing to do, I recall that back then there were only a handful of people releasing shareware typefaces, maybe a couple hundred souls at most. Looking around the web today, you can find tens of thousands of freeware and shareware typefaces designed by a wide number of designers. On one site there are listings for 1200 individual type designers and another site showcases a study estimating the total number of unique typeface designs in the world to be an astounding 500,000 typefaces! How long do you think it will take Microsoft Word to load with that many fonts installed?

But SynFonts has been more than just a typeface design project for me. It has been my experimental test bed for trying out new technology and theories almost since day one. Every time I would get artist's block or buy some new software package I would invariably find my way to redesigning some aspect of the site or producing some new interactive catalog. Better to experiment here than on a client's project, right?

When the web came along and I started really getting involved in developing HTML, I noticed that it was different from anything else that I had ever worked on before, not only in the infuriating sense that nothing

A Potted History (continued)
1997

With the site in need of an update and the electronic downloadable catalog even more out of date, I decide to revamp every aspect of SynFonts. I redesign everything from the web site and electronic catalog to the printed catalog, t-shirts and advertising in an attempt to unify the brand experience. While the site did not win any major awards, it did gain a reputation for being one of the best examples of a type web site on the Internet from several independent sources. In order to receive more information from my users, I place a form that invites feedback as an option on the homepage.

The use of plug in technology is still being explored. The first iteration of Macromedia's Flash technology (called Futuresplash at the time) is released and I incorporate it into the site. The Futuresplash plug in is so small that I decide to test whether people are ready to be required to download a small plug in to reach content. When it turns out that they are almost violently opposed to the idea, I implement alternative content immediately.

I decide to try my hand at building e-commerce directly into the site. I succeed in creating an application that provides secure connections, but I have no luck at building online fulfillment for the orders that are taken. I end up becoming a slave to my e-mail and phone line, watching them for orders wherever I am and whatever time of day it happens to be.

A Potted History (continued)
1998

The Internet had spawned an unexpected boon in free advertising, but the company name "SynFonts" places me near the bottom of most lists – most of which tend to be alphabetical. To counter this, Chris MacGregor and I start a new company called "About Type". To simplify the ordering process on the SynFonts site and to make a stronger value proposition for font sales, I reduce sales to collections of typefaces that are sold in bundles of ten. People come in expecting to buy one typeface for $39.00 and instead end up buying it for $49.00 and getting nine more for free. Since most of my sales are made out of an immediate impulse need for the client and not from repeat orders, this also increases the average sale and the happiness of most customers at the same time.

I decided that, since most people were not using the plug in content, it really didn't make sense to build it into the site. To keep things simple, I removed any interactive content from the site and reduced the previews to a very simple GIF image use only. This sped up downloads and ensured nearly universal browser compatibility. The original 1998 redesign highlights only these collections. While this technically allowed me to show the items for sale, it doesn't allow anyone to view an individual typeface. I redesign the site to showcase each typeface individually and upload the site again mid-year.

Late in the year I make a career move and take a break from freelancing. I move to Atlanta, Georgia and become an Interactive Creative Director for Caribiner International. The move allows me new opportunities in exploring digital media that I would have never had as a freelancer.

ever seemed to work perfectly, but also in the way that as a project, my site was never really 'finished'. All I had to do to release a bug fix or new update was to simply re-upload the affected pages and my updates were complete and implemented worldwide.

I redesign the site as often as I have time. This usually translates to about once a year. In between these updates, I do a lot of tracking of information and little tweaks of the layout and functions that make up the site. But the biggest challenge is always those times when I have to reinvent the whole design. Since neither SynFonts nor the type design behind it is a full-time occupation for me, I spend only a little time working on the site each year, really just a handful of hours each month. The times that I usually end up doing the updates strangely coincide with periods in my career where I have a bit of spare time between clients. But these redesigns are almost always more fun than work, so I always look forward to them.

The following is a pretty good account of the process that I had to go through in order to create the latest update for the SynFonts site.

Time for a Redesign

In late 2000 I decided to rectify the problem that had been going on with the SynFonts web site for almost a year. Since early 2000, the site had consisted of a redirect page that sent traffic to a reseller of my typefaces. I had been too busy on a couple of projects that were going on at Talisman Creative to do anything about it until this time. For the latest redesign of SynFonts I had several challenges ahead of me. There was the idea of rebuilding the reputation that I'd had for having a site that provided an entertaining and rewarding interactive experience. Previous versions of the site had received awards, and I kept getting ego-swelling e-mails that constantly reminded me that my placeholder site needed replacement soon.

I had been experimenting with building better technology into the site that would allow for more comprehensive viewing of the typefaces that I had to sell, I felt that the GIF images and JPEG files that I had been using could be improved on with the right technology. I really wanted to implement an interactive type viewer, allowing people to pull up a font they were interested in buying and grow it, shrink it, and change the font weight so they would have a better idea of what the typeface looked like in detail. But I didn't want this to be just any type viewer, as there are already several of those on the Internet. I wanted to create it in such a way that it would be easy for me to update the next time that I had typefaces to add, and I also intended to make sure that the average end user didn't have any plug in hoops to jump through if they weren't so inclined.

I wanted to make something that was completely modular and would facilitate a site re-design without a complete reprogramming. Creating a completely modular site might also create a revenue stream by allowing the possible sale or lease of the technology to another type design company or font reseller.

I also wanted to create a site that would surpass most, if not all, of the sites that other type companies had. With the many high-caliber sites that have sprung up in the past few years, this would be a pretty daunting task. There were some big names that had finally managed to produce truly outstanding web sites that incorporated some kind of type viewer engine. Each of these had some sort of shortcoming that left me wanting more. Some sites had limited functionality, allowing the entry of a single line of text and no ability to view the font in detail. Other sites had very complex technology (server-side scripting that generated gif images on the fly), poor display technology or were hard or unsatisfying to use for some reason. I wanted to do better.

The main challenge was that all this had to be completed with little or no additional investment beyond the standard hardware and software costs for equipment and programs that I already owned, and not much of an investment of time. Any time devoted to this project would have to be stolen from other projects that

A Potted History (continued)
1999

This year marked the beginning of a very difficult time in my life and since SynFonts is such a personal venture, the happenings of my personal life impact the site also. My father had recently passed away and that had a great impact on me, and later this year my mother would also pass away.

With the combined stress of my parents passing and the stress of the new job, any major site redesign had to take a back seat to life for a while. While I continued to use this time to make small changes to the site, adjusting wording and link placement to determine how they affected sales and traffic, the site remained visually unchanged for the remainder of the year.

2000

Early in 2000, domain name problems caused the site to disappear off the radar entirely and for a while there is no site. After the problems are resolved, I am in the middle of a new seemingly 24-hour-a-day interactive start-up called Talisman Creative that doesn't allow me enough time to get the site up and working again. In its place I uploaded a simple redirect page to one of my resellers.

By late 2000, the start-up company had thoroughly crashed and burned and I am left with a hole in the web where SynFonts used to be. I decided to update the site again, this time, re-implementing Shockwave and recapturing some of the excitement of the earlier electronic catalogs that have been missing for the last two years.

were going on at the time in a way that would not compromise any deadlines for those other clients. At the time that I developed this site, I was working on three other projects for clients of Talisman Creative, and one that I had pulled in on the side as a favor to a friend. I was pretty busy.

Learn from Your Mistakes

Sometimes, the best place we can go for inspiration is in a very unlikely direction. We occasionally need to look in the rear view mirror in order to see what lies ahead. I know many designers who look to other designers' web sites and design review magazines for inspiration when they are starting a redesign.

However, that approach often has its problems. For one, if you are looking elsewhere for inspiration, and try too hard to emulate what you think is "great design" it's much harder to generate a style that is all your own. Your work starts looking a lot like that of the designers that you are copying.

I find it very helpful to begin any redesign by looking at older attempts to solve the problem and making a critical and comprehensive list of everything that was lacking or problematic with those earlier attempts. Even if all you learn is that "everything I've ever done before is lame and I have to start from scratch!", you still walk away with the knowledge that you aren't guessing the truth; you've studied it and considered all your options and are starting from scratch for a sound reason. Many times, you may find that some of what you want to throw away is actually sound design and just needs to be tweaked, not thrown out.

Take this all into account and you'll probably agree that it was your average in-house project.

I had many personal goals and aspirations in mind as I began the new redesign, but the primary goal of the site was to allow people to browse through and closely examine the 31 typeface families that I have to offer. On the surface this is a simple task, made possible by a number of technologies. But if you look around you will notice that there are only a handful of type company web sites that allow for any kind of online preview of type online, and most of those are so simplified or limited in function that they border on being useless.

So I sat down and started mapping out what the plan should be for this 2000/2001 re-design I was about to undertake.

The best place we can go for inspiration is in a very unlikely direction. We occasionally need to look in the rear view mirror in order to see what lies ahead.

Discovery and Design

I'd learned a lot of things in the evolution of the site up to this point (see the history sideline to catch up with a few highlights), and the site had lain dormant for a while as work and other things took over my time. I now wanted this to be a whole new site to try to regain some of the successes of former sites, as well as finally getting an interactive type viewer idea I had up and running.

Now, are you ready for a shock?

I made a really interesting discovery while writing this chapter. A discovery that showed clearly that my homepage navigation demonstrates arguably poor usability. What do I do? Justify my choice? Claim to be right anyway? Quickly change the design before the book gets released? Um... Nope. I said that I would lay myself bare, and that's what I'm going to do. I'm going to explain my choices and give you the chance to better understand why I came to the conclusions and created the designs that I did. It doesn't make my homepage navigation any more usable, but it will let you better understand how the choices you make can work for you and against you, and how you need to constantly re-evaluate those choices in the light of new information.

The process that I'll demonstrate is sound, but some of the navigation choices that I made while using it have hindered the usability for parts of the site. Though I had reasons for making every choice that I did, I realize now that I might have been able to make better choices in terms of usability.

But I also made some really good choices on the site, good choices that led to good design that *is* easy to use. The coexistence of these two aspects in the same site, makes it almost the perfect example of how hard creating a truly usable site is. This dichotomy is a great example for demonstrating that usability is more than just a dogma of blue links and standards, it is a vigilance that you must exercise in your designs even *after* they are finished, always attempting to enhance the user experience aspects of your work. In a way, the fact that it uses Flash is beside the point, and I believe that the example of good usability you'll see later on will show that it's not what you use but how you use it that determines usability.

Let's begin. And remember, I'm going to share the good as well as the bad, so pay close attention.

I Did it My Way! (My Development Process Explained)

With every interactive project, you can count on there being four phases during the development process. These are: **Discovery**, **Design**, **Implementation** and **Testing**. Each step in the process is instrumental to a good project and if you don't touch on all of them, your chances for failure will increase.

During the discovery phase, time is spent mining for information about the client. Questions are asked and assumptions are made and confirmed. This is by far the most critical stage of the process in the building of any project. It's during this stage that we will be ascertaining what it is that we are going to attempt to create.

I find that a lot of clients' expectations change during this stage. They change because we often uncover new needs that they weren't thinking of or needs that they can dispose of because they are unnecessary. This is illustrated by the idea that five years ago, everybody "needed" a web site. Did they? Really? Does a small mom-and-pop shop that sells quilts only to their neighbors really *need* a web site? Sure, it opens up possibilities in finding new business, but whether they *need* that web site should be reviewed with them to check whether it will answer their needs better than, say, a local television and radio campaign. For example, the discovery process might uncover that the only reason their quilts sell at all is because they feature a local sports club logo on them, and it's arguable that quilts featuring the "Hooker, Oklahoma Horny Toads" (I swear this is a real team!) might not sell well outside of Hooker, Oklahoma. By asking these questions you will gain their respect and do them a much better service in the long run.

During the design phase, I'm concerned with blueprinting a project and creating any wireframes or proof of concept tests that are required so that I'll have a comprehensive understanding when I start to build. It's this stage where I sit down and design sketches for a project. A larger project than this web site design might include the production of a Design Document that outlines the knowledge gained in the discovery process matched with the planned solution, but for a project of my own, I'd settle for stepping myself through the process.

During the implementation phase we build the projects that have been scoped out during the design and discovery phases. It's during this step where all the magic happens. But if the planning doesn't go right, or the project changes mid-stream due to "scope creep" or problems with technology then this is where costs can skyrocket as you run to catch up or add features. (A project can suffer from scope creep when unplanned additions are made during production that seemingly only expand the scope "a little bit" but usually end up doubling the size of the project).

The testing phase really shouldn't be considered a phase at all. It should be considered a lifestyle. Testing for usability needs to happen early in the design of a project, and often during the implementation phase. You don't need a prototype to test with, you can test with sketches on paper or screen designs that are semi-functional or non functional. Any testing in terms of usability is better than none. As we follow the development process, look for the many times that I mention that I am testing.

If you test always and often, you usually won't encounter many problems during the final testing phase at the end of a project because you will have found most of them during the design and implementation phase.

The final testing phase at the end of a project is a confirmation of the successes or failures of a project. If you've done your job right, this is where you get to say "see, told ya so!" to everyone who doubted your wisdom. But if you were wrong and you failed to test often enough during the process... well, at least you learned something.

Discovery, Part 1: So You Want a Web Site?

When starting the discovery process, I usually begin by researching into the business of the company that I'm creating the work for. This helps me determine whether they need me to do the work for them in the first place. With SynFonts, since the business is mine and I'm pretty deeply connected with every step of it, I knew what it is that I do, and I knew that my business needed the web site to be refreshed in order to do it. But I would still need to perform the steps of discovering what kind of web site that I should build.

First, I needed to find out what other type web sites had to offer so that I could determine how difficult it was going to be to make a site that would compete on an equal level with the competition. My preliminary study uncovered a few sites that had advanced far beyond what I had ever presented on my site in terms of technology. I found at least ten different sites that offered some form of type preview engine. But many of these sites, despite being ahead of what I currently had to offer, were either pitifully underpowered or utilized some archaic and painfully hard-to-use technology, but they at least had something online. I started to see the possibility for a new chance at designing the perfect type web site, one where a customer could not only preview and purchase type, but interact with it so that they were sure that the typeface that they were going to buy was exactly what they needed.

I also saw the opportunity for a new revenue stream. If I could build the perfect type viewer, I might also be able to sell that type viewer to the many font companies out there who had either no preview engine at all or had one that was lacking in some way. (Are you starting to understand the value of the discovery process yet? I just got a whole new business model by using it!)

Next, I laid down the ground rules for the design. I set minimum machine requirements, realistic browser requirements and many other requirements that I would follow during development. The only area that I would be willing to budge on was in the area of timelines. With this still being an effort that I didn't care to sink a lot of money into, I wasn't about to make the thing happen at any cost.

It's at this point that the design of the site takes a radical turn from all the other updates. While the other updates were mainly site designs that may or may not have included the use of a plug in for delivering content, this would be a complete design for delivering a new way to preview type online.

Always Ask Questions!

Many times just the act of asking these questions will alleviate many usability problems before they happen. Some sample questions to ask about pretty much any project might be:

- "What kind of computer will this have to play back on?"

- "Who is going to use the site?"

- "Does my design allow the easiest possible access to the information for the type of user that will be using the site?"

- "How could I accomplish my goals in a different way by using a different technology/old technology/more cutting edge technology?"

- "How would I design this project differently if I had double/half the budget that I have currently?"

- "Why is the information laid out in the way it is?"

- "Have I asked any of the site's audience how they would use the information? What kind of design would suit them best?"

- "What can I add/eliminate from the design to make things simpler for the user?"

- "Is my ego designing this project?"

- "How would I design this differently if the site was for a competitor?"

- "If I replace all the text with a foreign language, can I still tell what the links mean?"

- "Is it possible that the specs for the design are wrong?"

- "What is the worst possible way to design this site, and how is my design better?"

- "What are the most common tasks that someone will be doing with the site, and can I redesign to make those tasks easier?"

- "What would happen if suddenly the client added/subtracted five navigation menu items?"

By all means, don't stop with these! Since clients, work styles, and projects are never the same at every company, each list of questions should be different to match them. For example, if your client often makes changes only after seeing the project go live to the public, one good question to ask them would be "can we implement a soft launch instead of a public release so that we can better ferret out any content changes?"

Flash is 99% OK

Discovery Part 2: (I Want, I Want...) Setting Goals and Expectations

I wanted to set the goals and line up any problems I might encounter so that I could address them in the design. Every project I work on usually begins with a line of questions similar to this, each one digging deeper into the issues at hand. The process usually leaves me with the knowledge that I need to put a scope on a project before I begin work and helps to predict some of the roadblocks that I may encounter, but occasionally this opens up new questions that sometimes lead to project changes before the development process begins and sometimes a decision that the project might not even be needed. If you walk away with only one lesson learned from my chapter, this is it... Ask questions *before* you begin your work! Even if you are also the one who is answering the questions and people make fun of you for talking to yourself.

Here are the questions I asked myself, and some answers.

1. Which Technology Do I Use to Build the Type Viewer Engine In?

There were a lot of options available that had not been around when I had last tried to created a type viewer for the web site in 1997. I seriously considered the following:

- **Macromedia Director**: Director had a lot of things going for it. For one, it has the capability to *kern* type. But there was no way that I could place a plug in requirement that is as large as Shockwave has just to view type. I had gone down that road before and I knew that it wasn't the answer I needed. Kerning is the specific spacing between each letter on a page. Since most end-users will custom kern a single line of display type, this is fairly important and it pained me to lose this feature. Director also allows for easy control over the color and size of individual letters, and gives

the power to change which typeface is being used, the text that constitutes a block of text, and many more capabilities that no other technology could offer at the time that I was developing this site.

- **WEFT**: Among the many other options that are available that I considered are web embedded fonts. Using web fonts allows for someone to actually embed the font into a web page. The problem with this approach is that even though the potential customer is viewing the actual font in use, they have no real control over the use of the typeface, so they cannot try and use it in their own particular application. In effect, this method doesn't really provide much more usefulness than a GIF image would for the result that I was after. Currently WEFT (Web Embedded Font Tool, produced by Microsoft and originally introduced in 1997) is in version 3.0 but, according to the Microsoft site, still exhibits some display peculiarities on certain browsers.

- **Server-Side Scripting**: There was also the consideration of server-side scripting. Since there are already a couple of sites doing this I had some samples to look at, but the problems with this approach were twofold. First, I had no practical experience with the technology required to build something using server-side scripting that could do anything as robust as what I was after. The other problem is that the applications that I have seen using this technology are pretty bland and featureless. From a user perspective, you would enter text into a text entry box on one HTML page, press a button, and wait for the server to generate an image and have the page reload before you can see the result.

- **Macromedia Flash**: Flash is not unlike Director, but it has one major difference. While

Director started out life as a program for making CDs and kiosks, Flash was designed to make small, quickly downloadable vector graphic files for web use. Unfortunately, both Flash version 4 and 5 (the versions that I was using during the development of this project) both have dismal font support, so using either would make my job a whole lot harder.

2. What Was the Installed User Base for Flash and Director?

Were they even big enough to support building a site so heavily dependent on one of these two technologies? When I started seriously thinking about this project in August of 2000, estimates of the installed user base for these two technologies was ranging between 70-80% for Flash and 40-70% for Shockwave for Director. I gathered these estimates from several sites available on the web, including Macromedia's own estimates and those from other sites like *Statmarket.com*, and many others easily found by doing a *google.com* search.

3. What Changes Should be Made to the Interface Design for the Site?

Starting from the earliest design I could find, I listed several points to readdress in order to make sure that I wouldn't trip myself up by not learning from past mistakes.

- I should create a standard self-explanatory interface that would not rely on metaphor or exploration to be used sucessfully.

- It should require no required plug ins — instead, plug in content should be optional.

- The design must be modular so I can add content or redesign easily.

- The design should be light and airy, not dark.

- Text should be easy to read, preferably black text on a white background.

- No frames...

- Any static GIF version of the site should have a full character set of any typeface represented in a GIF preview.

- The site should feel fresh every time someone visits it.

- When compared to any other type design site, SynFonts had to hold its own. It had to be a world-class site.

- Because I still do not pay for advertising, the site had to offer something different enough to bring people in on its own merit by word of mouth.

- The site had to involve a revolutionary type preview engine that would convince other foundries that they should seriously consider purchasing the type viewer technology that I would build into the site.

4. Were There any Predetermined Branding or Design Guidelines that I Would Keep from Previous Versions of the Site?

- I wanted to return to using my older logo design as I felt that it was better than the one that I had been using.

- Some of what I had been reading in the area of color theory was that blues and greens make people more comfortable, and that more comfortable people are more likely to trust a site and spend money on it. While I had green in my colors from the beginning, I felt that the green was too military and a little harsh and dark. I don't have the exact articles that I had been reading at the time, but there are several on the web today, including these two brief overviews:

http://www.uwec.edu/Help/Webpub/Color/meanings.htm

http://www.creativepublic.com/visitors_area/using_color_vis.html

5. Were There any Goals that Specifically Related to the Type Preview Area?

- Since I wanted to try and sell the technology to other type companies, it had to be easy to implement in an existing radically different design.

- The technology should feel natural, not forced. The use of Flash or Director should seem to be a natural extension of the web site and not feel like technology for technology's sake. The plug in download process had to be painless.

- The content had to be viewable at the largest possible size (preferably full screen) to allow the users the highest access to inspect the details of each typeface.

- Since many people don't view the theft of typefaces to be "stealing" (although it is to me!), the type viewer had to utilize some kind of copy protection for the typefaces, the fonts could not be easy to extract. (Find out more about typeface theft at *www.typeright.org*.)

With all these considerations being placed on my list of concerns, it seemed that the first thing that I had to do was decide on the technology. I had ruled out everything but Macromedia Flash and Shockwave and now I had to make the choice between them.

After looking at the numbers of how widely the Flash plug in had spread (one source, StatMarket, quoted a number as high as 88.23 percent for an installed base on the Netscape browser) and considering that Macromedia had worked deals for its inclusion in nearly every browser from that point on, (as of the release of this book, Macromedia states that Flash *is* installed on 98.3% of *all* web browsers!) I decided to choose Flash over Shockwave, even with the shortcomings it had with font control.

Technology for Technology's Sake

If there is one major problem running through most early attempts at plug in technology on the web, it is that they seem to have been driven by the urge to use the technology, not to solve some problem that a client may have. I have heard many people say things like, "Wow, I just can't wait to try out the new XYZ plug in technology. I saw a demo at the XYZ tradeshow last week and it looks awesome!" Then these same designers or developers try and sell it into every job that comes in until they build something with it. Often they might not even ask if the use of the XYZ technology is the best way to solve the problem.

Discovery Part 3: Defining the Target Platform and User Profiles

Insuring a sucessful user experience is a mix of many aspects; things like **Design**, **Style**, **Mood** and **Content** all add into the mix of what a user will walk away with when they are finished using your site or project. These things are pretty hard to quantify. How do you exactly define what the "mood" of a site is? Sure, you can say that it is "dark" or "festive" but those are hardly quantifiable concepts. These are issues that exist squarely in the area of "art" and tend to be subjective qualities.

But there are other aspects that also play in to a user experience that *can* be quantified, things like who the intended audience actually is, and what kind of target platforms they may view the web site or project on. By defining these quantifiable aspects of a project, we can often make the job of creating the more subjective qualities much easier.

Great Site, But Who's Going to Use It?

With any web site, predicting the audience's browser of choice is impossible The very nature of the Internet involved building on the kind of open standards where almost any kind of computer *could* be used to access a web site. This kind of moving target makes it very difficult to design web sites, and almost every designer cringes after hearing the words, "Please design to the lowest common denominator," which almost universally means, "Make it slow and boring." But this doesn't ensure that your site design is the best design for your audience. You might be doing a disservice to your users if you design for the lowest common denominator if your user base is a high-tech audience full of early adopters.

However, in this case I can easily narrow the estimated hardware profile down by first profiling my customer. If I were designing for a client's web site I would check, re-check and triple-check any assumptions made about the users of the site, performing a pretty thorough line of questioning and study to determine who the average

users are. However, since I had been running the site since 1995, had been a professional designer since 1988, and had been selling my typefaces and talking to thousands of my customers over the years, I figured that I knew my customer base pretty well and that a truly exhaustive user-profiling step would be unnecessary.

Over the years I have compiled an understanding of what kind of user stops by SynFonts, and more importantly what kind of user is more likely to become a customer. My customers tend to be graphic design professionals, or alternatively someone supporting a graphic design professional. This tells me the following:

> My customers will tend to be between the ages of 20 and 50, using a faster machine with a lot of RAM, in a cross-platform environment. They generally have a higher than average connection speed. Since they often have to transfer large files, they require a high bandwidth connection or access to one.

> My user's computer is also probably pretty capable in the arena of color and resolution (anywhere between 1024 x 768 and the spacious world of 1600 x 1200).

Design Part 1: Information Architecture

Now that I had a good idea of what I was going to create, I could begin the process of building the blueprints and designs that I would follow in constructing the site. I had to determine how the information would be divided on the site. Historically I had always broken this down into some form of the following links: An e-mail link, News (or Journal), Order, Offline Order, Download, and some way to choose the various typefaces – occasionally under a sub-group like "Fonts", listed individually. There were sometimes additions to this list, but these were the basics.

Flash is 99% OK

Next I asked myself if these basics were valid as far as the next generation of the site was concerned. I broke out each link and assaulted it, making myself defend the reason for having each link remain on the site.

- **E-Mail** – I had to have an e-mail link. This was the one real connection I had with my customers now that I was using a third party for sales. If there were any problems, I wanted to maintain an open line of communication with the end user of my typefaces.

- **News (or Journal)** – While I would need some sort of area to make announcements, the inclusion of news (or even worse, my Journal) as a main navigation item on SynFonts was unnecessary, I decided to move the more personal news to my personal site where it belonged. The font-related news could be served up from a link on the home page if it was important enough and then it could be dropped as it became irrelevant.

- **Order** – This link's reason for being is self-evident. I had to have a place that people could go to in order to, well, order. But I decided to ask myself if it was necessary anyway. How and when would people likely order typefaces from my site? Would they order when they were browsing? Yes. Would they order immediately after stopping in? Could happen, they might have to go get approval before they order, they might come back after looking for a credit card.

One of the things that I have noticed in the few professional usability studies that I have been involved with on other sites is that people don't generally do what you think they will do. They look all over for different ways to accomplish their goals, so the more ways that you can give them to accomplish their goal, the better. It's OK if they don't do things the way that you think should be done. Your only job is to make things as easy as possible for them to figure out how to accomplish their goals.

Thinking about it that way, I decided I should probably have two or more separate ordering areas. One in the main navigation for people stopping in to buy immediately, and one for the impulse buy when looking at each typeface. The more order links that I could place on the site, the better.

- **Offline Order** – Is there a reason for a separate link for offline ordering in the age where I want people to order type online? Absolutely. My largest orders have traditionally come in over the phone, people asking about buying two or more licenses at once and asking for a discount is a good example. Also, the addition of a link for people to order from a human being alleviates the concerns that someone might have with giving a credit card to a computer.

- **Download** – There are many reasons for keeping the download area. I can use it to house the section containing the free sample typefaces. (This often gets me free links on font sites and generates a lot of traffic for me.) I can also house any promotional materials that are old but interesting to collectors, and I can provide links to a password-protected area where customers can download the typefaces if they have trouble with the online ordering section or if they order from me by telephone.

- **Fonts** – This is always the toughest area to define. How do I allow the selection of over 30 typefaces easily? Do I make it its own category or stay with the separate links that I implemented in the last update?

The overall site map looked like this:

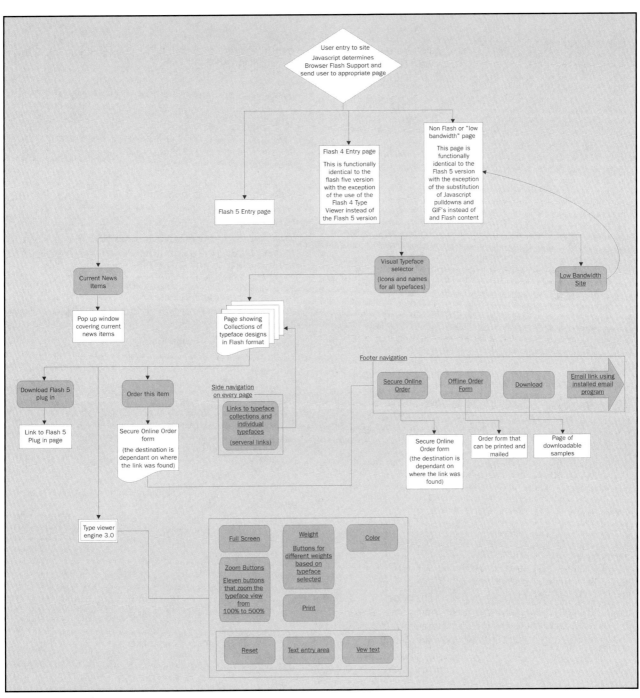

SynFonts Site Map.

Design Part 2: UI

Determining the site's main navigation is one thing, but once you have it, where do you put it? It's obvious to me at this point that I have to carry some sort of "footer" navigation that exists on all pages, so that no matter where a user might be, they can access all the areas of the site including the ordering sections. The navigation will need to be pretty easy to use. I decided to use text navigation as the basis for all navigation on the site outside of the typeface selector on the home page. (I'll go into this more later.)

Text navigation is pretty small in size, would be required for the non-Flash site anyway, and had been working well during the last update. Additionally, on larger, high-resolution monitors sometimes the default browser font is larger than normal. Text links would allow the design to scale if the user wanted it to; a Flash-based navigation would be more difficult to scale effectively.

In the previous release, I had allowed some goofy naming conventions that I thought were "cool" to get through to the published site. Specifically, I called the single font collections "Hit singles" and the collections "Compilations" which made sense at the time... (bad decisions always do) but I now wanted to make these more literal. I renamed these two headings to "Select a collection" and "Select a typeface" so that people would not need to decipher what my categories meant. This change made a world of difference in how simple the navigation felt.

Mom, Please Keep my Peas out of my Potatoes, I Don't Like my Food Touching.

I made the conscious effort to divide the content from the navigation on the screen and to build the site in such a way that the ordering process would be as available as possible to the user, so that whenever they felt like ordering, the order mechanism would be visible. On the standard screen size, no matter how hard you try, you cannot escape the many ordering methods that are placed around the design. If you have

the site up at full screen, the order information is at both the top and bottom of the visible page. If the site is displayed fully, or scrolled down to the bottom of the page, the real estate devoted to ordering increases.

The visible difference between the content and the navigation makes the identifying the two rather easy. Especially when the content itself has its own navigation built in.

Since this layout sticks closely to a standard T-bar style web design with site navigation to the left and top of the content, users have little to figure out in the way of how the site is laid out. With the challenge of using the type viewer ahead of them, the less that I challenge them outside the Flash file, the better.

I received nothing but positive comments about this layout in the testing that I did before release, and can assume from the relatively high average of 9 pages viewed per unique visitor on a Windows machine and 14 pages viewed per unique visitor on a Macintosh, that the users visiting the site aren't having much problem with the navigation of the page design.

The Good, the Bad, and the Beautiful: The Implementation Phase

The implementation phase of the process is where the magic of a project often happens. For it's in this phase that the dreams all come true, the plans and blueprints turn real and something gets created from nothing. But also in this phase are some real chances to make a project fail. If there are unseen problems with the technology, this is where you'll discover them. And if the plan has any holes, this is where you will fall down one.

It is imperative that you continually test everything that you are building during this phase: test for usability and for bugs. It's going to be a lot easier to change your design here than it will be later on if you find out that users don't understand it.

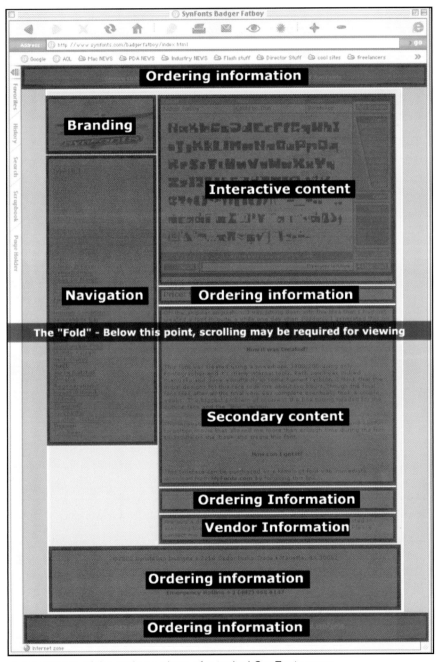

A breakdown of the main sections of a typical SynFonts page.

Flash is 99% OK

The type viewer that I have created has a lot of fans and is very easy to use. But the typeface selector I made for the home page is arguably a good example of poor usability. And since we can learn a lot more from a bad example than we can from a good one, this oversight in usability transforms into an example of how easy it is to make good choices that lead to bad usability.

Designing for cool is kind of like showing your artwork to your mom in high school. If she doesn't like it, it doesn't matter – she's just un-cool and her opinion doesn't matter.

Let's start by covering the process of building the SynFonts Type Viewer. Within this, I actually go through a sub-cycle of design and implementation, just like I did for the entire site concept as a whole.

The Good... (Forget About Cool. Think Simple!)

The truth is that I've loved simplicity for a long time prior to starting this project, but simple is often very hard to accomplish. Cool design is often relatively easy to create. Designing for cool is kind of like showing your artwork to your mom in high school. If she doesn't like it, it doesn't matter – she's just un-cool and her opinion doesn't matter.

To create something usable, you often need to suffer the slings and arrows of harsh criticism from people telling you that what you think works just great is actually very hard to use. You also have to work out whether you just need a few tweaks or an overhaul.

Building a Better Type Preview Engine

If I had unlimited resources to use in its creation, what would the perfect online type viewer consist of? It might look like some combination of Quark XPress, Microsoft Word, Illustrator and Photoshop, all wrapped up and blended into a giant mix of type controls that would be selectable from a drop-down menu that would allow you to choose the interface that matches your working style, so that you can play with the typefaces as you would be in real life. Sounds great! But is that really perfect?

Well, no. The challenge of building something this complex is tantamount to a lifetime commitment of redesigning every time one of these programs gets a new version. And that's without thinking about any of the platform issues. The problem of building this is so immense that it is realistically impossible. There are other reasons, but these are enough to stop this idea here. No person I know of has attempted such a project and I don't think I want to be the first.

Actually, the perfect type viewer would be closer to a device that did the top two or three things that these programs allowed the user to use type for, in a simple interface that would not require much study to use.

The Iterative Design/Implementation Phase for the Type Viewer

To outline functionality, I started by listing out features that I think are important and then asking questions of a couple designers in the office where I was working at the time.

- "What besides the things on this list would you like to be able to do to preview type online?"

- "Would you remove anything from this list?"

- "What is your favorite type web site and why?"

An early test of the type viewer before including different font weights was considered.

My list of what the user should be able to accomplish:

- The user should be able to enter a line of text.

- The user should be able to zoom the text to facilitate the review of each character.

- The user should be able to print a sample.

The responses that I got back added some things that I had overlooked:

- The user should possibly be able to play with colors.

- The user should be able to select different weights (Bold, Italic, etc.)

- The user should be able to kern the type.

I had ruled out kerning because of the plug in problems, so I couldn't add that one, but I would need to add a way to navigate through the typeface weights for each font. The color addition would be a lot of fun as well.

OK – the list of what I need to do is pretty simple, and by this time I had already started building prototypes to see if I could make some of these things happen in Flash.

Above is an early test of the type viewer that was built when I was not thinking of including a way to select different weights for each family appear in the same Flash file. Weights in this design would have appeared in different windows, as would print functions.

As I built these prototype files, I tried to test them as often as I could. I would set a co-worker down in front of the computer and then watch them as they used the demo. I might ask, "How would you zoom the text to make it larger?" but usually I would not say anything and let the user tell me what they thought they were supposed to be doing with the device.

It's really important that you think about each element on your design. Common sense will tell you a lot about the way that things should be designed. All you have to do is listen!

If you look at the design above you should easily spot what I could not see at the time. The zoom buttons make the image larger when you move your mouse down. If you apply a little common sense to this, you notice how counter-intuitive it really is. Making something bigger should require an upward movement.

Flash is 99% OK

Another early version of the type viewer shows some of the additional navigation elements coming together.

This version has a much better zoom tool, redesigned so that the numbers climb instead of descending. And as they climb, they appear larger, giving a visual cue that things get bigger as you click higher.

This iterative process continued for a couple of weeks, and each time I would add, remove, or change features in the test file. During the testing process, I was often working with files that were only partially functional. When this was the case, I would only show the file for feedback if I could be in the room with the tester while they used the file. This prevented any kind of misunderstanding about whether the problems with a file were bugs or usability problems.

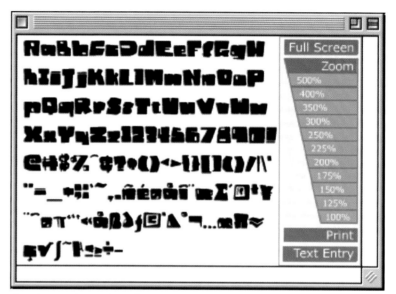

Another early version of the type viewer, with additional navigation elements.

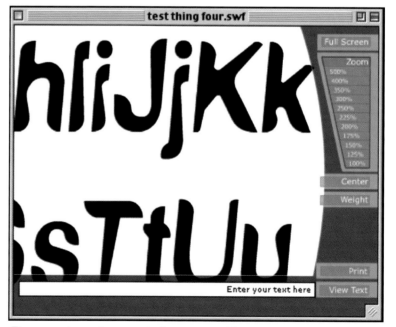

The same type viewer as before, zoomed in.

Eventually the final navigation was boiled down to the following:

The final type viewer.

View Text (and Reset)

I had a lot of problems with the method of implementing a way to view user-entered text. Flash offers both the ability to grab and move an object (the text) and the ability to make a text field editable, but the problem is that both of these require selecting the text with the mouse in the same way. I tried making buttons that switched between the two and also creating a button that caused the user input to happen upon pressing the button. Neither of these was very easy to use. Eventually, I asked myself what exactly it was that I was trying to accomplish. The answer was that I wanted the user to view a "string of text" in a certain font of their choice. After looking at the problem like this, I saw how I could separate the two and make the user input area separate from the text that the user might need to grab and move and the problem would be solved. After watching a lot of people make use of this, I can say that most people easily figure this step out.

The *reset* button was added after I noticed that people would try to reset the page by clicking on the different weight buttons. Once the *reset* button was added, people stopped clicking on the weights to reset the character set.

Zoom

The zoom tool was changed many times during the process, and I tried a lot of variations on the basic feature, making things happen on rollover, with a scrollbar, on button presses and by sliding up and then down... but the method that worked the best was to have a series of single click buttons that were each marked with a percent number.

Weight

When I thought about designing a method to select the different weights, I considered making it into a pull-down list or some other way that would not limit me in terms of space. I ended up with a series of six buttons that each had a letter indicative of a weight on it and that would allow for visual selection. Some of the typeface files could be rather large, so if I could eliminate making people click and load information they didn't want, then I could save them some time and effort.

Color

The ability to change the color of the typeface almost didn't make it into the interface. The actual effect of this is of little value to the selection and review process of buying type. But it does factor in a lot of fun value that people liked to play with. Choosing between fun and function is always difficult, especially when you consider that the color selector added about 20k to the total size of the type viewer. The engine was getting fat and this could send it over the edge if I wasn't careful.

When I added this feature, I sketched a couple of examples of how one could select colors. I again played with sliders. But after thinking about it, all other selection items on the type viewer are simple buttons, so these should be too.

I found the basics for what I need online in an open source forum. As is often the case with open source material, it was only really good enough to get me started, but that was better than inventing the process and code from scratch. The color selector I found provided me with another dilemma. Since there were so many colors to choose from, I had to either reduce the numbers of colors drastically, which would reduce function and fun, make the buttons really small, or have them pop up in some way. With so many buttons on the screen, they would drastically reduce the available screen real estate dedicated to the typeface.

I decided to place all the color controls on a pop-up window within the Flash file. This was easily accomplished and gave me other options.

It allowed me to include the ability not only to change the type color, but the background color as well. When I sat this down in front of some people, the results I got were all smiles. The only problem is that since you have to "launch" the color selector, it is easy to miss. But since the functions are not essential, it would hurt little even if over half the people who used the site never knew it existed.

Print

From the user viewpoint the print button is easy as pie: All you have to do is press it and the computer will do the rest, walking you through the standard printing process that the user's computer is configured to perform. But from my point of view... this was a major pain to make happen. Macromedia designed a really poor print system with this program. I have no clue why a vector program is so poorly equipped for printing, but hey, there's always the next version, right? In order to print the files at the correct aspect ratio, I had to make the files a certain size, otherwise the print would be stretched and out of proportion.

Full Screen

One button that was not originally in the plan was the "full screen" button. The full screen button was added when I was doing my personal testing on various platforms and screen sizes, I noticed that while the site functionally worked at 640 x 480, it was harder to use the type viewer than I wanted it to be. The addition of the full screen command allows the user to open the type viewer into its own window that is large enough to view even on a small monitor.

The color controls in action.

Incorporating Copy Protection into theType Viewer

Stealing typefaces is a big concern. Since typefaces are software, and software has a worldwide piracy rate of 40% (and in some places as high as 80%) there is great incentive to implement some kind of copy protection.

Even though I can't stop everyone who wants to steal type, I wanted to make it harder for them to do so. This is important to the aspect of selling the type viewer to other foundries who would also be concerned about typeface theft. If I implemented no copy protection for the typefaces, I wouldn't sell one single copy of this.

The structure of the type viewer places the typeface information outside the grasp of downloading, so nobody should be able to crack the files and extract the fonts free of charge unless they are some kind of computer hacker.

Another kind of stealing happens when people start taking advantage of the situation. Because I had created such a capable engine, you could conceivably set your type, do a screen capture, and not have to purchase the font. Since I can't stop that unless I reduce the functionality, I decided to add a watermark image behind the typeface. This way, to get an image of type set using the engine, some sort of image editing would be required... Since my average customer values their time, this might make it cost them more in time than it would to actually purchase the typeface.

The Bad (A Good Look at the Un-success of the Homepage Usability)

Remember earlier that I said I made a really interesting discovery while writing this chapter? That I had discovered that a small piece of the site was a good example of poor usability? Well, of all places for that example to be, it was dead center on my home page (...doh!).

I'm not saying that the home page is a failure, far from it. I've gotten more compliments on its design than I've received suggestions that it is hard to use, and the stats on the web site indicate that more people get past this homepage design and find content on my site than any other design that I have released. But the fact that I still get people who indicate that this design "drives them crazy", "is too much like a video game" or just "is very difficult to use" tells me that I've missed the mark somewhat with the design.

I'll start this section off with the process that led up to the current design, and then follow up with a critique of some of the missteps that I made and choices that I should have made differently.

The Homepage Design, 2001

I had recently begun to work on designs for my personal portfolio site and thought that sharing some similarities between the two in terms of layout and style would be a good idea. I often provided links between the two sites, so I figured that if the design of the two felt similar, people would not be presented with a clash of design styles when moving from one site to the other.

The look and feel that I put together for my own site was very simple and clean and I had already received good feedback on the design, so I decided to try and follow it as a general guideline. The main feature on the homepage was a predominant bar that cut horizontally across the middle of the site with a single focal point for an image to be placed.

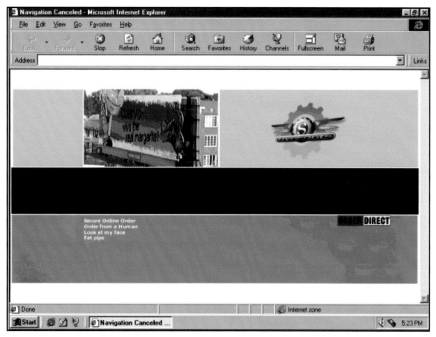

SynFonts homepage, 2001.

I wanted to create something that was both easy and fun to use. The homepage sets the mood for a site and I wanted the navigation to have a sense of fun above all else. People should enjoy the experience of their first visit to the site and an attractive and entertaining interface would be one way for me to achieve that on the homepage. But the site still had to be easy to use or I would lose customers.

I not only wanted the user to have fun when they got to the site but I wanted them to understand right away that the web site used rich, interactive content. If I could present them with some content on the home page that would be representative of the Flash content that they would find deeper into the site, it would be less likely that they would miss it later on: they would be looking for it.

In the review I had made of the previous updates to the site, I noticed that most of the designs I had used stopped the user at the homepage (or sometimes at a splash page and *then* at the homepage) and made them click their way through a short maze before they saw any typefaces at all. If I could solve this problem and allow them to select typefaces immediately when they arrived on the homepage, I could save people a lot of time and effort. I wanted a cleaner design, so a long list of typefaces was out, but there had to be a way that I could provide a direct link to every typeface I have without having a lot of clutter. The initial thoughts that I had were that the interface would be some sort of elastic "zooming" interface: each menu item would grow and shrink as the mouse rolled over it.

Since I had decided that this site would be heavily dependent on Flash because of the type viewer on the content pages, I decided to explore the ways that I could build the homepage with Flash; but should I build the whole page in Flash or just a part of it?

To Flash or Not to Flash, that is the Question!

I decided to make the homepage straight HTML with small Flash elements included in it. All I had to do now was determine what should be Flash and what should not. Too often Flash designers forget that they don't have to build an entire site inside one single Flash file. This is actually one of the main reasons that Flash has gotten such a reputation for bad usability. Building a whole site into one single file almost always destroys many of the features that are built into the browser: the back button, keyword searching, and so on.

After some thought I decided that the best thing to do was limit the Flash that was being used on the homepage to the typeface selector alone. My thought was that if this was the only area on the screen that was animated and interactive, that people would be less likely to become confused by the workings of the interface.

Keep in mind that I wanted this to be a fun and exciting interface – generally things that are fun and exciting have to be thought about when we use them, and making someone stop and think is pretty counterintuitive in terms of usability. I wanted to make sure that the thinking was happening where I wanted it to happen, not because animations were distracting people.

Don't Break my Back

At the time of this writing, all web browsers treat a Flash file as if it were a single item, not the rich content that it really is. Even though you may have twenty pages of information in your Flash file, the browser only sees the one file that you have embedded on the page. Therefore a user hitting the back button will not be taken back one page, but instead is taken out of the site completely any time they hit the button!

It is precisely this kind of disregard for standard controls that raises the hackles of usability experts like Jakob Neilsen. And the more that Flash designers disregard these standard controls, the more that usability experts will think that Flash is 99% bad, so do what you can to ensure that you don't break the back button!

Currently, there are a couple of ways that you can ensure that you don't break the back button. One way is to split your site up using HTML, placing separate sections of your movie on different HTML pages. Since this solution uses standard HTML, it is the most likely to work everywhere, regardless of the browser or platform used. Another way is given in this tech note on the Macromedia site: *http://www.macromedia.com/support/flash /ts/documents/swf_back_button.htm*.

But it requires a lot of internal work to be done with your Flash file. Finally, at the time of this writing, the new version of Flash MX is supposed to have built-in support for the back button (is that cheering I hear?) so this may not be an issue for much longer.

Flash is 99% OK

The Synfonts homepage, with animated typeface selector highlighted, before it was redesigned.

To get the "zooming" look that I was after, I was going to have to create a Flash file that overran the bounds of the area that I had cordoned off for the typeface selector (in the screenshot above, this would be the black horizontal bar). I couldn't make this work unless the whole site was in Flash. I either had to change the concept for the type selector or build the whole page in Flash. I didn't want that, so I searched for possible alternatives for the typeface selector interface.

Steal Your Way to a Great Flash-Based Web Site (Well, Sort Of...)

Having a limited set of skills should in no way hinder you from having a great Flash site, especially in these days of open source Flash files. Back in the days when Director was the development tool of choice and Flash and the Web were just a dream, programmers were very protective of their code. Many would only give away their code to other developers at a high price or not at all. Giving away one's code was akin to leaving the barn door open. (I still have Director code that I wouldn't give away to save my life!)

But the age of HTML and JavaScript changed many developer's viewpoints on this. Since people couldn't easily protect their code from theft, they started signing it and distributing it for notoriety and bragging rights. This eventually built up a community that fed off this new open source effort. By the time Flash programming

hit the scene, there was a new history of sharing. That in turn caused the creation of many code-sharing sites.

Redefining the Homepage Navigation Using Open Source Code

When I started looking, I found no less than twenty different open source navigation Flash files that I thought might deliver the kind of general interface that I was after. The effort of finding these files took a good deal of time and testing, but the end result took far less time than starting from scratch would have taken. Additionally, since the files were in effect finished testable interfaces, I could even set people in front of them and see how well they worked, or post them online and get feedback from friends or prospective users.

I narrowed my choices to two that I felt solved the problem the way that I wanted it solved. Both of the two effects were pretty fun and I thought they would work pretty well, so I went ahead and began modifying the test files so that they fitted within the site design

The first consisted of a series of squares that grew and shrank as the mouse was dragged over them; not exactly as I wanted them to, but close enough. But I didn't feel it was exciting enough:

Growing/Shrinking source code.

Hindsight is a wonderful thing and I think this might have been an easier interface to use. It's likely that had I chose to use this as the typeface selector, I probably would have never received a single suggestion that my site was hard to use. The choice that I did make has turned out to be pretty controversial as a usability issue. I ended up choosing a scrolling interface.

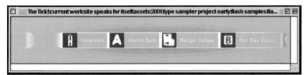

The final choice for the typeface selector – scrolling interface.

While looking for open source files, I actually came across several scrolling interface widgets, but none of them worked exactly as I wanted it to. This was easy enough to fix, even with the stern warning in the open source code that if I changed anything I would probably break something and make everything stop working. The downside to open source material is that, even though you may find a gem, it is often in the rough, and will require a lot of polishing before it will shine brightly.

The problem with a scrolling interface is that the idea behind it is to make your user "chase" after the button that they will have to click on. If the user is adept, this won't be a problem. But if they are lacking in hand-eye coordination, this could be a problem. If the rate that the buttons scroll at is too fast it will hinder the selection of a button or worse, make it impossible. If the scroll rate is too slow, it might make the selection of a button take an unnaturally long time and your user could find the process frustrating.

Where can I Get Good Open Source files?

The following sites are great for finding open source Flash files. But that isn't all. You can also find great music, sound and general Flash design resources and around the clock help from the various forums and boards.

Flash kit
http://www.flashkit.com

Flash Planet
http://www.flashplanet.com

Extreme Flash
http://www.extremeflash.com

Virtual FX.net
http://virtual-fx.net

Flash Guru
http://www.flashguru.co.uk

Were-Here forums
http://www.were-here.com

There are many, many more resources online and the list keeps growing every day. The chances are that whatever you want to accomplish, there is somebody who has either built it outright and released it as open source, or at least constructed something that you can learn from or build into a finished piece yourself.

Just a note on open source files: in some cases, the files may be open source, but will contain disclaimers that prevent use for commercial purposes without payment to the author. Please make every attempt to follow the wishes of any open source author whose file you use or learn from.

Flash is 99% OK

Here's a response that I received from one of the people that I asked to help me test out an early version of the site that implemented this navigation:

> *"I do have one comment – when you first see the home pages, the font names scroll so fast it's almost like a video game to slow them down and select them. Maybe that's what you want, in which case, it's fine. It not, you could slow it down a little." – Daniel Will-Harris*

This interface was a controversial decision for me because of feedback like this, but I decided that I would use it on the site and replace it only if I got negative feedback from a greater number of users after the site was launched. (Again, I wanted fun and entertaining and not all people will think the same things are fun or exciting.) But deeper into the site, because I wanted the user to concentrate more on the content than the Flash, the interactive type viewer has no movement.

Designing From Wisdom and NOT the Drunkenness of Power

Just because you **can** do something does not mean that you **should** do it.

No matter what, when you introduce a non-standard way of interacting with a web site, chances are that you will have some people who stand around and stare blankly at the walls trying to figure out what the heck to do with it. Introducing them to a small piece of interactivity at an early stage will awaken their mind to the idea of looking at the web site more closely for other interactive areas. Using my site as an example, the finished home page navigation starts moving upon loading and is the only thing moving on the page, which draws attention to the idea that you might have more to click on than simple blue links.

So Was the Homepage Really ALL THAT BAD?

When I put this homepage design into action, I wanted to create a fun, yet easy-to-use way to make a visual selection of one of my typefaces. It's arguable that I have created that, but it's also arguable that what I have created isn't fun at all, but is merely an unusable roadblock to the real web site.

...and the Beautiful (Wrapping it all up with HTML)

With the type viewer design completed, I now began the process of building the actual files. The Flash files were almost complete due to the fairly comprehensive testing phase that I conducted, but I had yet to build the HTML files that housed the site.

I dragged out the finished design files and started breaking them down into HTML tables. I hadn't designed anything radical, so the tables went together pretty easily. The only hitch was that, in one of my early builds, I posted for feedback on the design (not the code), I had not yet tested the file in Netscape and it completely blew up on one of the people that I had asked for opinions.

The basic layout of the homepage was modified slightly from my original design at this point. I changed the dark band to a lighter color and refined the placement of the information on the page to be more pleasing to the eye:

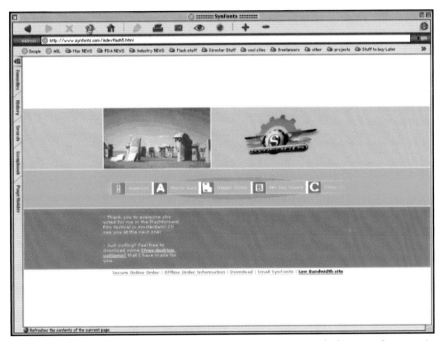

The homepage, with minor modifications made to color, and element placement.

Because of the assumptions that I had formed about the user, I decided that a "liquid" or "stretchy" web site would be best, stretching to fill all the space that the browser made available. That way I could make the site look like it was designed for all resolutions and not just for a single monitor size. Personally I dislike sites that lump everything in the left side of the screen or confine all the content into a small box floating in the middle. And the sites that create a pop-up window and remove my browser controls get on my nerves even more.

The Problem with Ego

I have sat in too many meetings where there was a serious suggestion made that the best way to deal with a problem encountered in the area of user design was to "force" the user to make things easy for us! I heave heard top notch designers actually state "If the user doesn't like the way it looks they can just go download (IE, Netscape, this plug in, that new technology) and reset their resolution to 800x600. And we can always tell them that if that doesn't work, they should buy a new computer." Think about this for a minute. Would you shop at a store that treated you that way?

Flash is 99% OK

Looking at the World Through Rose-Colored Monitors (The Benefit of "Liquid" Designs)

If web site design is an art, then the user's screen would be the canvas. But unlike a regular canvas, every user's monitor is different and unpredictable. For a designer, this is a pretty big problem. After all, one thing designers are concerned with is making their work look good. If you don't know what you are designing for, it's pretty hard to make something look good. The answer is to design web sites to behave like liquid, flowing to fill all the available screen real estate.

Before the web became popular, interactive designers had a much easier job of designing for a computer screen. They could re-set the resolution of the monitor if they needed to or black out those areas that they didn't use. They didn't have to worry about taking the browser window into account or that there might've been other open windows or applications on screen competing for attention. The screen real estate was something that the designer could control.

But when designing for a web browser, an interactive designer has to take into account that the resolution their site may be played back at will most likely be different for every viewer, and not only that, but it may be viewed at more than one resolution by the same user if that user resizes the window while on your site. The challenge for a designer is to ensure that people with different monitor resolutions get the best possible experience, no matter how high or low the resolution of their monitor is.

I find that when designing for the Web, you should always ask these following questions:

- What does the site look like on a monitor with a low resolution?

- What does the site look like on a monitor with a high resolution?

- What happens if I resize my browser window?

Looking at the possible resolutions that my site might be viewed on convinced me that I had no choice but to design the site to scale to fit any resolution monitor. With any technology other than Flash, this would have been a very big problem, but one of the impressive abilities of the Flash plug in is that content created for it can be scaled without losing quality.

This can happen because Flash uses vector graphics. Since an image created with vector graphics contains only the information that describes what the image looks like, the computer will redraw the image at whatever resolution is required based on the design. This is different from other web technologies like JPEGs or GIF images. These two technologies are based on raster graphics. Raster graphics are made up of individual pixels and can only be displayed at one size without becoming distorted.

> *Whenever possible try and design for the greatest number of platforms and resolutions.*

Of course, the ability of vector graphics to scale will only do you good if you allow your Flash file to scale when you create it. Many Flash designers set preferences in their HTML pages that make the Flash movie play back at only one resolution, or worse, build the whole site in a single Flash file that sits in a small window. If you do this, you are severely limiting yourself. A user with a larger resolution monitor or visual impairment may not be able to read the text on your web site.

Whenever possible try and design for the greatest number of platforms and resolutions. Even if you have a good idea of what platforms and resolutions your users will be equipped with, there is always the possibility that they could be coming in from a different location. If you can accommodate a wide range of resolutions and platforms without compromising the design for the intended target audience's platform it can only serve to make the site available to more people.

Monitor resolutions are only going to get better as time goes on. If we try and make sites that allow for scaling text and images, we will be able to avoid becoming obsolete as resolutions pass far beyond those of today.

The Mad Flasher (Learning Firsthand How Many People Have Flash)

I now had to address the issues that happen behind the scenes. I needed to answer questions about what I wanted the user to handle in terms of installing and redirecting themselves to a Flash or non-Flash version. During the first test of the site, I had set the limitation that I was only going to use Flash 5 files. Implementing Flash 4 wouldn't make much sense anyway since version 5 was the current version and had been out for a few months. Well, that's what I thought anyway...

> *Making things easy for the users was getting more complicated for me every day.*

Welcome back to the land of user feedback. I began the testing of the type viewer with a small release to a handful of people whose opinions matter to me, and even though this small test was only released to about twenty or so people, about half of those who responded commented on the lack of Flash 4 support. I didn't realize how many people would be opposed to updating.

I had built the test site to load a different page when people didn't have Flash installed. Now, with the suggestions coming back in stating that I should really consider Flash 4 support before a public release, I had to solve the problem of implementing not only a Flash 5 version of the site, but also a non-Flash version *and*

a Flash 4 version. Making things easy for the users was getting more complicated for me every day.

I knew that Macromedia had a way to export as a Flash 4 file without having to reprogram. Well... they almost did, anyway. The scripts that I used were not Flash 4-compliant and, try as I might, my attempts at changing them to work in Flash 4 did nothing but waste my time. Eventually I just went ahead and rebuilt the files using Flash 4. However, Flash 4 did not allow me to change the color of the typeface programmatically. If I wanted a color changer in the Flash 4 version of the site, I would have had to fake it my making a couple of hundred versions of each typeface and then switching between them. This would take too much work. I was beginning to regret my choice of using Flash over Director.

I threw myself into the project at hand and produced a new Flash 4 version without color support in a few days. Then, I tried to find a good, easy way to let the user select which version of Flash to use. But the problem was that no matter what I did, if I required the user to select anything before they got to the home page, I would just be wasting their time. I wanted the process to be automatic.

I went out looking for a solution to the problem and I found that there was a great script online that solved the problem. A great and very talented developer by the name of Colin Moock had written a Flash detection script that used JavaScript to detect the version of Flash that you have installed on your browser and send the visitor to the appropriate page. This was great – it answered the problems that I had with making the user take an extra step. With this script installed, I could send those who had the Flash 4 version to the Flash 4 site, those who had Flash 5 to the appropriate page for their plug in, and those who had no plug in to another page that answered their needs. Finding this script was a lifesaver.

Colin's excellent script and instructions on how to use it are located at www.moock.org/

159

Flash is 99% OK

I implemented Colin's script into the site easily and moved on to other issues. Since I was acting as my own programmer and I don't know database programming, I chose to build the whole thing in straight HTML.

The Look and Feel of the Non-Flash Site

I would need to create some sort of non-Flash navigation and layout that would take the place of the type selector on the homepage for the non-Flash site. I worked up a couple of designs that used images, but since I had read that Flash had surpassed 75% in its browser install base and that it was climbing daily, I chose to use a simple pull-down list colored with JavaScript. I figured that most people wouldn't see this anyway, so why waste a lot of development time on it?

As you can see, the non-Flash version of the type-viewer page doesn't offer the interactive abilities of the type viewer, but it still does a good job of displaying the typeface to the visitor who may not have a plug in enhanced browser.

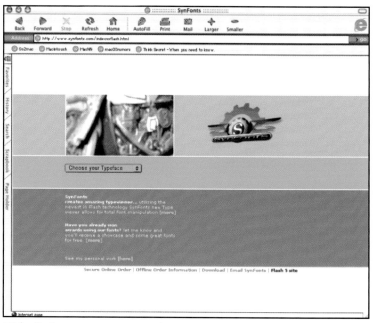

The site homepage, as seen by users without Flash.

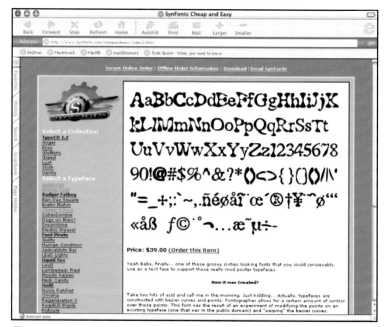

The type viewer page, for users without Flash.

I'm Finished... Or am I?

Well, that's it. The work that went into the development of the site is done. The files are ready and the content is in place. I'm ready to go public.

But wait, I almost forgot to tell you about the last step in the project development cycle...

Test, Test, Test

Do you remember all those toys that you broke when you were a kid? Close your eyes for a minute and get back to that feeling that you had while you were breaking them. Got it? Great.

During the testing process, that's what you have to do. As you have seen throughout the process I ran several tests, some were concerned with usability issues, some conducted to pinpoint bugs and problems, and some to determine whether the design I was working on was pleasing to people other than myself. Had I not done so much testing throughout the process, I would be stuck with a massive amount of testing at the end and probably a lot more work to do in making fixes and squishing bugs.

But regardless, at the end of a project, I always run tests to see if the completed work is ready for release. And this project was no different. After I was finished with the production of all the various elements of the site and the content had been added, I held a final preview to try and knock out bugs and spelling errors.

Because I don't have a fully equipped testing lab, I really can't test a site as thoroughly as a larger web shop might have, but I have managed to set up a pretty good testing setup. This isn't hard, and doing something similar will assist any web developer to test their work.

Home Browser/Platform Testing Labs Made Easy

First things first... go out right now and buy a new Macintosh, the current version of Connectix's Virtual

PC and spend some time looking over the Web for old browser installation programs. *http://browsers.evolt.org* is a good place to get probably any browser you can think of, and is part of the evolt case study (Chapter 5).

With this setup, you can test the functionality of your web site development on almost every conceivable browser and platform combination. The Mac will generally allow you to install almost any version of any browser concurrently without any conflicts. If you add Virtual PC (software that emulates a Pentium-class machine) you can install every single version of the Microsoft Windows operating system and have different versions of each setup to use a different web browser.

This system is not perfect, but it takes up far less desk space than a rack of computers would, and the Virtual PC programs display accurately and can be run concurrently for testing on multiple platform/browser combinations at a single sitting. (Try doing that with a PC equipped with multiple operating systems!).

Additionally since the PCs are emulated they run much slower than a modern machine will, allowing you to test for performance problems that often only happen on a slower machine. With preparation, you can test a web site for display inconsistencies or performance problems in a matter of hours.

Everybody Loves LOG!

After uploading the final version of the site I went back in and determined the effectiveness of what I had created. I've been using user logs to determine success since 1996 and I value the information that I get out of them. These logs show where users are coming from, what they do while they are on your site and where they go when they leave. They show you so much about your users that even if you don't do any user testing you can make you site better just by reading them.

Flash is 99% OK

Since these logs are essentially traces of activity performed by computers talking to one another, they are impossible to read without a program to interpret them.

In 1996, few hosting companies offered log analysis for free. I used to have to download the logs and run them though an offline reader to make head or tail of them, but now many companies offer log reading as a part of their hosting packages. If your company doesn't offer a log analysis tool for free, you should switch hosting services. This information is too valuable to live without.

> *If your company doesn't offer a log analysis tool for free, you should switch hosting services.*

Now for some interesting news: after a lot of suggestions that I build the site in Flash 4 rather than Flash 5, only 13 percent of people at the time of release landed on the Flash 4 homepage.

Interestingly, my suspicions prior to the time of the design were correct about Flash finally being ready for prime time – only 10% of all visitors landed at release had either no Flash or a version prior to 4. Of course, these numbers are changing every day. Currently they show that while almost all of my visitors have upgraded from Flash 4 (only 4% visit with this older version of the plug in) my average for non-Flash or those whose Flash plug in is prior to version 4 is remaining steady at 10%.

By looking at these logs I can assume that soon my need for a Flash 4 site will have dwindled to close to nothing and I can discontinue support for it completely.

Is the Site a Success?

The site has been successful on every level that I hoped for. I've gotten larger type design companies interested in using the engine on their site and actually sold development copies to smaller companies to develop on their own. The visuals of the web site turned out to be very pleasing and helped to generate more interactive work for me with other companies. And of course, the site is no longer on hold, so I'm selling type again.

Additionally, the site was a finalist in the e-commerce division of the Flash Forward film festival that took place in Amsterdam in October of 2001.

I think it's a success overall. Here's a review from Typographer.com (*http://typographer.com/2001_01_ 01_spotlightarchive.html*):

> Site of the Day – SynFonts
>
> *SynFonts has been around a while, but their recent site redesign is worth a look – clean and crisp with interesting use of Flash technology, plus there's some free fonts on there if you rummage about enough! Take a peek at the type viewer, easily the best example on the web at the moment and puts the big guys to shame. – Copyright (c)1998- 2002 David John Earls, All rights reserved.*

But was it a success in terms of usability? This prompts a slightly different answer: yes and no. Yes, the type viewer was a success in terms of usability, and the pages that it sits on are easy to navigate. But the scrolling navigation on the homepage, while fairly easy to learn, is not globally easy to use. When I made the decision to use that scrolling navigation, I also made the decision that I would be open to changing it if I continued to receive negative feedback. Now that I'm still receiving it, the next change made to the site should include some further exploration around this issue.

Speaking of changes that are yet to be made...

What Comes Next?

Whatever you do, never rest on your laurels if you want to continue to succeed in life.

Now that the latest version of the site has been out for over a year and I've had the chance to review and study the effectiveness of the site as well as get a lot of feedback on the possibility of releasing the technology to other type foundries, I'll probably plan only minor updates to the look and feel for the time being, with those changes being on the further development of the navigation on the home page. The site's design is clean and attractive enough to postpone the need for any major redesign for a couple more years unless design styles change radically or technology offers a good enough reason for further updates sooner than that.

> *Whatever you do, never rest on your laurels if you want to continue to succeed in life.*

Future Changes to Content

The content on the site, however, will need to be updated soon. I've just added 30 additional typefaces to the foundry and will be trying to sign up more new designers as time goes on, so I may need to change the typeface navigation on both the home page and the typeface display pages to accommodate other categories and choices.

Future Changes to the User Experience

While I have been using a third party to sell type on my site for a while, that is not a very elegant solution and brings in the problem of a pretty good-sized disconnect in the look and feel between my site and the vendor site. I would eventually like to move to an embedded e-commerce system so that I could more closely ensure that the user experience would remain more uniform throughout the browsing and purchasing process.

Future Changes to the Type Viewer

The type viewer itself needs updating, and now that I know more about Flash I can work more on reducing the size of the files and implementing changes to make the set-up of the engine more "drag and drop" so that I can sell it as a package more easily. Eventually I would like to get this to the point where it's polished enough for non-Flash-using designers to be able to implement it into their font sites without having to buy Flash. This is going to be tough, but not impossible, now that Flash MX has hit the shelves offering the capability to build much more complex tools that are very simple to use.

As I watch more people use the type viewer, I learn more about the things that I should change. I've got plans to modify the color chooser to use tabs instead of buttons. More than half the people I watch never try to change the background because they don't realize that the button changes what they are coloring.

I need to build a navigation element that will allow the user to choose different typefaces in full screen mode so that the user does not have to close it to select a new typeface.

In the last year I have received a lot of requests for PDF catalogs to complement the current print feature that I have in the type viewer, but I will have to figure if that is necessary after determining how much more capable the printing features are in Flash MX.

Flash is 99% OK

Conclusions

After updating the site for the past eight years, I can honestly say that I've learned a lot about what it takes to keep up a web site as a long-term project and not as a hit-and-run job. Being the one who receives the feedback from the design and user interface gives me lots of reasons to do a good job in those areas. After the first time I had someone yell at me for forcing them to download a 240k catalogue back in the 2400 baud AOL days, I decided that I would strive to make the user experience as pleasant as I could manage. The simple truth is that I like my customers and I care about whether they enjoy their experience while they are visiting my site. Businesses fail all the time because they fail to connect with and please their customers and I don't intend to fail.

Continually improving the web site has cost me a lot of time in the past eight years. If you add up all the effort that I've put into the development and testing of the web site, It probably amounts to more than I have spent developing the typefaces that I sell on it. But the payoff is that I get to walk away with a better understanding of a lot of aspects that I otherwise wouldn't be able to get hands-on experience with.

Can a One-Man Shop Compete with a 3000-Person Web Firm in Terms of Usability?

I think the answer is a resounding 'yes'. Much of my experience working in and around a variety of agencies has taught me that, even though a company may be a juggernaut, most of the effort that is put into the development of any site depends on the efforts of only a handful of people. And of those people, most of the weight of the interface design depends on the designers and junior designers anyway. I've joked with companies that were very serious about sites that cost an arm and a leg that ended up being built in a week by a couple of people. In the end it all comes down to the talents of the handful people working directly on the project. The designers, programmers, project managers, content, and strategy people all play a part,

but the fact that they have 3000 co-workers usually doesn't.

The area where larger companies do have the upper hand is in user testing labs and experience using them. Most of the larger companies have heavily invested in testing labs for both bug testing and for observing user testing. These are powerful assets, but the truth is that they are still only as effective as the people who are using them.

If you lose the interest of the audience, it doesn't matter if the links are blue... the people have all left.

Think about it. A job comes in, it goes through the process, and the team presents their work to the usability lab. All the lab can do is make suggestions on what the best design is and what they would do to make it better. You can accomplish most of the same results by doing some testing of your own and keeping an open mind while you do it. Test with your family, your co-workers, friends and anyone who will listen. Team up with a group of internet buddies and test each other's sites, make everyone agree to provide a full written page of feedback and have them fill out a list of standard questions. If you dedicate yourself to the process of making your designs usable, it doesn't matter how limited your own resources are.

Use this as a chance to get ahead of the curve. There are many other books on the subject of usability – you can buy and read them all – Jakob Neilsen's *Designing Web Usability*; Steve Krug's *Don't Make Me Think*; *Tog on Interface*, by Bruce "Tog" Tognazzini; *GUI Bloopers: Don'ts and Do's for Software Developers and Web Designers*, by Jeff Johnson – and many more.

However, whatever you do, don't follow them by rote. Good usability is **not** about blue links or some methodology that happens to be in vogue. Good usability is about designing the right site for the right audience. That includes concerns about style. If you lose the interest of the audience, it doesn't matter if the links are blue... the people have all left.

Come Get Your Free Usability Diplomas!

A good usability expert doesn't know anything.

What I mean by that is that the usability experts that I have worked with that have impressed me don't come at a problem pretending to know the solution, they ask questions and form their opinions only after they know the whole picture. If you behave in the same way, not defending your design to the death but instead yielding to constructive criticism and user feedback, you can improve a lot of what you create and save a lot of money on hiring usability consultants.

A good usability expert doesn't know anything.

There is no way that anyone could write a comprehensive book on usability. There are too many variables: race, religion, language, sex and sexuality, profession, upbringing, and all the things that make us who we are individually cause us to comprehend things in different ways. A smart young kid raised on video games has a different outlook and different needs than, say, a migrant worker that has never seen a computer. Writing a checklist of do's and don'ts that would cover every possible user situation would result in a set of books that would make the Library of Congress jealous and would be out of date as soon as society changed in any way.

With that being said, here is my best attempt at making a list that can make you a usability expert.

1. Think through everything you design as many times as you can afford to before, while, and after you design it. You are smarter than you realize.

2. Ask all the questions that you can – of yourself and the user. The more you know the less you have to guess.

3. Think hard about the fact that your design might be wrong. Doing so will let you create something better.

4. Design for your audience, not for yourself. Unless your audience is made up of Flash designers, don't do cutting edge Flash design.

5. Test, test, test!

Basic Flash Design Rules

I can't tell you how to handle every situation that you may encounter on every project, but I can give you a set of guidelines to follow when working in Flash that may save you some of the headaches that you may otherwise encounter. These guidelines are by no means definitive, but these are good rules that will generally aid your Flash-based web site designs if you follow them.

1. Make the interface simple and straightforward.

As the designer of a site, you have a lot of knowledge that the end user may never have. If you don't have a blueprint of the site on paper, you will certainly have one in your head as to how all the information fits together when you design the interface. Your job as interface designer will be to make the experience of discovering the information easier for the end user. The more straightforward you make the interface, the less the user has to guess about what things may mean.

Flash is 99% OK

2. **Try and keep the Flash on your site compartmentalized.**

A site that is entirely built in Flash may seem like a good idea, but breaks many browser functions. Many designers, including celebrated designers that have a cult-like fan following, often create sites that are completely based inside a single Flash file, these are fine only if your users are other Flash developers trained as you are.

3. **Don't restrict the viewing size of your Flash movies if at all possible.**

Many people set a static and non-changeable pixel resolution for their Flash web sites. While this does keep your site looking exactly as you want it to, it also means that it will show up as a teensy tiny little square of unreadable information on my 1920x1440 resolution monitor. Flash is a scalable vector technology; so let me scale it if I want to. Do you really think it's better to force me to change the resolution on my monitor in order to read your site? Do you think that's going to make the user happy?

4. **Don't use tiny fonts.**

One of the current styles popular with "hip" web site designers is to use 6, 7 and 8 point bitmap all caps text. These designers are attempting to create a trendy pixilated 80's videogame like design. I'll be the first to admit that it looks cool! But trust me on this, just don't do it. To explain why, I'll write the reasons here, really small:

YOU SHOULD NEVER EVER WRITE COPY IN SOMETHING THAT IS SO SMALL BECAUSE IT WILL USUALLY CAUSE THE USER TO HAVE TO GET OUT OF THEIR COMFY OFFICE CHAIR AND GET REALLY CLOSE TO THEIR MONITOR IN ORDER TO READ THE INFORMATION ON YOUR SITE. THIS MAY CAUSE AN UNUSUAL AMOUNT OF ANGER IN YOUR USER, CAUSING THEM TO PLACE YOUR EMAIL ADDRESS ON SPAM LISTS OR SEND YOU AN 'I LOVE YOU BUT I CAN'T READ YOUR SITE' VIRUS OR POSSIBLY EVEN JUST PLAN ON NEVER VISITING YOU, EVER. USABILITY TIP FOR THOSE OF YOU WHO ARE DILIGENT AND SHARP-EYED ENOUGH TO GET THIS FAR: THERE IS A REASON THAT THE SMALL PRINT IN LEGAL DOCUMENTS IS PRINTED SO SMALL – THEY DON'T REALLY WANT YOU TO READ IT!

5. **Avoid hidden (rollover to reveal) navigation like the plague.**

It makes for a very clean design if all your navigation is hidden, but it may also mean that people won't know where to click to go somewhere.

6. **Try not to use Flash for the navigation for your site unless you provide a backup for non-Flash enabled browsers and devices.**

This is one of the rules that I have followed since day one. Never, ever require plug in use for any site where the plug in is not directly delivering the content... Even then, you should attempt to add alternative content if at all possible. An example of this would be providing Windows Media files and Quicktime files on a site where you are delivering video content. If you do this, the user can decide which to use.

7. **Drop the idea of an intro movie and animations between button choices.**

These only serve to slow your site down. I don't care if you are the number one Flash designer in the world, your animations cannot ever be exciting enough to waste my time every time I click a button or stop by your site unless these animations are part of the content itself.

8. **Test, test, test.**

Test your code for bugs, test the interface for usability issues, test the colors you use for colorblindness... just test everything! This should be self-evident, but often it is not. The more that you test your site or creation, the more likely that you will find any errors, bugs or usability snafus before a project sees the light of day.

I don't care if you are the number one Flash designer in the world, your animations cannot ever be exciting enough to waste my time every time I click a button

I once found a button glitch that I had never seen before in one of my projects that was over three years old. I had opened this project hundreds of times in client demos, and on top of that, the project was professionally tested for days before it was released when it was created. Yet somehow a bug got past the gates.

9. Poor man's user testing.

Even if you can't afford professional usability testing, test with your mom or some other older family or staff member (and DO NOT tell them what they are supposed to click on!) You'll be surprised how much you can learn from this simple activity, it's probably the best poor man's user testing available. The viewpoints of older members of society will often point out problems that are overlooked by younger users who may be more capable in their skills of computer and Internet use.

Usability testing is invaluable; you only have one set of eyes and one brain. Sometimes it takes someone else to point out the obvious to you because you have been made numb to your design by working on it for so long.

That's it for this chapter. I hope you've found something useful in here, and I also hope you've seen how Flash is not the enemy. You can be usable with or without Flash, and you can be unusable with or without Flash. But if you remain open to criticism and changing times, you won't find yourself with an unusable site just for the sake of using a "cool" technology.

Where Can I Find Other Flash Usability Tips Online?

Macromedia.com
http://www.macromedia.com/software/flash/productinfo/usability/articles/
(This link may change. You might also try searching for "Flash" and "Usability" on the Macromedia site if it does.) This is Macromedia's collection of articles that relate to usability – it's probably going to be more current when you read this than any list I can assemble here, but some of the content is not specifically Flash-based. Still, all of the reading that you find here will help you out and even if an article here isn't specifically covering Flash issues, you will still walk away with something useful.

Flazoom
http://www.flazoom.com
Run by Chris Macgregor, this site can occasionally be a little like watching an episode of Mystery Science Theatre 3000 because of all of the banter and site-blasting that goes on in the reader-provided site reviews, but Chris is a top-notch usability expert who writes a good amount of the commenting on reviewed sites himself and when he does, the reviews are top notch. In addition to writing many very useful articles, which he publishes here, Chris is responsible for authoring Macromedia's Flash Usability white paper. This is the definitive source for Flash usability opinion.

Jakob Nielsen
http://www.useit.com/
Hey, Jakob was the one who said that Flash is 99% bad. He's got a lot of really good points. And the best place to find out what the "other half" thinks is to visit his web site.

Don's Usable Objects of Desire

The modern financial network – God what a marvel! Without the modern financial network in place around the world, I don't know that I would be able to cope with life! I visit cash machines at least five times on any trip that I'm on and they allow me to be absent minded with my money. No matter where I am anymore (in the US and most places abroad) I have access to my account funds. Second to this is the way that credit cards work (not the high interest rates but the fact that I don't even really "need" money anymore in most occasions), and Internet bill payment – I no longer have to worry about missing bills because I'm traveling. This monetary network where my funds and bills are accessible anywhere allows me to be "at home" wherever I am.

The modern high-resolution digital camera – While almost all cameras are inherently unusable (how many times have you asked someone to take your picture only to have them stare blankly at the camera unsure of what to do or what button to use), the advancement to digital is what I'm really impressed with. Modern digital cameras have reached such a high resolution that they are finally offering images as good as those achieved by film. This allows my to take as many pictures as I want without the added expense or trouble of going to get the film developed. Because of this, my camera is almost always with me and gets used for hundreds of pictures that I would have otherwise missed. Since the images are digital, it even saves me the step of scanning in a photo if I want to use it in my computer or send it over the Internet.

Also:

802.11 wireless networking – By using Apple's "Airport" technology, otherwise known as 802.11 wireless networking, I no longer have to wire my house to get computer networking set up. I simply walk around and log in to the Internet from wherever I am in the house. Friends and clients with the right software and hardware (and most of my friends and clients have both) simply open up their laptop computers, log in to my network and they too are able to surf and check e-mail anywhere in my house. No hassle of finding an ethernet plug or telephone line and being tethered to a wall six feet away.

The Schuberth motorcycle helmet – The Schuberth offers a one handed flip open design that allows you to have discussions at a stoplight or petrol station, easy to use vents that can be operated one handed while the motorcycle is being operated, and a couple of other mostly standard items. The real feature that makes this helmet stand out is that it has a built-in sun shade. Much like the "blast shield" on a pilot's helmet, this item flips down with a smooth one-handed operation and replaces the need to risk your life by pulling over to put on or take off sunglasses.

Watson 1.1 – This OS X application is quite possibly the most wonderful Internet application that I have ever used, bar none. Its simple information based interface allows quick browsing of Internet based information without surfing to a different web site to find it. For that reason, it probably has a very short life. After all, if I don't have to go visit moviephone.com, a popular movie listings site in the US, then I won't be viewing moviephones advertising and they will go out of business. But until the rest of the world catches on to Watson and tries to stop it, this will be one of the staples that I use to find "real information" on the web. The technology works with plug-ins that allow searching for different kinds of information, for example, there are modules that search just for movies, flights, UPS shipments, recipes and much much more. While the interface is not the "best", it is a quantum leap from having to search out some other site using a browser and then learning their navigation and working your way through to whatever information you are after.

Also:

Firewire – The plug design makes it easy to plug in and the technology behind it allows hot plugging of devices; I no longer have to shut down my computer to attach a hard drive. Additionally, the self-powered feature allows me to travel with a small pocket sized drive with as much space as I currently need that requires no power supply and will work on almost any machine with a Firewire port (most modern computers in my business).

Streetsigns – Because of the language barrier, almost all streetsigns regardless of the country that are in have evolved into symbols that tell you at a glance what to do or where to go. Though there are exceptions, this is true almost everywhere that people drive cars.

evolt.org
workers of the web, evolt!

a d r i a n   r o s e l l i

www.evolt.org

A founder of evolt.org, Adrian Roselli is Vice President of Interactive Media at Algonquin Studios, located in Buffalo, New York.

Adrian has almost 10 years of experience in graphic design, web design and multimedia design, as well as extensive experience in interface design and usability. He has been developing for the World Wide Web since its inception, when he should have been finishing film school projects. In addition, Adrian is also a board member of the American Advertising Federation affiliate in Buffalo (Brainstorm), and a co-chair of IDEA, a special interest group focusing on the web and multimedia.

You can see Adrian on the evolt.org site and lists, as well as other sites and lists, under the handle "aardvark." Nobody knows quite where the name came from, although he assures us it's a terribly boring story.

If you weren't doing this, what would you be doing?

I'd still be trying to find my way in film, theatre, graphic design, multimedia, or something else. I need something that has a blend of technical and creative aspects, but it takes a while for me to settle into it.

Which living person do you most admire?

Egad! Can't say I've thought of that. I'm way too cynical to have heroes in living people, I like to wait until they've been dead a couple hundred years or more and admire the idealized persona.

On a scale of 1 (Amish) - 10 (Star Trekkie), how geeky are you?

Probably an 8. I'm a design geek, but not an operating system geek. I'm a browser geek, but not a cutting edge browser geek. I certainly dress like a geek.

What's your favorite building?

Ask that of a former architecture major, and you'll get an answer only after days of reflection.

What is the best typeface? Why?

London Underground. Based on the Edward Johnston typeface that was designed for the London Underground system in the early 1900s, P22 is the only foundry that's got it right (and legal, I understand). It's a strong face that's legible at any distance and at any size, but not at all overbearing. It's very friendly and very refined. It doesn't need to tell people it's the best, it might not even believe it, but it knows it's a winner. It calls me on weekends, too.

What's your favorite book? Piece of music? Type of pizza?

• The Hitchhiker's Guide to the Galaxy by Douglas Adams.
• Music, well, that's hard to say. I've been on a Chris Isaak run for a year now, though. But if I were trapped on a desert island, you could probably play Bolero over and over without me killing you.
• Pizza? Broccoli and pineapple.

If you were a superhero(ine), who would you be?

Batman. Not the movie Batman, not the cartoon Batman, not the campy 50s Batman (although he's cool). The Frank Miller Dark Knight Batman. Only I'd smile more.

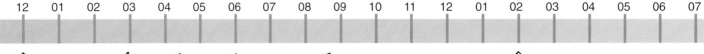

12 01 02 03 04 05 06 07 08 09 10 11 12 01 02 03 04 05 06 07

December 14, 1998 The original e-mail that got us all revved up to form our own thing is sent by Dan Cody.

March 12, 1999 The evolt.org mailing list, thelist, is launched on MajorDomo.

April 1, 1999 Beta version of the first evolt.org web site. It was lavender.

June 1, 1999 The original evolt.org site is launched.

August 17, 1999 Browsers.evolt.org is brought up as the manifestation of two years' worth of browser collecting.

February 19, 2000 First gathering of evolt.org members in real life, Washington, D.C.

Evolt.org is one of those communities that was formed in response to a need. Many web developers on the MonkeyJunkies list run by Wired Digital were looking for something different, something that they had some control over, and in many cases, something that wasn't specific to the United States of America. Being a list of web developers who wanted a different kind of list, we all put our money (time, in our cases) where our mouth was, and so began the first steps to creating *evolt.org*.

With some 25 people banding together, we all felt that there weren't any places for developers to go to share their insights and experiences without someone trying to make a profit off the information or otherwise trying to direct its growth despite what the members wanted. There were other mailing lists for web developers out there, and many members of the MonkeyJunkies list belonged to more than one. But when you're not the person in charge, it's hard to be certain they have your best interests at heart, which is a suspicion that seems common to Internet culture. This doesn't mean any of these lists or communities were bad or inadequate, but we wanted a place to foster this idealized, 'by developers for developers' environment, made up of volunteers and donated equipment.

Some of the points of our creation have been lost in the ether of the Internet, which is something we don't mind so much. Ultimately, we had a number of talented people volunteer their skills for the creation of, first a mailing list and then, a web site.

The goal was simple: create a resource for web developers that was run by web developers. No banner ads, no parent corporations to answer to, no restrictions on direction other than those set by the

Some of the evolt.org *admin team from our trip to South by SouthWest (SXSW, a film, music, and interactive conference and festival) back in March of 2001. Visible are (top row) Scott Dexter, Martin Burns, (middle row) Rudy Limeback, Dave McLean, Erika Meyer, Emily Christensen, Marlene Bruce, (bottom row) Dan Cody, Adrian Roselli, Jeff Howden, Elfur Logadottir, and Bob Davis.*

No banner ads, no parent corporations to answer to, no restrictions on direction other than those set by the community.

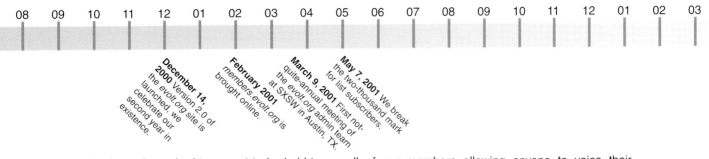

08 09 10 11 12 01 02 03 04 05 06 07 08 09 10 11 12 01 02 03

December 14, 2000 Version 2.0 of the evolt.org site is launched, we celebrate our second year in existence.

February 2001 members.evolt.org is brought online.

March 9, 2001 First not-quite-annual meeting of the evolt.org admin team at SXSW in Austin, TX.

May 7, 2001 We break the two-thousand mark for list subscribers.

community. As such, we had to expect to be held to a higher standard than most. It's one thing for a web developer to blame implementation flaws on bosses or faceless corporate parents. But when you claim to be a resource for web developers by web developers, you have no such excuses. After all, if you host articles on designing pages that adhere to the HTML standards, and your own pages don't even validate, then you've potentially disqualified yourself as a resource. It's as if your English teacher told you that "ain't" isn't a word, shortly before telling you, "It ain't time to leave," during your mad end-of-class dash to the door.

At the same time, the lack of a boss or parent organization pushing us for new development often causes our haphazard process to falter as people's day jobs and real lives often take precedence when it comes to allotting time for work on the *evolt.org* behemoth of projects. We try to work for our members, but sometimes our members understand our plight too well, so they're too forgiving when something doesn't get done right away.

We have a chaotic structure, with no defined job titles or specific tasks. Sure, some of us gravitate to specific duties, but it rotates regularly with interest, time, and capability. Sometimes it takes us a couple of days to find out who is best suited to do a task, and as you'd expect, that poor guy or gal is usually taking a day at the beach while their mailbox starts to pile up with frantic requests for feedback, files, access, or even the rare ingredient for a recipe.

Despite all this, we all feel passionately about what we do, and have no problems voicing our frank opinions on proposed changes, features, content, or anything really. Recently, in fact, we've opened up a new list to

all of our members allowing anyone to voice their opinion on the short- and long-term direction of *evolt.org*, with topics ranging from fundraising to pay for bandwidth to article submission guidelines. This influx of new perspectives, derived from everyone from coders to writers to designers, has proven to be a boon to our future direction as ideas are tossed out that some of us original founders might never have considered.

We wanted to be a multinational organization from the start, partly because we had a few non-American members when we first started *evolt.org*, and partly because we recognized how few resources existed for foreign web developers. As our membership has grown, our intent to be multi-national has started to manifest itself in our new subscribers and article authors. While *evolt.org* is still 50% made up of Americans, we have an amazing diversity of users. At the same time, we're a bit spoiled because they are seemingly all English speakers who work on the Web, meaning they already understand how to interact with US-centric designs and language. We do, however, continue to attempt to appeal to developers in all countries.

The Original Site

The original *evolt.org* site was launched in early 1999 and lasted until our 2nd birthday in December of 2000. It was a great start, but was intended to be those first steps out, to get our feet wet and experiment with our idea of creating an online resource for web developers beyond just a mailing list or a developer 'zine that was always a few weeks behind the curve. We had already been going strong as a mailing list, but it took us a little while to get our web site off the ground. We wanted to see just how well we would be received.

I must admit, I wasn't prepared for how quickly things took off. Initially, we weren't sure if readers would just submit articles without us specifically asking them to, and for a little while, that was true. For a few weeks, our poor readers were subjected to our ramblings and yammerings, and either for the sake of their sanity, or taking pity on us, the articles started showing up. Now with over 800 articles on the site, and unsolicited submissions coming in nearly daily, we've managed to create a constant stream of material coming in from around the Web and around the world.

The initial goal of the site was to provide a place for web developers to provide articles for their community. These articles would be on display on the site and categorized in a number of "centers". Each center name was chosen in an attempt to categorize all the disparate aspects of web development, somewhat based on how other sites broke information up, and somewhat based on our own ideas of what made sense as a structure. We knew up front that many articles would probably qualify to be in more than one category, but we didn't implement a relationship in the back-end code to allow articles to exist in more than one category. We decided to save that for later development.

We also created a special category called "Suggestions" which allowed anyone to post an "article" that was a suggestion on improving the site or the community in general. Posting these as articles on

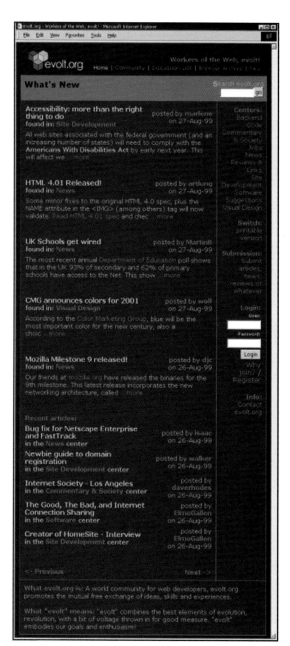

The original evolt site, with its primary colors on black background. Note the right-hand navigation bar.

the site allowed people to comment on the suggestions and take a community approach to addressing concerns or brainstorm ideas. I'm not sure if any other sites were doing this at the time, but it seemed like a good way to hold us accountable by lighting a fire under our feet. Some of these suggestions proved invaluable, while others were, well, interesting. The ratings system, the number of comments displayed in each article on the home page, some personalization features, and even category ideas have come from the suggestions queue. Since the creation of a mailing list covering the future of *evolt.org*, as well as a mailing list dealing with developments on the site, this category has fallen into disuse for the most part.

> *Now we always try to find common words to express ideas on the site, instead of trying to create a site-specific language of our own.*

Of course, the mailing list itself was the first time *evolt.org* bared itself to the world, and as such, was the face of *evolt.org* for some time. All the mailing list signup information, however, resided on another server and in a very basic design as output by the list management software, a modified (by Dan Cody) version of MajorDomo named MajorGumbo. This obviously made for an inconsistent experience as an *evolt.org* member went from the mailing list archives and signup pages to the site.

The original design of the site was a conglomeration of bright greens, blues, and reds sitting on a field of grays. These colors made for an easily recognizable site, but one that often received complaints for everything from text size to color scheme. Given the fact that all the borders were achieved with multiple-nested tables and all the text styling with a fleet of <font>s, it's a wonder we didn't get more grief about our site coding. Of course, back then, we were just following the trends in web development.

One of the things we learned about that initial site, beyond the color scheme and the site coding, was that the term "centers" for categories confused some our readers more than if we had just used the word "categories". How this escaped us I'll never know, but it was our first lesson in the problems of abstraction. When we rebuilt the site, we briefly discussed changing it from "centers" to "categories," so briefly, in fact, that we just did it almost without thinking. Now we always try to find common words to express ideas on the site, instead of trying to create a site-specific language of our own.

Much of the initial design was done by our (at the time) preferred method of getting things done - someone just went and built it, and usually that someone was the person who not only had the skills to do it, but had the time available as well. Back then, we didn't really perceive ourselves as having specialties, and some of those specialties we assumed probably weren't accurate (I was nearly made the database designer for the site, and believe me, that would have been amusing if not disastrous). There was an initial beta version live for a couple of months before the color scheme was overhauled to what you see here. That was in mid-March of 1999, about the same time our mailing list rolled out as well. The true first version of the site rolled out on June 1st of 1999, just in time to start directing our burgeoning list subscribers to a central resource for both posting and researching all the web topics they cared to address.

Some further testing on that first version showed us that there were significant rendering problems with the site in Navigator 3.x. Of course, this was in early to mid-1999, when Navigator 3.x was already becoming a forgotten browser. This demonstrated that even early on we were concerned with allowing any user to visit our site, regardless of their browser.

That was really about it for testing. We all spent a lot of time revising content, names for links, and technical issues, but for the most part, the design was accepted pretty readily. We knew some issues would pop up, but we also knew that we had been looking at it for so long that we had to just roll it out to the community and see how it was received.

> We had been looking at it for so long that we had to just roll it out to the community and see how it was received.

Home Page

The home page of the site was a pretty basic concept. The five most recent articles were displayed with an abstract. This abstract consisted of the first 200 characters of an article, which often proved problematic in cases where links or other tags appeared near the end of the 200 characters and weren't closed properly. Every time an article was submitted, an administrator had to ensure that the 200 character truncation wouldn't cut something off mid-tag, which when it did happen, produced some interesting and bizarre results on the home page (a form of interactive art, if you will). We knew this was something we wanted to fix for the next version of the site, so for a while we just lived with it. We knew other content management systems handled abstracts differently, but for an all-volunteer effort, moving it out quickly sometimes outweighed usability convenience for the small group of administrators.

The next five articles avoided this problem altogether by not displaying an abstract. Every article link included the title, the author (as a link to the author's bio page), the center in which the article was found (also a link),

and a "*more…*" link in case the user didn't think to click on the bright green title.

The home page also offered a search feature, a list of all the centers, as well as the ability to view a printable version of the page, a link to the article submission page, and the login form. Of course, with the login form was a link with some very smart wording: "*Why join?*" This brought the user to a page on the history and idea behind *evolt.org*. And of course the obligatory contact link was below all this.

This relatively simple collection of items in the navigation made up the entire site navigation. It seemed to serve us pretty well, although, based on user feedback, many users never seemed to catch on to the idea of just clicking a center and surfing through all the articles within it.

Another concern we had early on was how long it took the home page to render. This first version of the site was using Access as the database, and we started to push that to its limits with all the data we were pulling for the home page for all the traffic we were getting. Since everyone in this profession understands the value of a fast-loading page (or, more accurately, the loss associated with a slow page), the code monkeys among us set out to create a static version of the home page to reduce the strain on the server and the database, which resulted in a faster page load time. The only drawback was that approved articles didn't appear on the home page immediately, they had to wait until the next static version of the page was drawn.

Article Page

The navigation on the article page was the same as the home page, with one notable exception. Below the contact link appeared a list of the titles and dates of the last five articles posted by the author whose article you were viewing. Below that, another link allowed you to see all the articles posted by that author. One advantage of this was that readers might continue to

 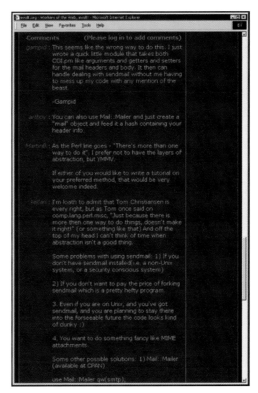

Two shots of the article page.

explore the site through this, since most likely none of these articles appeared on the home page at the time.

Beneath every article there was a place for members to contribute comments to the article. What we feared might grow out of control, and spiral into something with the traffic and complexity of Slashdot, actually turned out to be a refined forum for commentary on the article at hand. This first iteration of the comments feature only showed the user name of the person who posted the comment. Often, authors or other members would check back on an article just to see comments that had appeared since their last visit, but there was no way to tell when a comment was made. It didn't take much feedback from users to realize we had left out an important piece of information on each comment.

Most other comment features on sites consisted of threaded discussions, or just flat lists of comments. We decided the threaded discussion approach was redundant considering the mailing list and the fact that we were always trying to push readers to participate in the list. This meant the robust threading and moderation systems found in something like Slashdot were unnecessary for us. We also wanted to avoid emulating the way that other sites like CNN hid their comments behind a link stuffed into the bottom of the page. We felt comments could add a lot to an article, even allowing authors and readers to keep it up-to-date, but that it would be no good if you had to click around in a mad shell game to find the commentary.

Code Blocks

One of the limitations of the old design, color scheme notwithstanding, was how it handled blocks of content such as code or very long URLs. Sometimes authors would post articles with blocks of sample code that had a hundred (or hundreds of) characters per line, not considering how they might render in the template. Often, members who didn't know that the comment fields accepted HTML would paste in one of the famously long URLs we've come to love from many of the media sites, causing the entire page to be pried apart for just the one chunk of text. Given that the design wasn't liquid, and given that the navigation was on the right, sometimes an article or comment would cause the right-hand navigation to get pushed off the screen. (This wouldn't happen if the navigation bar were located on the left, because the content of the page would continue off-screen instead). For a new user, this could be a bit disconcerting if they followed a link in to a page but didn't see any navigation and missed the dreaded horizontal scroll bar. This issue with code blocks became one of the things we wanted to correct in later versions of the site.

Liquid Design

One of the greatest advantages of the web is that it's something that your average dedicated print designer or software developer can't get their arms around. It's a fluid medium, and information can be experienced in as many ways as there are users.

In the traditional software world, a developer needs to know a lot about the user's system in order to tailor applications to the platform – things like amount of memory, processor speed, and even maximum resolution (in order to let application elements like forms fit in the user's screen). In the print world, a designer needs to know everything about the output as well. Knowing the dot gain of a particular paper stock or controlling the kerning of the copy on the page, both contribute to the experience the viewer has of the final product.

On the web, all that goes out the window. Users could be running anything from a text-to-speech browser to the latest version of Internet Explorer with JavaScript disabled. Their systems can be anything from the newest version of BeOS to an old Amiga, and monitors can range from old 14-inch bricks running 16 colors at 640x480 to a multiple flat panel set-up, each running at 32-bit and 1,600x2,000 pixels. Ultimately, the user has control, and no matter how much the designer or developer wants to wrest that control away, it just can't be done.

With so many users who leave their screen resolution at the factory default, to users who cannot change resolutions due to hardware limitations, to users who run at the highest resolution possible, there are a number of variations out there. Couple that with the fact that not everyone surfs full-screen, and most users have toolbars of some sort taking up space that could otherwise be used for web page display, and you've got an infinite number of possible dimensions in browser windows.

I've often suggested that designing for discrete screen resolutions was flawed in principle. Even if half of your audience has screen resolutions of 800x600, how many of them are surfing full screen without any browser chrome? – Probably not many.

So instead of leaving users at low resolutions with a scroll bar at the bottom of their screen (requiring them to constantly scroll left-to-right-to-left to read content or see ads), or leaving users at high resolutions with large amounts of white space outside of your content, developers came up with a "liquid" design approach. Layouts would scale their width to fit the window, either removing giant blocks of white space from the sides of a page, or preventing scrolling fits.

By allowing a page to scale up to any resolution, as well as down to nearly any resolution, you can ensure the user determines some very important aspects of the page: the readability of the content (characters per line), the ability to print pages regardless of the user's

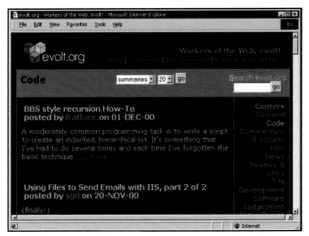 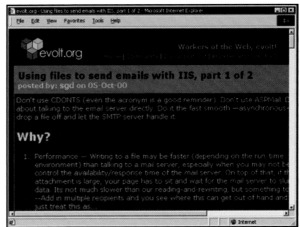

The image on the left shows how the page should appear in a 640x480 window. The page on the right shows a content page with a very long block of code, or a very long URL, further down the page pushing the navigation beyond the edge of the window. Most users would have no idea that the content was pushing the navigation out since, as you can see here, the content responsible for this was usually not visible until much further down the page.

window size, the bandwidth constraints (since images are often tiled, reused, or skipped in favor of colored table cells), and compatibility (if you design it correctly, you could even accommodate users on palm-top browsers).

There are some users who won't like this solution, however. Sometimes the user chooses to surf with a maximized window, and won't scale the window to a size that makes the text easier to read. While it may seem counterintuitive, these users rely on fixed-width sites to control text readability in lieu of scaling the window. They are, however, still your users, and this must be kept in mind when approaching a liquid layout.

Admin Pages

Of course, you can't run a site remotely without some way to administer it. Some of the parts of the site that got the most thorough abuse were the administration pages. These pages allowed the admin team to answer e-mails to the site, approve or deny articles, create new centers, or surf through the membership to handle passwords and the like.

> *You can't run a site remotely without some way to administer it.*

One of the most trying aspects of the initial site was the article submission process. Articles with code samples normally need to be 'escaped' (converted so that a section of example HTML would display as text you could read, and not get rendered by the browser and make a mess) to show up properly. In our case, these had to be doubly escaped in order to show in the `textarea` without being converted. So an admin editing an article with `&gt;` within it would have to make it `&amp;gt;` in order for it to display as `&gt;` in the `textarea`. Even though fixes were applied, many of the admins kept second-guessing the tool, the code, and themselves, which ultimately left a lot of us confused.

We also had the ability to respond to e-mails submitted to the site. Many of the admins, however, chose to respond through their e-mail client since the form was not as easy to use or as full-featured as their e-mail client. Typing into text areas that wrap at 50 characters and don't do quoting as an e-mail client does may have cost us the ability to track responses on the site. People who did respond through the admin section of the site at least had their responses archived as well as having the message marked off so nobody else would reply to it. This was a case where the admin team found a feature difficult to use, and so didn't use it. Unlike the article summaries, where the admin team sucked it up and made it work, this feature just wasn't used enough in the first version, because it was so hard to use.

What did we Learn?

We had started out on the first site more concerned with the community features than anything else. We hadn't considered usability as much as we could have, and so we kept stumbling across issues and re-assessing our decisions regularly. It also showed us that some readers wouldn't take an article on, say, screen resolution as seriously if it was not contained within a site that embodied the principles espoused within the article.

On one hand, we missed the boat on some seemingly obvious issues, but on the other hand, we learned that, as a team, we were capable of recognizing some of our own design and implementation flaws as well as responding to member suggestions. That experience would prove invaluable as we began our move to the second version of the site, something which we also hoped would remove all the remaining problems with the first version of the site. Yes, we really were that naïve.

We had been discussing many features for the next version of the site for some time, although we all had different ideas on how best to achieve them within a new design. However, we all wanted to be sure that whatever we made was bigger and better than version one.

The Current Site

When the time came to create a new site, many of us decided to sit down on our own to produce site designs based on our individual experiences with the old site, and where we thought it should go for the new design. We took this approach because enough of us felt we had good ideas on our own and wanted to present them untainted, and then see if we could pull the strengths from many designs into one. This resulted in an interesting array of potential solutions to some of our more pressing problems.

We wanted to code a site that:

- Was HTML 4.01 Transitional-compliant (*http://www.w3.org/TR/html401/*)

- Used CSS (*http://www.w3.org/Style/CSS/*) for all styling outside of layout

- Was accessible according to the Web Accessibility Initiative (*http://www.w3.org/WAI/*)

We succeeded on these points easily enough, since there's little room for subjectivity when it comes to those three goals.

> *We wanted a site that we could hold up as an example of good coding and modular design.*

Clearly we also wanted to create something developers could use easily, without confusion, and as efficiently as possible. We wanted a site that we could hold up as an example of good coding and modular design. This started to shape some of the designs on the table, with us overwhelmingly going with a design that Isaac Forman had put together. Unlike everything else we did, the debate on this selection was succinct (and yes,

Some initial (re)design ideas. The new look and feel is a lot more relaxed in tone than the first site.

my design offerings were terrible), and the revisions began as Isaac worked to address future goals and current technical limitations.

Choosing to go with a tabled layout and HTML 4.01 was based on the notion of allowing everyone to use the site in the same way. To ensure we were still accessible, we had to be sure the tables linearized well. Basically, this meant that the content of the page would still make sense if viewed in the same order as it appeared in the code. Using a text browser, like Lynx, during development helped ensure that we didn't split headers from related copy, form labels from their corresponding text boxes, or even scatter navigation all over the place.

A consistent experience from operating system to operating system, and from browser to browser, was considered very important for both branding and usability. If a member could be guaranteed to see the same site whether they were at work, at home, at the library, or even on a TV browser, then we could be assured that they could use the site the same way without any need to take time to learn how to use

elements of the site again. Granted, there would be differences, and the use of CSS for coloring page elements, for example, meant that non-CSS browsers would get a black and white version of the page, but at least users would see a similar layout and find navigation in the same place regardless of what browser they used.

Some of the other goals of the site weren't as clear-cut. We knew we wanted the site to address all of the problems we had run into with the previous site, but we often had differing opinions on the best way to address those issues. For instance, just choosing a color scheme wasn't a matter of running with the design, but went through numerous reviews to ensure we had both a "pleasing" color scheme and one that also offered enough contrast to users with visual impairments who still surfed with CSS-capable browsers. If a color-blind user accessed the site, we didn't want the text and background to appear as the same shade of gray, for example, so we wanted to balance these issues early on. Another decision was going with pixels as the units for type in the CSS, as opposed to a user-scalable unit like ems, percentages, or keywords. This decision, however valid at the time, is now undergoing review as we attempt to convert to user-scalable type that doesn't display bizarrely or inconsistently in many browsers. No matter how technically capable our audience, we don't want to force those who can't read the text to create user style sheets or disable CSS in order to read the content.

Of course, this design, as well as the coding, has had plenty of opportunity for stress testing as we've wedged new features and elements into the layout of the pages. The design has even grown now to seven sites from the original three, which we accounted for, which were:

Tabled Layouts

Our tabled layout decision was made, and the site was rolled out, well before the Web Standards Project (WaSP) and A List Apart's much-publicized (within the web community) move away from tabled layouts. The WaSP had instead taken a stance that declared old browsers to be bad for the web in general, and called upon developers to create sites that would display messages to users of older browsers telling them that they needed to upgrade to experience the site properly. We opted to maintain the tabled layout primarily because it still met all the accessibility goals we targeted, still validated as compliant code, and, unlike the WaSP message, still allowed users on nearly any configuration to see a functionally similar site. Not to mention, at the time the ALA site offered nothing the *evolt.org* site couldn't do, except it maybe could do it for fewer users. Now, this doesn't mean we disagreed with them as a group, but we didn't feel we needed to ditch the tables to be compliant and accessible, especially since we had done it *despite* the tables.

- *www.evolt.org* – the main site

- *lists.evolt.org* – listserv management and archive

- *browsers.evolt.org* – browser archive

As you'll see, the colors of those three initial sites mimic the RGB color triplet in our logo, with the main site colored green, the archive blue, and the list site red.

The sites that popped up later (and were saddled with different colors) include:

- *members.evolt.org* – our member hosting site

- *directory.evolt.org* – web resource directory

- *test.evolt.org* – our testing site

- *food.evolt.org* – our soon-to-be-launched food site

Before we get into each individual site, however, let's take a look at some of the more recognizable elements of the various *evolt.org* sites.

Style

By relying on Cascading Style Sheets (CSS) for all styling other than layout (which was tabled, as described above), we could guarantee a baseline experience for all our users, and then expect the CSS to address colors and type styling. We also ensured that the CSS was compliant and still addressed any known bugs with browser rendering, ideally ensuring that the CSS would be as effective in later browsers as it was the day we wrote it. The advantage to this wasn't just that it was easier to create alternative colors for each site, but also that it addressed our intention of creating the ability for users to customize the site themselves. If the user needed more contrast, or larger fonts, all they had to do was load another stylesheet to address those needs, and with an audience of web developers who just might try it, we made sure that the site was ready to accept any of these custom styles.

At the time of this writing, the site uses pixels as units for text sizing in its CSS, which, while giving a consistent experience across browsers and platforms that support CSS, doesn't allow the user to shift the typefaces up or down in size using the browser's native features. For now, a user with experience in creating user-defined stylesheets must create a local CSS file in order to override the CSS in the site. Ultimately, this is a case where we want to test all the possible units (or lack of units); still retain a consistent look; avoid any browser bugs while still being compliant, and do it all during whatever free time we can muster as volunteer developers. I highlight this particular flaw because it's one that we didn't think about until well after the site was launched, since none of us scale our type (except Rudy Limeback, the first admin to point out our flaw).

Giving Users Control of the Site

Part of the delay in rolling out the ability for users to change styles is in the complexity of the proposed tool. Initially, the idea was to have everything in the CSS inter-related. For instance, the color of the navigation bar on the right would also be the color of the <h1> on the article pages. Then we decided to allow the user to customize every aspect of the page, which made for a more complex method of allowing custom styles. Now we could no longer offer a handful of fields whose color and size attributes were distributed throughout the CSS file. Instead we had to allow every style in the CSS file to be an option for editing. With over 250 lines in the CSS file, that could make for a very daunting set of options.

Another factor was the desire to have the tool give immediate feedback to users. It's one thing to allow users to change every element on the page, it's another thing completely when your users can't see the effect without constantly reloading the page. We found in testing that users just wouldn't configure the page if

they had to constantly reload it, it just took too much time. Given this goal, the only option we had to allow immediate feedback was to use DHTML to redraw elements on the page, and at the time, our audience included enough users of Netscape Navigator 4.x that it was deemed untenable. The DHTML necessary to accomplish this task just would not work in Navigator.

Coupled with this was the concern of storing these custom styles for each user. If every user could include 250 custom lines into a CSS file for the site, and every user would need the ability to edit it, then we suddenly had to consider what sort of database hit the site would encounter to either pull a CSS file off the file system for use, or even pull 250 styles out of a table associated with that user. What good would custom CSS be if the user had to wait upwards of 10 seconds to render a page? And what good is the ability to customize it if the page of fields is going to take another 10 seconds or more to draw? We did explore creating static stylesheets from the database records, and only using the database to update these static files, but the development time was still too much of a burden for us to take on.

While we toyed with the idea of offering a `textarea` for users to enter custom styles, we realized we might not reduce database loads, and we might end up becoming tech support for the less experienced CSS coders who make up our membership.

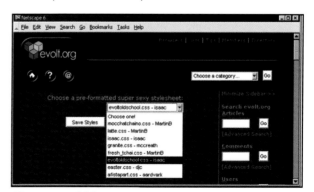

The preset CSS stylesheet selector.

The current proposed solution is much simpler, and once we finish it up and roll it out, we hope to see it used regularly. We have a series of sample CSS files on the server, and the user is presented with a select menu to choose the style they want to use to view the site. Allowing users to submit styles would still allow a user to customize the site, as well as removing the burden on the programmers to build the tools and the database to piece together the elements. Of course, if a user isn't conversant with CSS, they could also ask us as a whole to consider creating a style that addresses their concerns – larger typefaces, bolder colors, or whatever.

Style Guide

Another benefit of relying on both valid HTML and CSS for the site was that coding articles would become much easier for authors. Previously, if an author wanted to have different tags in an article rendered to match the site colors or style, they would have to class the elements to match the classes defined in the CSS of the original site. It also meant that authors who didn't like how their <pre> blocks displayed on the page would often take it into their own hands to adjust the size and color of these chunks of content (yours truly being the worst offender). We even had authors paste code in from HTML WYSIWYG editors (like FrontPage or Dreamweaver) because it was easier for them to simply attempt to mesh our styles with theirs.

By creating a site where all style was defined through CSS, and all HTML on the page conformed to the HTML 4.01 Transitional specification, we made it much easier to define to authors what was acceptable within an article. No <font> tags are allowed, and nothing else deprecated in HTML 4.01 is allowed. The <h1> tag is disallowed since that would be used for the article title on the page anyway. In the end, an author is allowed fewer than thirty elements with which to code an article, and so far none have complained about restrictions or limitations because they've generally recognized the need for consistency within the site. All of the allowed elements have styles associated with

them through the CSS file of the site, splitting the structure from the style, and authors are not allowed to embed styles within an article. So when a user does choose a custom style, all of the elements within an article will be affected. After all, what good is hard-coding your text as black if someone uses a style with a black background – Unless, of course, the article is terrible?

Curiously, I got stuck with the worst articles, and all those articles were mine.

Many elements allowed in the HTML specification aren't allowed in articles. For instance, <small> is not allowed because it offers no semantic or structural value to the text it encloses – it simply indicates that the text within should be rendered in a smaller type size. By the W3C's own specifications, it exists simply to style text so that it appears smaller, not to impart any meaning to the text within. Instead, if a user wants smaller text for some reason, we fall back to the CSS file to address it, although we still have not encountered a scenario where smaller text was absolutely necessary for the article. Also not allowed are <b> and <i>, since their cousins <strong> and <em> offer not only semantic value instead of style, but can even be used by some screen readers to adjust how the computerized voice reads the content back to the user. We, of course, style the <strong> in the CSS so it renders as bold text, and the <em> so it renders as italic text. There may be cases where a <b> might be preferred to <strong>, but we haven't encountered any yet.

The style guide also details how best to use some elements. For instance, not all authors are familiar with the <abbr> tag, so there is a block of text explaining what it does and how to use the title attribute to define the text being abbreviated. In the case of hyperlinks we also suggest that authors use the title attribute to tell a user if the page will open in a new window or the current window.

Of course, converting old articles to this new standard was nothing short of a hassle, and more of a nightmare for those of us who got stuck with the worst offending articles that embedded `<font>`s all over their content. Curiously, I got stuck with the worst articles, and all those articles were mine. Once converted, however, the need to go back and modify articles for new styles has fallen away, leaving us with a highly mutable site that can accept the styles of any user universally across all the content. These unconverted articles were part of the catalyst that helped us move away from embedding styling into our content, since managing it proved to be so time consuming when moving to a new design, and we didn't want to go through this again for the next version of *evolt.org*.

Blacktabnavbarthingie

One of the signature elements of the current *evolt.org* site is the black bar that extends across the top of the page with the *evolt.org* logo in a tab on the left side. This one element was chosen early on as something that would be consistent throughout all the *evolt.org* sites, regardless of what styles we might implement. It is also the only consistent navigation element from site to site and page to page. We hoped its consistency across (nearly) all browsers and platforms would not only help enable users to recognize it when seen on a stained Internet café screen, but even be an interface

benefit by becoming an anchor for the main navigation of the sites. Internally, with no real way to refer to the entire conglomeration of logo, links, and images, we just started referring to it (affectionately, I might add) as the "blacktabnavbarthingie". Searching on this in our public development archives alone should show many of the discussions we've had on its use and implementation.

Two key requirements of the blacktabnavbarthingie were that it had to scale with the sites, and that it had to accommodate any text styles and background colors the user might select through either custom user-defined stylesheets, or alternative stylesheets as offered by the sites. The liquidity was achieved pretty easily, allowing it to scale down to very small widths (the screenshot shown is at 640 pixels, and it still has room to shrink). The floating text navigation can easily scale up or down without throwing anything out of whack, and the select menu also has plenty of room in which to grow should the user need large fonts.

The edges of the blacktabnavbarthingie are aliased so it can sit on any color background. Granted, it makes the curves look a bit chunky in spots, but the advantage is that as we moved away from just one color scheme for the site(s), we had a navigation and branding element that wasn't restricted to just one page color. It also meant we didn't have to wait for someone to create a new navigation bar aliased to a particular color should we decide to roll out a new site or even just change a style on one of the sites. Instead, this little

This is the blacktabnavbarthingie. Well, what would you call it? Note the text links at the top right, and the sunken buttons under the title.

marvel of pixel engineering can sit on any color background without a halo from anti-aliasing to a matte color.

There are four key parts of the blacktabnavbarthingie. The main element, and the most obvious, is the *evolt.org* logo, which also acts as a navigation element to the home page. Given the ubiquitous nature of the tab as a navigation element, coupled with the upper-left placement of a logo as a link home, this one element seemed like a slam-dunk to us all – the logo would link to the home page of the site.

However, it wasn't quite that easy. Most people who frequent sites other than *www.evolt.org* (such as *browsers.evolt.org*, or *lists.evolt.org*) would expect it to bring them to the home page of the site. However, some people noted that the logo would be most appropriate if it brought them to the main *evolt.org* site, not just the home of that specific site. Then began the discussion of what the main *evolt.org* site was. Many people had different ideas of what it might be, based on their experience with *evolt.org*. While it's generally agreed that *www.evolt.org* is the primary site, the case can easily be made for *lists.evolt.org* being the main site, given that *evolt.org* started as a mailing list, and is generally most active through its lists. However, we decided that not enough users had this perception, and that the site sitting at the *www.evolt.org* address was the overall home page for the *evolt.org* family of sites and should be linked appropriately. This decision ensured the tab would act as the link to the *www.evolt.org* site, and the house icon would link to the home page of the site the user was visiting at the time.

Text Links

The concession we made was to reformat the text links that sit in the upper right of the blacktabnavbarthingie, free of the black bar itself. Initially, the text links were formatted as they were in the original site: *Home*, *Community* (a link to general information about *evolt.org*), *Discussion List* (a link to *lists.evolt.org*), *Browser Archive* (a link to *browsers.evolt.org*), and *FAQ*

(a link to a general *evolt.org* FAQ page). Given the new goal of representing all our sites (and the potential for new ones), the list of links was modified to point to each site individually, and currently reads: *Join* (the member sign-up page), *Browsers* (a link to *browsers.evolt.org*), *Tips* (a link to the Tip Harvester), *List* (*lists.evolt.org*), *Members* (*members.evolt.org*), and *Directory* (*directory.evolt.org*). The "*Join*" link goes away if you log in to the site, opening up a little space in the text links.

Unfortunately, over time we have found that the text links in the upper right tend to be missed by the average user. Not only was this clear when we received e-mail from our more vocal average users but, as it was mentioned here and there, many of us would do informal tests and ask people they knew who had seen the site if they had noticed the text links. Many had not.

Many users come to the *evolt.org* site out of search engines or somebody just passing the URL over to them, and never realize all the other sites and features that are offered by *evolt.org*. Given this insight, a design requirement for the next version is to integrate or highlight links to the other sites. Some design concepts for the current site included extra tabs, one for each *evolt.org* site. These ancillary tabs were to be smaller than the tab holding the logo, but given that we only had *browsers.evolt.org* and *lists.evolt.org* at the time, it didn't seem necessary to rebuild the header and possibly dilute the brand by including these new tabs. We also suspected more sites might come in the future, and after a while, the number of tabs might become too cumbersome, especially for a liquid design. Of course now we know that, even if tabs weren't the right way to go, we need some method to make the other sites more prominent in the design. Requirements for the future will likely echo the need to handle user-defined styles, liquid pages, and now a multitude of *evolt.org* sites.

Those Buttons

The three "buttons" beneath the logo are there to offer some access to the kind of meta-information you find on most sites. The first (with the picture of a house) is a link back to the home page. For a time, this was discussed as an option to let the user go the main *evolt.org* home page, while the tab itself would bring you to the current site's home page. The opposite of this was also discussed, and eventually chosen. For all the sites, the tab will still bring you to the *www.evolt.org* site, but the house button takes you to the home page of the site you are currently visiting. We felt that having a redundant link to the main *www.evolt.org* site on each page was a waste of real estate, and since the element was already there, we might as well use it to allow users to get to the home of the current *evolt.org* site. After all, at the time we had no other method to allow users to get back to the front page of, say, *browsers.evolt.org*.

The question mark takes you to the Frequently Asked Questions page, and the "@" symbol takes you to the contact page. We hoped the "@" would make users think of e-mail, which is a further abstraction from an e-mail link, and the question mark might make users think it was a place to get questions answered.

The beveled look was chosen in deference to the established UI principle that buttons are three-dimensional in nature, as demonstrated in various OSes and argued by interface folks like Bruce Tognazzini and Jakob Nielsen. Just as the tab has a beveled look, black links in a black field need some way to stand out as clickable, just as underlines in text denote hyperlinks.

Some of our users, however, and not just our international ones, don't quite *get* the symbols in the images. Some users think the question mark indicates that it's a link to ask questions and get them answered. Then they have no idea what the "@" symbol is for. Some don't see a house in the first image. Some people did raise these issues as concerns during

development, but our mistake was in convincing them it *was* a house or a question or an e-mail link, and not addressing the fact that others would take these symbols as something else as well. To address this, Marlene Bruce has proposed a new set of images that have the text embedded within them, removing any confusion about the message. The obvious drawback is that as images, the text can't be scaled up by the user, or modified in any other way through CSS.

Navigation by `<select>`

The final element of the blacktabnavbarthingie is the select menu on the right side, which allows a user to go directly to a section. In the initial site design, these links sat in the navigation bar on the right side of the page. With a need to reclaim that space, we opted to move the sections into a select menu. The decision was not made easily, given how many of us tend to disagree with the use of select menus as navigation, and given the number of quoted usability experts who shun them, such as Nielsen. But at the time, we didn't have a better method to offer similar capability within the limited space, so we thought we'd give it a shot and see if we could make it work. The addition of a "*Go*" button at least ensured that it did not rely on any client-side script to do its job, enabling users in just about any browser to use it. The "*Go*" button also meant users who just wanted to see the options wouldn't be whisked away to a new page just for looking or, worse yet, missing a selection and clicking the wrong one by mistake.

The position this menu occupies is analogous to the position the search option occupied on the old site. Luckily, users generally weren't phased by the fact that the search box wasn't there any more, and the select menu itself looks different enough from the search form (even though it is a pair of form elements) that users seemed to understand it pretty quickly. There was one time, though, when one of my friends, while doing some informal (and arguably improper) testing, clicked the select menu while the page was still loading thinking it was the search. Instead of a text field, he was greeted with an open select menu, but it showed him

Evolt.org is an all-volunteer resource for web developers made up of a discussion list, a browser archive, and member-submitted articles. This article is the property of its author, please do not redistribute or use elsewhere without checking with the author.

Here's what the blacktabnavbarthingie boils down to when you select the printer-friendly page.

the category he wanted to see, so he ended up just going to the category. In fact, he was pleased to see it loaded immediately as the rest of the page was still downloading, allowing him to quickly select a category and go without waiting.

The mirror element to the blacktabnavbarthingie is the black footer that appears on all pages. It has no specific function other than to hold a description of the *evolt.org* community and provide some design consistency with the top of each page.

The blacktabnavbarthingie and the footer are the only elements of the site that are designed not to be generally affected by any user-defined styles. The text sizes can be scaled, and the color of the text links floating off the bar may be adjusted, but the black color and white text is hard-coded into the HTML itself. This is to ensure that regardless of the browser and operating system configuration, the user always sees some consistency from system to system. When the site is viewed unstyled, the blacktabnavbarthingie is particularly bold against the gray background and white content area.

Printing

All of these features, of course, tend to be pretty pointless when it comes to printing. Printed pages don't need select menus, buttons, navigation, or cool graphics that aren't relevant to the content. They do, however, need the branding of the site. So the one exception where the blacktabnavbarthingie gets dumped is when the user uses the "Print this page" option. The resultant template strips the bar and

replaces it with a logo aliased to white, and a block of text briefly describing *evolt.org* as well as a statement about the copyright of the article.

> *Printed pages don't need select menus, buttons, navigation, or cool graphics that aren't relevant to the content.*

The printable page also allows the user to display comments and ratings, or remove them altogether. Of course, with any printed web page, the URLs from hyperlinks are lost. We discussed using the content system to automatically read anything in `<a href="">` and displaying it in brackets after the linked text, but the code to do that was so complex that we weren't sure we could get solid performance out of it when the site was being hammered, and it wasn't exactly foolproof no matter how strict we made our writers' guidelines. With the advent of CSS2 and attribute selectors, it will be possible for CSS2-compliant browsers to simply show the URL after the hyperlinked text. While browser support right now is low for this feature, we expect to make use of this for the next version of the site, and might even integrate it into the current version, just to offer the extra capability for those whose browsers support it.

During the writing of this piece, I've found that some users expect the text link we offer to do what it says – send the page to the printer. And so somewhere I suspect a user is still eye-level with his desk, staring expectantly into his printer, waiting for some article to pop out. While some other developer sites (such as Webmonkey, devArticles, eDevCafe, and others) use this very same text (or even an icon of what might be construed as a printer), sometimes following others isn't the right way to go. By the time you read this, it should have been changed to "Printer-friendly page."

Implementation

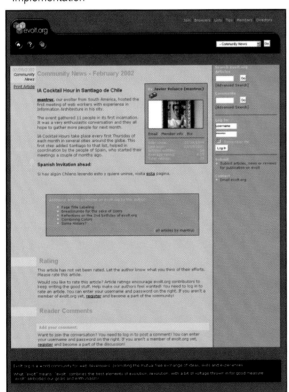

This modified screen capture of an article shows how the blacktabnavbarthingie and the black footer are independent of the table that holds the content. The three tables simply sit atop one another, allowing the blacktabnavbarthingie to display in the browser while the content is still downloading.

To allow pages to render more quickly for users, and allow for a more modular design, both the blacktabnavbarthingie and the footer exist in tables independent of the content table. These tables stack neatly on top of one another, and allow the blacktabnavbarthingie to be drawn on screen while the page content is still being downloaded and/or drawn. The only drawback to this is in the case of articles that have content that displays wider than the user's current window size. For instance, large images, very long URLs that can't wrap, or even extremely small window sizes will show an unfortunate side effect of the stacked table approach. Both the footer and the blacktabnavbarthingie can almost always scale smaller than the content table can. As a result, in these more extreme circumstances, the content table will extend beyond the right edges of the blacktabnavbarthingie and the footer. This can end up looking pretty ugly, but it's a tradeoff we've come to accept. This has dictated how we choose to display blocks of code in articles, as well as influenced the display of `<tips>` on *lists.evolt.org*.

The page at an extremely narrow width (423 pixels) shows how the blacktabnavbarthingie can scale down further than the content table. The same can occur if the content table is so wide that it scrolls beyond the window, while the blacktabnavbarthingie stops at the edge of the window. While this usually isn't desirable, it happens so infrequently that it's not too much of a concern.

User Testing

Of course, what good is all this work if the audience doesn't like it, or can't make sense of it? Even though we had some good information about our audience based solely on our list traffic, it was still imperative to make sure the site was still usable to them, and wasn't just a real-world manifestation of a couple of dozen wide-eyed developers who thought everyone must be assimilated into the cubes.

Because *evolt.org* is such a distributed a group, user testing was an interesting conundrum. It's one thing to sit with a co-worker or client and show potential issues in a design, or even gather together users of the site and watch them in their tasks. But targeting a worldwide audience of web developers left us unable to pull together a truly representative mix of users to do true user testing.

So we performed it on a user-budget.

Greeked Text

Jakob Nielsen long ago advocated the idea of using fake ("Greeked") text in layouts to determine if users could still guess what functions certain links performed. The process is generally simple: change all text links and text buttons to gibberish text, and see if the user can still sense the hierarchy and move around the site, possibly even completing certain tasks. A holdover from the print layout world, it also shows how a page full of copy might render on-screen with a layout as well, allowing developers to trouble-shoot layout hassles before the content comes in. Of course, it's important to change the Greeked text back to real text before you launch a site, something that a simple search for "Lorem ipsum dolor" on Google will show is often forgotten.

Many of us gathered co-workers, friends, and even family into impromptu and informal user groups. In my case, I was able to drag newer staff at my company into a room as a training session on performing user testing, and then later as a training session on site critiquing. By getting co-workers to act as both guinea pigs and usability auditors, I was able to gather insight into elements of the site that I had either taken for granted, or even completely missed. Others performed similar tests, often posting quick Photoshop mock-ups of changes, or posting comments made by friends about the site.

> It was harder to find hiccups in their understanding of the site because, as web developers, they are generally familiar with how to use sites and what sort of expectations designers have of them.

Some of this testing was done with "Greeked" text. Navigation elements were reduced to random letters and users were asked to identify each part of the site, or conversely, try to find specific parts of the site. Other testing consisted of setting tasks. These tasks ranged from finding an article on a specific topic, to becoming a member and submitting articles, to describing what *evolt.org* is.

For the most part, the users were able to quickly and efficiently identify elements or complete their tasks. It was harder to find hiccups in their understanding of the site because, as web developers, they are generally familiar with how to use sites and what sort of expectations designers have of them. Instead, little things stood out, like how many times they missed a radio button, or over-scrolled in the select menu.

Most recently, we performed another type of informal testing for the site; we deployed a survey. While not specifically geared toward usability of the site, we still asked questions about the site and how members respond to it (we were really looking for more general feedback, but what better place to piggyback some user experience questions?). Since the new version of the site had been live for more than a year when we asked for input on the survey, we knew users had had plenty of time to experience the site and think about what worked or failed to work for them. The danger with this long of a time span is that some users may have created workarounds for parts of the site that confused them, so we would have to rely on newer users to point out any of those issues to us.

Now that we've gone over most of the global aspects of the design of all the *evolt.org* sites, let's look at some of the features specific to each one of them individually.

Survey results

Some things we have learned in the survey include:

- Users have trouble recognizing that there are different categories of content on the site, and don't intuitively gravitate to the select menu to navigate through those sections.

- The text links in the upper right of the blacktabnavbarthingie get lost and are missed by many users. This lack of prominence for the other sites of *evolt.org* also causes visitors to miss them completely, or assume they are of much lesser importance.

- Authors were looking for more recognition in articles, something that gave them a place to toot their own horn and maybe drive traffic their way. This was expressed as an expectation for donating article content to *evolt.org*.

- The article searches don't always pull up the article a user wants to see. Right now, article content is not included within the search, so if a search term isn't in the abstract or the title, it won't show up in the search results.

- We should offer new ways to view `<tip>`s pulled from posts to the list. This is addressed a little further on in this chapter.

- Users want to see us organize the browser archive, ideally by operating system.

www.evolt.org

The primary site of the three core sites that make up *evolt.org*, this site is the home to all the articles submitted by users over the years, as well as limited member pages. All of the administrative features of the site live here as well.

The *www.evolt.org* site essentially has two kinds of users. There are casual readers who don't ever register for the site, and there are those who register with the site and are granted access to some additional features (I'll refer to them as members for this discussion, although if you ever want to start a week-long discussion on the *evolt.org* lists, ask what makes a member and what doesn't, because it goes beyond just having a username on the *www.evolt.org* site...).

Having this separation between casual users and members creates a bit of that barrier to entry, although it's really nothing more than providing an e-mail address and password. However, as folks like Derek Powazek and others who spend their careers tackling the intricacies of communities suggest, even this mild barrier can increase the value of the community by simply inserting an extra step before people can do things like post spam articles or start posting graffiti as comments on articles.

Home Page

The most-visited and most-recognized face of *evolt.org* is the home page. On it you can find the ten most recently submitted articles sorted by date, along with their abstracts.

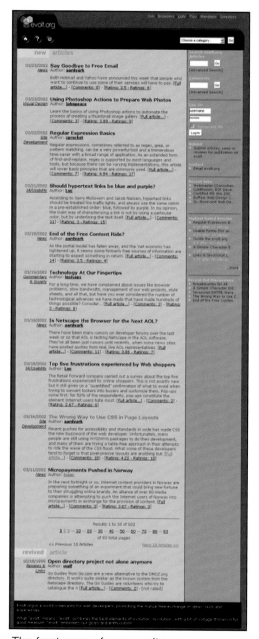

The front page of www.evolt.org.

Abstracts

02/06/2002	**Links & JavaScript Living Together in**
Code	**Harmony**
	Author: **.jeff**

It seems there's not a week that goes by that someone isn't asking about how to properly execute some JavaScript from a link. Unfortunately, they're not usually driven to bring their problem to others for help because they're trying to make their site as usable and accessible as possible. [Full article...] - [Comments: 9] - [Rating: 4.61 - Ratings: 18]

An article abstract, showing links to the code, full article, comments, and ratings.

Unlike those on the first version of the *evolt.org* site, the abstracts on the home page are no longer driven from the first two hundred characters of the article. Instead, the author now has the opportunity to create an abstract of the article as a whole, which offers readers a better opportunity to determine if an article interests them. Not only do authors appreciate the opportunity to tailor their abstract, it also allows the admins to stop worrying about counting characters in our heads. This abstract is also used as meta-information for site searches for articles, which means content that consists of more than the introduction paragraph can greatly help users find relevant content on a search.

The abstract also displays the date the article was posted, which offers a bit of a "freshness" guarantee when it comes to reading anything that may have changed in the past 24 hours, which on the web is not unheard of. We felt it important to let the readers see immediately what was new by date and quickly find out if they had missed anything. The author's name is also displayed, since not only does this piece of credit reward authors, it also allows readers to either skip articles or spot an something by an author who may interest them in some way.

Beneath the content of the abstract is a block of text telling the user how many comments an article has.

Sometimes an article with a lot of comments can be interesting to users who might otherwise skip it, and this gives users an idea of participation on that article. Members who are logged in are presented with the number of new comments since their last visit, if any.

After the comment count, some text tells a reader the rating of an article. Since ratings don't exist in a vacuum, it also tells how many total ratings the article has received. An article with a rating of 5 after one rating might not be as interesting as an article with a rating of 4.5 after thirty-eight ratings.

All of this information gives readers a good idea of what they might be getting into before they click the link and wander into the content of the site.

Sidebar

There are essentially two possible sidebars a user may see when they visit the site. The first sidebar is for visitors who haven't logged in, and the second is for members who have logged in to the site. Each sidebar has blocks of content and links that we charmingly refer to as "evolt boxen". These "boxen" contain information that is ideally pertinent to users on the site, and created based on feedback we've gotten from users over the past year. Granted, this sidebar is identical on all pages, but the first-time visitor, as well as those who mostly just scan the home page looking for new content, sees it as their first view of content on the site that isn't necessarily on the home page. We've gotten feedback from many users that they immediately look to the sidebar to spot new comments on articles (see below), new job postings, or even to watch the constantly rotating top-five article list.

Members who have logged in may also minimize the sidebar with a link provided at the top. This way a user who may already be running a browser at full-screen may remove the sidebar and eke out that much more space for content on the page. It does, however, have the drawback of not letting users see the options presented in the sidebar, such as search, without reloading the page in order to display the sidebar again.

Of course, with our liquid design, the width of the sidebar is not hard-coded to a pixel width, but instead it's coded to a percentage. At extremely large window sizes, it can be argued that the sidebar takes up more room than it needs to since all the text and input fields stop well short of the full width. However, if we coded it to a fixed pixel size, we felt it looked too awkward, and allowed the content area to splay out that much farther.

The normal and logged-in right hand side navigation bars.

Search Options

In each sidebar, the user may search for articles at any time. We quickly found, however, that as articles received comments, sometimes the comments held as much value as or more value than the articles on which they commented. Since the article search feature didn't search comments as well, a separate search was created to allow users to search on the contents of all the comments on the site. The long-term plans include one search that allows users to search comments, full article content, posts, and tips, all through one search form. We are, however, restricted by the fact that some of these information stores exist not only in different formats, but in different physical locations as well. Being all volunteers with all donated equipment means that generally we use what we can get. For most sites, this wouldn't be an issue at all, since the average corporate site has one integrated architecture or at least one common data store. But since that's not the case with us, it has very real impacts on things as simple as the search feature.

Members who have logged in have an additional search option available to them. They may search on members of the community, with the results showing the member page for that member. There is also an option available to perform a more advanced search. Clicking the link takes the user to a more robust search page, which I go into more detail about below.

Comments

Another feature available to members who have logged in is a listing of new comments on the site since their last login date. Sometimes the number of comments exceeds the listing of five allowed in the sidebar, but there is an option to view any that don't fit in that list. That option also brings up the comment search page, allowing the user to further delve into comments on the site.

In the sidebar, the title of the comment, and the date and time of the comment are provided, as well as a link to the article with which it appears. The author name is also provided with a link to the member page of that author. One feature we added to these entries was the entire text of the comment within a title attribute on the title of the comment. We found, however, that in the case of long comments, these title attributes not only dramatically increased page size, and hence rendering time, but some browsers that showed the title attribute as a Tool-tip would cause the text to flash on and off if there was too much content (more than about 250 characters, and generally restricted to Internet Explorer on Windows). The solution to this was to truncate the comments after the first 200 characters, reducing the potential for large comments affecting page load too much, as well as alleviating the flashing that some users experienced.

Not all users care only about the latest comments, however, but are more interested in articles that are getting a good deal of activity over a period of time instead of since they last logged in. This is the *Recent Hot Discussions* list. I've found that once one of my articles makes it into that list, the comments start rolling in as people come by to see what all the commotion is about. It's also helped rekindle discussions on long-forgotten articles simply by drawing attention to them – after the seal is broken by that first new comment, of course.

An additional feature of the comments is that authors are notified by e-mail when an article they wrote receives a comment. It makes much easier for the author to give immediate feedback if the comment is a question about something in the article. Those who leave comments on an article also receive an e-mail notification when the article on which they comment receives another comment. It's really not as confusing as it sounds.

Highest Rated Articles

All users are presented with the opportunity to see the top five highest rated articles on the site. This listing appears on every page and shows the title of the article along with the rating and total number of ratings.

Articles in this highlighted area tend to get more traffic, and once an article breaks into the top five ranking, it also tends to get a sudden boost in the number of people rating it. Generally, an article doesn't last too long in the number one spot, and the top five list has pretty good turnover. Interestingly, once an article makes it into the top five spot, more people go to read it, and are more likely to rate it. At that point, it generally drops a couple of slots in the ratings. The dynamic of this is still new to us, and a little hard to track, although some side bets do happen among admin members once a new article makes it into the list (or sometimes before it's even approved).

Job Postings

Another feature requested by users is the listing of recently posted jobs. This list shows the five most recently posted jobs as links to the article itself. No other information is offered. This feature appears to be working satisfactorily since traffic to the jobs posting of the site has fallen off as users instead glance at the listing to look for anything new.

Common to all these links to articles is the fact that they are all truncated at twenty-two characters. We chose to do this because the sidebar was getting so tall as lines of text wrapped that some users in my test group (again, lots of co-workers, friends, and family) never scrolled down enough to see the other options further down the page. We chose twenty-two characters because at our most common user configuration, Microsoft Internet Explorer 5.x or higher on Windows 95 or higher, that was about how many characters fit in the same width as the text input boxes used for the search. This way everything in the sidebar could have a generally consistent width, allowing a user to more quickly scan the contents of the sidebar for general areas and individual links. Of course, using pixels for font size units in our CSS makes this more consistent across browsers and platforms.

Since the title attributes for every link have the full article title, it's a simple matter for users to hover over a link to see the tool tip that contains the full article title. In all our testing, no users had any problems with truncated titles, and many had come to learn that the *evolt.org* site makes extensive use of titles, so hovering over the links paid off for those users when they experimented with the mouse.

Log In

The initial state of the login form shows the user what is expected of them, reducing the need to document how the login form works or even label the fields. The username field contains the text "username," making its purpose clear. The password field contains the word "password," although it is displayed as asterisks since the field itself is of the password type. While we initially displayed the fields with labels, we found that our audience was savvy enough to recognize that the two fields, with the text within them, were the username and password fields to log in. On a site geared toward the general public, this wouldn't be such a good idea. Without discrete labels for the fields, users could easily get confused. However, we are fortunate in that our audience is generally more accepting of letting us experiment a bit. Their experience with web applications also makes them more readily recognize a login form for what it is.

For users with JavaScript enabled, the fields automatically clear themselves when either one is first selected by the mouse, saving the user the hassle of deleting the label text before entering their own login information. While there were initial concerns that this might confuse users or even punish those without JavaScript enabled, we've found that the opposite is true. General web users might get nervous at first if they clicked in a text field only to have all the text disappear, but it doesn't seem to have slowed our users at all, and during some of our forced testing with co-workers and staff, we've found they catch on to it almost immediately.

An added feature of the login process is that it reduces the frequency with which users have to log in. The login form allows them to store their login information on the computer as a cookie so that on subsequent visits, their login information is remembered and they are considered logged in. For regular visitors on computers they use exclusively, this means that they essentially only have to log in once.

Overall, this is a case where considering our audience and testing their responses showed that traditional usability rules could be bent, or even severely mangled. If we had just relied on standard users, or even common assumptions about users, we might not have been able to make the form elements as smooth as they are. It's worth noting that I resisted both the omission of field labels and JavaScript on the forms, but after being slapped around by the results, I had to eat my hat.

Membership Options

We also allow members an opportunity to maintain their member profiles through a link in the sidebar, as well as the ability to log out. This ability to log out is especially important for users who may not be on a computer that they own or use exclusively.

Revived Articles

A recently added feature on the home page is something called Revived Articles. After the ten most recent articles, there is an eleventh article that has been randomly pulled from the database for display on the home page for every visit. The article must be more than one year old in order to even have a chance of appearing here. This is an attempt to allow more recent visitors to see older articles that they may have missed, and hopefully remind them that the site is more than just the ten articles on the home page.

While not expressly requested by users, we felt that some wonderful articles weren't getting enough exposure. With many users never venturing beyond the front page, a busy week could mean a great article only lasted on the home page for a few days. We also felt that many articles that were authored before the new version of the site deserved exposure to the ratings feature, possibly giving them a fair shake at appearing in the coveted top five list.

revived article

10/31/2000 **Stock Photography Resources for**
Visual Design **Web Designers**
Author: isaac

Try to design and build a Web site using poor images and, more often than not, you'll end up with less-than-optimal results. We can't always be lucky enough to have clients providing us with CDs [Full article...] - [Comments: 22] - [Rating: 4.13 - Ratings: 8]

A revived article.

Right now, the drawback is that it sits at the bottom of the page, which is where regular users know the older content sits, so not as many people are scrolling down to see it. It also isn't highlighted in any way other than a headline. We had hoped to see an increase in traffic to old articles, maybe even seeing old articles get more ratings or comments. As of now, the logs and sidebar aren't bearing that hope out, although plans are in the works to draw more attention to those articles and also create a better method for selection as well. One suggestion is that different people with expertise in the different sections of the site comb through the content and identify high-quality articles that deserve to be floated to the top for visitors to see. Of course, this is still a subjective approach, and requires time from volunteers to complete, so this will still be open to modification as we move ahead with it. We've also considered changing the display settings so each article gets perhaps a full day on the page, as opposed to a random chance for every page view.

Rendering Time

As all of these features were rolled into the home page, the static HTML page that we would generate in the first version of the site suddenly became problematic. It's one thing to create a static page so everyone sees exactly the same thing, but in the case of the new site, users see a version of the home page customized to their login information.

Now a different solution had to be found to keep page serving and drawing times as low as possible, while still serving up completely unique pages for every visitor. Query caching is now used to minimize the execution time of the home page and still allow for relatively fast page execution times. This simply means that the results of the call to the database are held in memory on the web server until a specified period of time is up, or until another pre-set activity occurs. This way, the database doesn't feel the strain of every visit to every page on the site, which would severely impact on performance.

Articles

The meat of the *evolt.org* site is the member-submitted content. With over 800 articles in less than three years, with all but a few unsolicited, there is an amazing amount of knowledge stored within the site about nearly every aspect of web development.

Most Viewed Articles of 2001

1.9 million page views for 2001

Top 5 referrers:

- *www.google.com*

- *google.yahoo.com*

- *slashdot.org*

- *google.de*

- *http://radiodiscuss.userland.com/myUser LandOnTheDesktop* (RDF Feed)

Unlike other developer sites, the *evolt.org* site allows anybody to post anything web-related for the benefit of, or targeted assault on, their peers. And it's not just the articles that are valuable, but also the comments associated with those articles. The *evolt.org* site works almost as a peer-review site, allowing experts on a topic to post a thesis, while others in the community rate it and comment on it. While we never quite thought of it that way when creating it, it's one of the few sites where a web developer can post an article to be viewed by a community of other web developers, with the full knowledge that some people may tear it apart. Most of the other corporate-owned developer sites have staff writers or freelance writers they call on, and some developers tend to feel that if they aren't in the trenches every day, their articles are purely academic.

Most popular articles (the URL for each article is *http://evolt.org/article/gh/* plus the number in the table.)

Page Views	Title	URL ID	Author
21,386	Using Apache to stop bad robots	*18/15126/*	Daniel Cody
18,494	Your clients need a Content Management System	*20/5127/*	Martin Burns
13,654	Sending HTML e-mail from HotMail	*17/16466/*	Jasen James
10,990	Writing Smart Web Based Forms	*17/10199/*	Matt Warden
10,572	Real World Browser Stats Part II	*20/2297/*	Adrian Roselli
9,870	Netscape Themes Contest	*22/2906/*	Daniel Cody
9,147	Using CSS to create rollovers	*17/16676/*	Simon Coggins
8,990	Liquid Tables	*20/2321/*	Rudy Limeback
8,669	Developing User-Friendly Flash Content	*4090/9601/*	Chris MacGregor
8,482	Flash Interface Usability	*4090/8968/*	Merien Kunst

Highest Rated Articles as of February 16, 2002

These numbers change regularly, sometimes daily. Eight of the ten highest rated articles are regularly on the list, however.

Ranking	Title	URL ID	Author
1	Real World Browser Size Stats, Part I	*17/2295/*	Adrian Roselli
2	Inside the evolt.org Rebuild: The HTML and CSS	*20/5816/*	Adrian Roselli
3	Your clients need a Content Management System	*20/5127/*	Martin Burns
4	Usable Forms (for an international audience)	*4090/15118/*	Isaac Forman
5	To Hell With Bad Editors	*25/6096/*	Adrian Roselli
6	Accessibility: The politics of design	*4090/5034/*	Alan Herrell
7	Some Caveats with Using Frames	*22/293/*	Adrian Roselli
8	Does Netscape 6 Break Your Table Layouts?	*17/4427/*	James Aylard
9	Using Apache to stop bad robots	*18/15126/*	Daniel Cody
10	Liquid Design for the Web	*20/15177/*	Adrian Roselli

Highest Rated Articles as of February 18, 2002

Ranking	Title	URL ID	Author
1	Real World Browser Size Stats, Part I	*17/2295/*	Adrian Roselli
2	A Simple Character Entity Chart	*17/21234/*	Adrian Roselli
3	Inside the evolt.org Rebuild: The HTML and CSS	*20/5816/*	Adrian Roselli
4	Your clients need a Content Management System	*20/5127/*	Martin Burns
5	Usable Forms (for an international audience)	*4090/15118/*	Isaac Forman
6	Structured Writing – An Outline	*20/19664/*	Joel D. Canfield
7	To Hell With Bad Editors	*25/6096/*	Adrian Roselli
8	Accessibility: The politics of design	*4090/5034/*	Alan Herrell
9	Some Caveats with Using Frames	*22/293/*	Adrian Roselli
10	Does Netscape 6 Break Your Table Layouts?	*17/4427/*	James Aylard

Elements of an Article

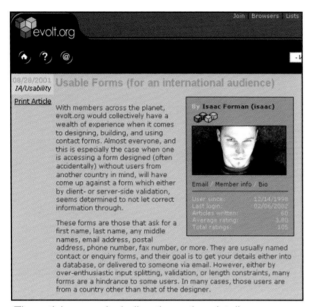

The article page, including the author details section beautifully embedded in the corner.

The top of every article tells the user not only the title, but also the section in which the article appears, the date of the article, and the author. There is also a link to view the printable version of the article.

One of the problems we've had with the date format is how our international audience reads it as opposed to our American audience. If an article is published on February 6th of 2002, its date is shown as 02/06/02. However, this can confuse users who don't use the month/day/year format. The format we used on the original site was day-month-year abbreviation, so that the date offered above would have read 06-Feb-2002.

Surprisingly, we completely missed this change when we were converting the old site to the new site. Our international admin members and developers didn't seem to notice it, either. While recently it has come

back up as an issue raised by some of our members, we are surprised that this lasted for a full year with almost nobody complaining about it or otherwise pointing out our blunder.

We do have the capability now, however, to allow members to select a date format they would prefer to see. This date format would be used for all dates generated by the site for that user. Ideally this will be in place by the time this book is in your hands. If not, forget I said it.

Author Information

One of the things our authors had asked for is shown above – more recognition within articles. While we had thought about it for some time, and even had wide-ranging discussions on what would make up author or member pages, our survey showed that people really just wanted a place for recognition and maybe a brief biography.

Our hope was that if authors felt less anonymous within articles, that perhaps they'd be compelled to write more (or even start writing). We also hoped it would give the site a more professional look, mimicking what we see on the corporate developer sites, and since we can't pay authors, allowing them to promote themselves seemed like a fair trade.

Just as *evolt.org* goes for brand recognition by trying to get links to our site and stuff cubes into the pages of members, authors try to increase the visibility their own brand within the *evolt.org* site. This system, while not expressly defined as such when we started building it, offers a form of reputation management. This is a concept Jakob Nielsen first approached four years ago, but which has largely been ignored or unrecognized when it is implemented.

With sites like *Amazon.com* and Epinions allowing readers to rate the value of goods or services, readers can effectively determine the reputation of an *evolt.org* author through comments and ratings. The author now has the ability to manage their own reputation through the author information presented to readers. Not only can readers see how much an author has contributed, but how well rated an author is. Authors are given incentives by this public information to create more articles of a higher quality. Of course, a well-chosen author photograph can help with that reputation. So, what are some of these author stats? Glad you asked.

Cubes

We had recently rolled out a method to show readers how prolific an author was, but it proved not to be adequate for our authors. This original method was integrated into the new author area, however. This author space at the top of every article includes the author's user name, real name (if the author chooses to display it) and a link to their e-mail address.

The number of cubes is proportional to how many articles the author has written.

Below that is the original idea we had to offer authors more credit – a string of colored cubes that indicate to the reader how many articles the author had written. We found pretty quickly in testing that the cubes themselves didn't mean much to users beyond the fact that some authors had more cubes than others, so we provided an article explaining what the cubes mean, and linked the cubes to that article in our FAQ category. Hovering the mouse over the cubes tells the user that author has written between X and Y articles. This information, in addition, is replicated below with an absolute count of articles by the author. We opted to leave the cubes because it offers a faster method to see at least generally how prolific the author is simply by the number of cubes, and it sits at the top of the page, offering an immediate idea of the author's volume of written work.

Photograph

Given that our authors are our members, we wanted to ensure they had control over how much personal information they would share. Many authors had requested the ability to include photographs, and many felt that this kind of feature relayed a sense of legitimacy to the user, as if the site were more of a professional magazine. Many authors had no interest in posting photos of themselves.

We decided to allow authors the ability to upload and display photos, but not make it a requirement. Initially, we had concerns about how best to allow photos and what sizes we could accept. In the end, in an attempt to limit the amount of work to be done (thereby rolling this feature out sooner) and provide a consistent experience for both authors and readers, we settled on a fixed size for all images.

We had concerns that some authors wouldn't do the work necessary to find an image and modify it to fit such an odd size, but many of our members on our site development list said they'd be willing to create an image regardless, and even thought of it as a challenge. We quickly found that authors were not only uploading images, but also becoming quite creative in their subject matter and design. Some authors even rotate images regularly depending on mood, weather, or other unknown circumstances. My own first experiment was a terribly big animated `.gif` of a tactical nuke launcher from my favorite video game. Of course, after a number of complaints, I replaced it with a much less interesting "Scene missing" image. It seems we had quickly discovered that users wouldn't stand for large files or annoying animations.

During some more impromptu testing, feedback I received indicated that this little feature seemed to give the article, site, and author much more credibility in the eyes of readers. Of course, an author can quash that credibility by posting a bizarre image just as much as an author can raise the credibility with good quality photos. Or an author may creep out readers with glamour shots.

Links

There are three links in the author block, which were intended to be relatively self-explanatory to our members. The first is an e-mail link, allowing a reader to interact with the author directly. An author has the ability to hide their e-mail address, which means this first link may not appear for all users to see. This modicum of privacy also affects the member's information page (which we'll get to shortly).

The second link points to the author's "member" page on the *www.evolt.org* site, as opposed to a page on the *members.evolt.org* server where a member may have a web page.

The last link of the three is simply an anchored link to the bottom of the page where the author's biography appears.

Baseball Stats

The small table beneath the photo and threesome of links is a sort of qualifier to the reader of the author's involvement within the community and general quality of work.

The "User since" and "Last login" lines are, ideally, self-explanatory. This allows a reader to get a feel for how long the author has been around the community based on join date. It can also offer an idea of participation by noting the last time the user logged in. However, a user who has the site remember their login and who has also set the site as their home page, could certainly appear more active than other members even though they may do nothing more than visit the site when their browser fires up.

More along the lines of baseball statistics, however, is the presentation of total articles the author has written, the average rating of all the articles, and the total number of ratings across all articles. It's one thing to tell a user that an author has an average rating of, say, 5 out of 5. It's another thing to tell the user if that rating of 5 is from one person or forty-five people. On top of that,

it's also useful to know if that average rating of 5 is from one article or a dozen articles. This helps identify one-hit wonders as well as those who never seem to get ratings.

There is some concern, of course, that an author who is a recent member, or one who hasn't logged in for a very long time, could be viewed as a less-than-ideal author or member. The same can be said for the average rating. While not intended as a method for members to keep tallies of each other, it can certainly be used by some competitive authors to ensure they are ahead of their worst *evolt.org* enemy in both articles written and overall rating. This isn't necessarily a bad thing – right now there is an informal battle between two of our most prolific authors as they compete to stay ahead in total article count. Bets are welcome, just contact me.

Biography Box

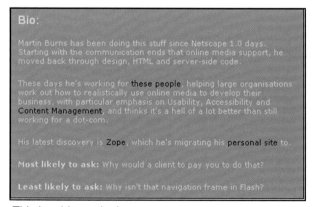

This is a biography box.

At the end of every article is an opportunity for the authors to push themselves as a lovely and talented resource. This value-add not only serves to give the articles more of a magazine feel by lending the perception of credibility, but it also offers the author a place to advertise in exchange for writing a free article on the site. Just as the two canines in the now famous

New Yorker cartoon (by Peter Steiner) discussed, "On the Internet, nobody knows you're a dog." Here is where authors can demonstrate that they are not, in fact, dogs – unless they are.

In addition, this box provides a place for an author's other articles to be offered up to the reader. Five articles are chosen from the author's collected works on the site, barring articles currently in the top five highest-rated articles, or articles appearing on the home page. Not only does this offer the author greater exposure, it offers readers who are pleased with an author's work the ability to read more on whatever topics the author has posted.

Article Preview Mode

Of course, the author info box at the top of the page could be a hindrance to the author if they decided to include images, code samples, tables, or other large blocks of content early on within the article. To help prevent this, we've offered the opportunity for the author to see how the author box would impact on the article content within the template of the page before

Previewing an article you're writing before you submit it can help you see if your bio is going to be a nuisance.

submitting it for review. This places the responsibility of formatting back on the author – the person best suited to make adjustments to the article – as opposed to the admin team, which could result in a delay as the article is reviewed, the author is contacted, changes are suggested, and somebody remembers to finally approve it.

Comments

Comments allow many members of the community to weigh in with their opinions on an article. This is the first step to helping members qualify authors and articles, as well as presenting a forum for discussion of the article in general. Luckily, we haven't been inundated with Slashdot-like chatter, so we've been able to keep a relatively simple system of comments in place, as opposed to threaded discussions that can go on for hundreds of messages.

Each comment presents the name of the member who posted it, as well as a link to the member's page. Only logged-in members may leave comments, so there is some level of accountability in comments. Each comment also shows the date and time posted, the title of the comment as entered by the user, and the comment itself.

Since many of the *evolt.org* admins are fans of blogs (or addictively maintain their own), they had noticed a trend in allowing people to link to specific entries in their blogs, entries that would otherwise be buried in the middle of a page somewhere on their site. This feature was the addition of an icon or text snippet that indicated to the user that they could use that as a hyperlink address. Clicking the link, or following the link from somewhere else, moves the reader to that specific comment within the article.

Given our audience's familiarity with blogs, we felt we could get away with a very simple chunk of text to allow readers to link to the comment: "link". And so far, we seem to have guessed correctly. For those readers who might not know what it means, and might be on a more recent browser, the title attribute for the link is a bit more descriptive as "Permanent link to this comment".

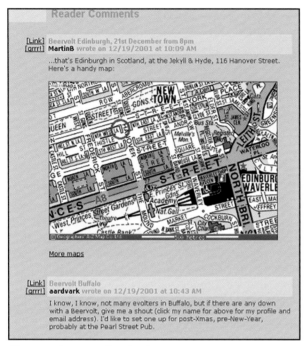

Comments page showing how you can include more than just text in a comment. Note the 'grr!' and 'link' links.

Of course, it is possible that a comment will appear that is inappropriate, irrelevant, or just plain bizarre. The *evolt.org* admins can't patrol the site looking for these, so members who are logged in have the ability to register a complaint with the comment right from the offending (or offensive) comment. So we were presented with the problem of relaying this option as a very short link that would sit below the *[Link]* option.

After much discussion, we opted for something out of the ordinary. Instead of a link that said "complain," or some variation on that, we fell back to something more guttural, more primal. We chose a link that says "grrr!" It's completely silly, but surprisingly effective. We even had one person registering a complaint who commented that he guessed that it was a complaint link after he pronounced it to himself. This user was not using a browser that showed the title attribute, which offers more information with the text, "Submit a complaint about this comment." So far all the users we've asked have correctly guessed the purpose of the "grrr," so we've opted to leave it as is. The nice thing about seeing a "grrr" in your inbox as a site administrator is that it's always refreshing to see the complaint wasn't about one of your own comments.

Blogs

One of the more recent trends of personal home pages on the Internet is the advent of blogs. "Blog" is short for weblog, a personal online journal where people enter their thoughts for the world to see. Many of them are updated daily, or even more frequently, and the topics range from web development (an obviously popular topic) to just about anything at all.

It's almost a joke that you can recognize your average blog by its layout – three columns with the left column acting as a link to the blogs of friends, a center column holding the real content, and a right column holding links to favorite sites and blogging tools. Part of this is because many blogs use the same chunk of code to run, and most users aren't as interested in completely rebuilding the interface as they are in filling it with information.

Many web developers frequent blogs maintained by more visible developers in the industry who maintain links and reference material on everything from standards and accessibility (like Jeffrey Zeldman) to CSS (such as Eric Meyer).

Instead of a link that said "complain," we fell back to something more guttural, more primal. We chose a link that says "grrr!"

At one point we experimented with the ability for a user to hide comments simply by clicking on the title bar of the comment. However, for the browsers that did support this, we found in testing that users who tried to click an e-mail link but missed it would inadvertently hide the entire comment since the entire title bar of the comment was an active link. This issue outweighed any of the benefits of allowing users to hide comments on the page, or so we felt.

Half of the respondents to our 500-person survey said they never leave comments for articles. In general, half of them said they don't feel qualified to speak on the topics they read, while the other half tended to say they didn't have time to leave comments. Only two respondents said they weren't aware that members could leave comments on articles.

`<label>`

Thanks to tags introduced in HTML 4.01, the text labels for each radio button are wrapped in a `<label>` tag. This means that while a radio button generally provides a very small target for the mouse, the user can click on the text label to toggle the radio button as well. Unfortunately, support for this tag isn't as high as we'd like, but as support rolls out, the ratings will prove easier to use, as with all forms on the site that use checkboxes and radio buttons.

Ratings

In addition to comments, ratings allow users to register their satisfaction with an article without having to write up a reason. Between them, comments and ratings give us the closest thing to peer-review that I've found for our industry, so many users employ them in conjunction to determine the value of an article. This doesn't mean there aren't any others out there, but based on member feedback, *evolt.org* has the best combination of comments and ratings to provide immediate information on quality to readers, as well as allow readers to weigh in easily.

Every member has the ability to rate an article on a one to five scale. When logged in, the member is presented with a selection of radio buttons on a scale of 1 to 5. Each radio button has text accompanying it that describes what the number means in plain English. If a member has already rated an article, then the corresponding radio button is pre-checked. The member can, however, change their rating simply by clicking another radio button and submitting the form.

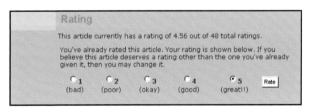

Rate this chapter...? Ratings are given from 1 to 5, where 5 is great, and 1 is really not.

Authors are, of course, unable to rate their own articles.

Rating the Ratings

Recently, it was proposed that we change the scale from a five-point scale to a six-point scale. The goal was to force users to choose toward good or bad, instead of sitting on the fence by rating an article a three out of five. However, we were unable to come up with a method to convert current rankings to a six-point scale, while still representing those numbers, which would be decimal numbers, to members with radio buttons so they could change their rating. Also, a change in text descriptions could drastically alter the rating a member gives an article, and there would need to be a change to incorporate a new number in the scale. Let's say I rate an article as "good", a 4 on the current scale, and the scale is converted so that 4 is "okay" and 5 is "good." Should my rating automatically be a 5 to conform to the word, or should the math place my rating at somewhere between the two, regardless of the word? While there are other questions associated with this conversion, this one question has given us the most trouble since there are strong opinions on both sides.

Of nearly 500 respondents to a question asking members if they leave ratings, 60% said they don't, and fully 10% of those users didn't do it because they either couldn't find the ratings, or didn't know how they functioned. It seems many readers come to the article,

read it to the end, and don't read any further down the page. The remaining 90% of users who don't rate tended to not rate articles because they either didn't want to take the time, or didn't feel comfortable rating an article on a topic they don't know inside and out. A good number of respondents who don't rate articles said that they don't log in, and they don't plan to take the time to log in just to rate an article.

Given that from these stats probably 94% of our respondents are aware of how to use the rating system and what it means, I think we've managed to make a good feature usable by the majority of our audience.

A new rating bar is in development now that shows a graphical representation of the ranking. So not only would an article receive a rating with a numeric value (such as 3.75 out of 5), but also a graphical bar showing where that decimal value would fall between one and five. While this isn't a major usability boon to the site, both methods allow both left- and right-brainers to quickly get a feel for how an article ranks just by looking at either the number or the bar. The image shown is actually us admins walking through different versions to test out how it might work. As you can see, we chose to use the comments feature on a test article.

Code Blocks

This section talks a bit about specific coding techniques, so if you've got a weak stomach when it comes to `<textarea>`s, you might want to keep on walking.

Good, you're still here. Now, given our previous experience with formatting large blocks of code on the site, we wanted to find a way to allow the page templates to handle blocks of code gracefully, without obscuring navigation or other elements (such as the content) by pushing it off-screen. Given that the site still kept its navigation on the right side for the second version, we still had to concern ourselves with navigation disappearing. Also, with the stacked

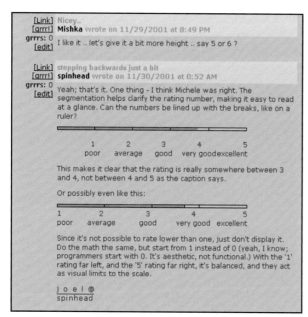

New style ratings display system using a bar. Here the bar itself is being discussed on our test site.

table approach to the page layout, that blacktabnavbarthingie and footer wouldn't grow to fit the content table, which would make for a very ugly page.

We also weren't in a position to modify code samples submitted by authors. Given that a user could come in at any resolution, any window size, and even have any text size, there was no way to determine what the character count would be per line in order to ensure no users see the dreaded horizontal scroll bar and missing navigation. Even if we had settled on a specific character count, we would now be faced with the unenviable task of asking authors to modify their code so that no line of code went over, say, 60 characters. And if the author refused or couldn't be contacted in a timely fashion, we'd be stuck making those changes. Without an admin conversant with the language used by the author, that would be impossible.

Faced with all these issues, we needed to find some way to present code blocks that wouldn't be a barrier to accessibility and wouldn't break the site. It also needed to render similarly in as many browsers as possible. This is a case where the style of the site was going to take precedence over presentation of the information, even though there were valid concerns about users being able to navigate when the links were off-screen, as well as users that would have to scroll back and forth to read every line of an article.

We settled on the `<textarea>` element. The use of the `<textarea>` is one of the cases where it can be argued that *evolt.org* breaks from its goal of using only code that conveys structure and semantics while validating and still allowing complete accessibility. This is an element generally reserved for gathering information and submitting it via a form. We, however, had decided to use it as a container for content. The `<iframe>` element was tossed aside because it would be too difficult to manage content in multiple pages, and scrolling `<div>`s created via CSS wouldn't work properly in too many browsers to make it viable, so the `<textarea>` was about it for options available to us.

Given all these concerns, we set out to make a code container that wouldn't be a barrier to the user in any way and would still integrate with the design of the site.

Using CSS, we styled all `<textarea>` elements that would hold code so that the background color matched the page, and the text color matched the rest of the content. Overall, the `<textarea>` was to have the same styling as its inline cousin, `<code>`.

While the discussions of implementation progressed, the members of admin quickly polled each other on what they did with code blocks from other sites when reading technical articles, and in general we found that most of us copy the code and paste it into our editor of choice. Given this information, we opted to make the

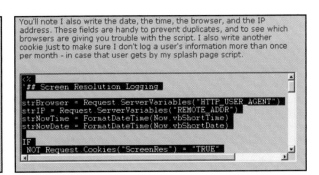

The code `<textarea>`, *before and after clicking, which selects the entire contents of the box for copying and pasting into whatever you like.*

`<textarea>` perform for people like us by automatically highlighting all the content of the `<textarea>` as soon as the user clicks on a scrollbar or in the content of the box. This way users could easily copy code off the page without having to scroll all over the `<textarea>` to be sure they got it all. Those users who didn't have JavaScript enabled just wouldn't see this feature.

This doesn't mean we solved all our problems, or that it's an ideal solution. There are users who have complained about its implementation for various reasons. Some of these complaints are from users who want to see all the code on the page without having to scroll little boxes of code, others are from users who prefer code linked into new windows so it doesn't clutter the content. Overall, however, we feel that we've addressed the issue pretty well, even though we revisit this every few months, just in case there's a better solution. To date, we still haven't found another method that serves the same purpose without distorting the layout of the page or otherwise making blocks of code take over the page. The next step may include using the abilities of CSS to create blocks of code that scroll for those on CSS-capable browsers, but function as `<pre>` blocks for everyone else.

Thankfully, authors are spared the concern of integrating `<textarea>`s into their code. All an author has to do is present a block of code within a `<pre></pre>` block, and the site (powered by a thousand screaming monkeys) converts the `<pre>`s into appropriate `<textarea>` blocks.

Member Pages

The member page consists of the photograph (if provided), e-mail address (if the member allows it), membership date, last login, and a brief biography (also if provided). Essentially it contains all the member information that appears within an article. It also has a link to search the `<tip>`s archive for all `<tip>`s written by the member. This member page also shows all the articles published on the *evolt.org* site by the author,

along with the number of comments and the rating for each article.

Members can maintain their page through a simple form that allows them to upload images, edit their biography, and determine whether their e-mail address is hidden or not.

Our long-term plans include making this more of a member self-aggrandizement area. We'd like to allow members to post favorite links, work experience, skills, possibly even résumés. Hopefully these features will make an *evolt.org* member page really valuable, as it potentially provides employers and others with a place to find resources on the web.

Article Submission

Of course, none of these articles could exist on this site if the authors couldn't find some way to get them into the system. And that method has to be as simple as possible, but still allow us to gather enough information from which to create an article. Every member who is logged in is provided with a link in the sidebar to submit an article.

The submission page has room for an article title, abstract, and the body of the article itself. The author can also choose which category it belongs in based on the options available in a select menu.

For a time, our article submission page seemed to get more questions directed at the mailing list than articles. Every week a couple of "articles" would come through that demonstrated that some users didn't understand the distinction between posts to the mailing list and articles on the site. We addressed this with some intro text explaining what the form was for.

That helped a bit, but then we noticed we were getting a lot of submissions from people who were trying to contact the site administrators. So we added to the explanatory intro text, telling readers that there was another form to use.

Submitting an article? Remember to read all the notes!

> **Much to our surprise, people seemed to be reading the copy, but only after the hyperlinks were added. It seems the hyperlinks caught their eye and caused them to scan the text at the top of the page.**

Hoping to leverage this newfound interest in instructions, we took the opportunity to provide links to our general writers' guidelines (which address how to write the content), our instructions on how to write job postings, and our code style guide (which addresses what HTML is acceptable to use within an article). The code style guide details what tags and attributes are allowed in articles, and has helped reduce the number of articles we get that are foaming with `<font>` tags and otherwise just copied out of an editor, `<head>` tags and all.

Just to be sure it wasn't missed, we linked to the code style guide again above the article content field. Just to be sure.

Searches

Every page on the *evolt.org* site allows a user to search both articles and comments. Logged in users can also search for members. The sidebar of every page contains a simple search form that consists of no more than a textbox, submit button, and link to an advanced search. As of this writing in early 2002, there is a unique form for each of the three searches. In the future, once we have enough time, we hope to integrate the comment and article searches into one, allowing users to perform quick searches from one search form, while

Once we linked to both the list sign-up page and the contact form for the site, nearly all submissions to the page that weren't articles stopped. Much to our surprise, people seemed to be reading the copy, but only after the hyperlinks were added. It seems the hyperlinks caught their eye and caused them to scan the text at the top of the page.

the advanced search form presents the user with further options.

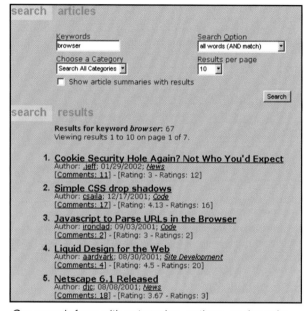

Our search form with categories, options, and results.

The advanced search allows the user to control how many results are returned per page, what sort of Boolean operators are used in the search, and what category, if any, the search should be restricted to. There is also an option to return results with summaries or without.

The results are ranked by the number of keyword hits in the article title and summary, and offer not only the title, but the author, date, category, and even number of comments and overall rating.

The advanced search for comments allows the user to see the entire comment in the results, as well as to sort comments by date, author, category, or article. Since so many useful bits of information exist in comments on the site, this makes it easier to get to the information than searching for articles that may have the comment

for which the user is searching. Once the comments and article search become integrated, the forms will offer more options to allow users to choose what sort of results they want.

The member search simply presents an input box to enter the name, and the ability to restrict the number of results per page. The results show the username, member name, date the member joined, last login date, and the total number of articles. They also show the number of comments given to articles, as well as the number of comments received on articles. The username links directly to the member page.

> *Most of the layout of the fields on the form, as well as the options provided, was determined by our own experiences with building and using on-site search engines across the Web.*

Most of the layout of the fields on the form, as well as the options provided, were determined by our own experiences with building and using on-site search engines across the Web. We found that we almost always want the ability to narrow searches, restrict the number of results per page, and create complex Boolean searches. We simply had to make it all function and provide the options for our users.

Unfortunately, while the form itself seems to make sense to our users, the results that users get aren't always what they want. The results we generate now for the general article search are based only on title and summary, so they aren't always ideal. The comment search, in fact, was a response to users who complained that they were unable to search for comments on articles.

Other Widgets

Of course, a lot more goes into making a site usable than just stuffing buttons into the users' line of sight. We had to make sure people could get to the pages to begin with.

In the original site, an article's URL was the path of the template with a series of variables appended to it as a query string. Basically, anything after the "*article.cfm*" in the URL was a piece of code that the web server used to determine which article to show. Unfortunately, it looked complex, and was hard (OK, impossible) to remember. Search engines had (and still have in some cases) trouble indexing pages with query strings. They just wouldn't do it since a spider could get lost in a site just bouncing between views of the same content. During the redesign, we wanted to create a URL scheme that didn't block search engine spiders, and that made it easier for users to create links to the articles. This approach has been used by a number of sites to mask query strings by replacing the ampersand with slashes, as well as other characters in the query string.

So a link to a popular article from the first version of the site might look like this:
http://evolt.org/index.cfm?menu=8&cid=293&catid=22.

Not only did this link prevent some search engines from indexing the content, it offered no clue to the user about what the link might contain. With a static site, the URL often indicates the structure of the site simply by showing the file structure leading to the current page. A more useful URL might show the user something about the file, like its path or title. For example, the following URL suggests to me that the page is in a section about design, even if I can't see the title of the article itself:
http://foo.foo/articles/design/42.html.

The next version of the site now not only allowed the old URLs with query strings and all, but it also presented a more palatable method to enable linking to a page. By replacing the standard query string characters and including the title as part of the URL, the

new address to the page would not only allow search engines in, but would make a more useful hyperlink for those who were presented with just a hyperlink. This new directory-style URL would prove to be much easier to manipulate as well. Since the URL was essentially a fake path, we didn't have to move hundreds of files

Spiders

Many search engines utilize "spidering" by sending "bots" or "spiders" out to web sites to read and store the content they find. These spiders and bots, which are the same thing, are just stripped down web browsers that go from page to page, site to site, storing all the content of these pages within the master database of the search engine.

While each search engine spider is different, in general they use the structure of the page, number of links pointing to a page, and the content of the page to determine how relevant a page might be for a given search term.

Unfortunately, with so many site owners trying every technique possible to get their sites listed, often by "spamming," or submitting pages with content unrelated to the nature of the site or other techniques, spiders became more wary of just inserting anything and everything they found into their database.

Spiders also found that they could easily get trapped in dynamically-generated sites, perhaps looping through the same pages simply because the URL looked different, even if it was the same content. As a result, it used to be hard to get pages indexed that had any characters after the file name, such as "?" or "&", both indicative of dynamically-generated pages.

around, we simply had to make sure the web server knew to pass URLs of that format to the content system serving the articles.

Here's the same URL as above, converted to the new format:
http://evolt.org/article/Some_Caveats_with_Using_Frames/22/293/index.html.

Of course, this is a longer URL, but it does offer some more information to the user on what the article is about. The *"index.html"* portion could be removed without any adverse effects. Also, because the title section of the URL can be anything, these URLs can be changed to not only be shorter, but also contain information that could appear in referrer logs. For instance, if posting this URL to A List Apart, it could be changed to: *http://evolt.org/article/ala/22/293/.*

This would show up in the page logs and we could identify, independent of referrer, that this page was called from a link on A List Apart, or by somebody who may have copied the link from that site to paste elsewhere.

Link Rot

Very few of the web sites that were around in 1994 are around today, and for those that are, the addresses of some or all of the content has changed. However, if you go to one of my first personal web pages (still lurking in a forgotten directory on a forgotten server as digital flotsam brings visitors), you'll see a page of links where all the links go nowhere.

This is link rot.

Whenever a site doesn't maintain its links by checking them, or the site being linked just moves things around without letting anyone know, you get link rot. Any link left on the vine long enough will rot.

Many organizations combat link rot by creating filler pages at the old addresses of moved pages. These pages tell the user that the page has moved, and offer a new URL for the page. Since an organization has no control over who might link to a page, it's generally a good idea to offer some means to move a user to where they want to go, or at least offer a friendly error page with suggestions on how to find the moved content.

We did, however, note that many of our members on our mailing list regularly pasted links to the articles within their messages. Many of these URLs extended past the 72-80 character limit of most e-mail programs, and were split across two lines.

To create even shorter URLs, a keyword URL scheme was created that allows site admins to assign a keyword to an article so that it can be found via a much shorter URL. Not only does it make the URL indicate even more clearly to the reader what it might contain, it also fits in e-mail posts without wrapping, and is portable enough that we can use it even if we decide to change our content system simply by placing an alias in the directory. Ideally, the URL is also short enough so you can remember it to scribble on a white board when trying to convince a wayward client that frames might be bad.

The above article could now be accessed via the following URL: *http://evolt.org/frames/.*

For users who might try pasting different keywords into the URL, instead of generating an error page, the search page is called with whatever they appended to the URL inserted into the search box with the results of that "search" as well.

Of course, with so many inbound links to the *evolt.org* site coming from pages that may not have been updated in years, we had to ensure that both the old and new methods of calling articles worked. There's really no point in creating easier-to-read URLs if it prevents all old links from working.

That wraps up the main *evolt.org* site. Many of the elements from that site are replicated on our other sites, but each one has its own unique features and abilities. So let's take a look at what we've got...

lists.evolt.org

The second of the three core sites of *evolt.org* is the *lists.evolt.org* site, which handles all the mail subscription options, administration, archives, and most recently, the tip harvester. Initially, these pages were the standard default black text on default gray or white background. Obviously, we wanted to bring these pages into the overall brand, so the initial list introduction pages and sign-up pages are incorporated into the design. The actual list archive pages were driven out of the plain white templates for nearly a year, but that was to allow the list software to automagically build the archives and maintain them. We're now using CSS and compliant HTML 4.01 to draw these pages, bringing them closer to our overall design, although they still lack many of the more familiar elements of the *evolt.org* sites.

The search engine for the list archives is Google. We found that having an on-site search engine didn't produce accurate enough results, and required constant updating in order to get the latest posts. So we simply built the search field to submit to Google with a site-specific search. Nearly all of our users are familiar with Google, and after seeing search results in a Google page, they understand how to navigate among those results.

Tip Harvester

Another feature of *lists.evolt.org* is the tip harvester. On the *evolt.org* mailing list, "*thelist*", off-topic posts are discouraged, but sometimes they seem necessary. For a chatty or off-topic post, the member posting it must

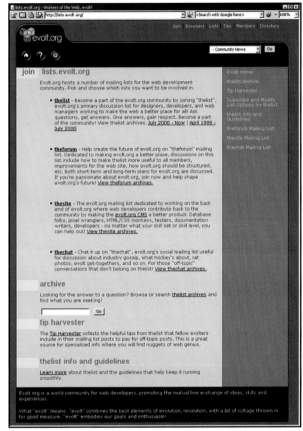

lists.evolt.org *front page, where you join evolt lists and search the archives. There's also a link to the tip harvester.*

include a tip related to web development in order to make it on-topic. While a great idea, it was borrowed from the monkeyjunkies list and its "objunky" payment for off-topic posts. Each week, a script goes through all the posts from the week and pulls out all tips encased in `<tip></tip>` tags. If the author includes an "`author`" attribute, the tip gets associated with that name, otherwise it bases the author on the e-mail address in the message post. If the e-mail address matches a member in the database, the tip gets associated with the member, and a search can be run to return all `<tip>`s from a particular member. A tip author may also include a "`type`" attribute, and if a type exists in the database that matches it, it can be

associated with that type. The result is a database of tips that can be search by type, author, or date.

The only catch with this is displaying it. Trying to find a way to display all the tips in a given week has been difficult. The original method displays all the tips for the week as one `<pre>`-formatted block of code. Obviously, for very long lines of text, very narrow windows, or very large text sizes (or heck, how about all three?), the page layout can start to fall apart as it pushes the right-side navigation off the screen.

This isn't, however, the only issue we considered when we began to explore a new way to display tips. We wanted to allow users to search tips based on category, user, or date. So a script was created that walks through the entire weekly archive and pulls the author, type, and date information out of each tip and stores them individually in the database. This allowed authors to start getting credit for `<tip>`s, some of which are gems in themselves, as well as allowing users to search through the tips on more than one criterion. The new view also offered a page for each tip with a link to the author's member page (when a match was found),

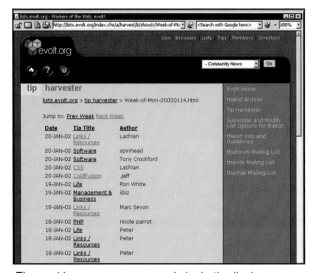

The tip harvester in action, showing a week's tips.

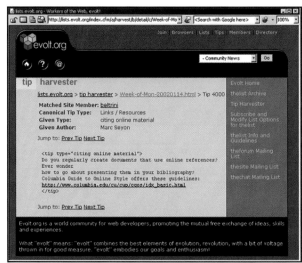

Tip weekly summary page and single tip display.

as well as an assigned tip category, and both the author and category assigned by the author of the tip.

After rolling out this new method of displaying tips, we quickly received feedback from some members who preferred the older method – the week's worth of tips as one giant block of <pre>. It seems some readers preferred to open the page and do a quick search within the content of the page to see if anything popped up that they were interested in. Displaying one tip per page made it impossible for them to scan the body of the tips to quickly see if there was anything of value – they had to click and read *every* tip. So now we were faced with the problem of displaying an index to both sets of tips, the individual and the week's worth.

The current solution has the tip harvester page showing a calendar and links to the default tip page by date, as well as the old digest version:

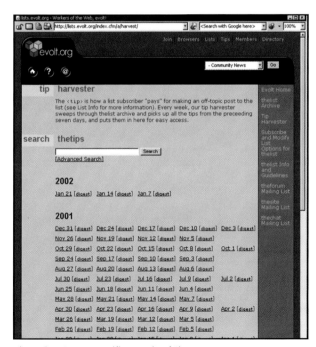

Jumping to a specific week of tips.

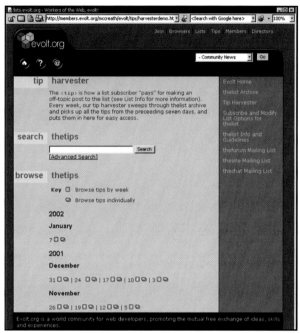

The tip search function.

A proposed solution has a similar layout with icons representing the two different views possible. At the time of this writing, this new view is still going through review and modifications. Not everyone can agree on whether or not the icons we're proposing indicate that one is a link to a collection of tips and the other links to just one tip at a time. We also want to ensure the icons can sit on any color background should we allow readers to use custom styles on the page, possibly changing the background color to that of the icon.

The tip search is internal, and allows readers to search on keywords, the author, or categories. During tesing, it seemed to work fairly well. We've also informally polled readers and found that they are generally satisfied with it. This search can be called from the *www.evolt.org* site, and the link from the member pages on *www.evolt.org* that brings the reader to all tips posted by a member simply calls the search based on author and no other criteria.

browsers.evolt.org

The *evolt.org* Browser Archive is the product of one man's obsession (mine) with cross-browser testing. It started out as a CD for my own use and creating its directory structure was more important than creating a single index, or even organizing the archives beyond their folder names. Of course, releasing that to the public forces one to rethink how it's all organized.

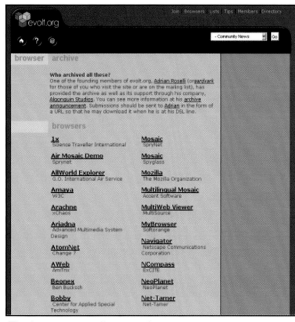

The browsers.evolt.org *main page.*

At the time of this writing, there are 115 unique browsers in the archive, often with multiple versions of each. Each of these browsers supports at least one operating system, yet the home page offers no indication of which browsers run on which operating systems.

As the user delves into one of the browser pages, they are often presented with a directory-style view with a readme file as well as folders to different versions. This

readme file is an artifact of the original CD version of the archive and contains the manufacturer's URL and some information on the browser pasted from their site.

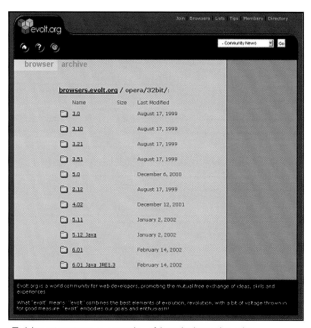

Folder structure a couple of levels into the site.

The layout of the pages mimics the directory structure of the original CD, and as such, adding a new browser to the archive is as simple as creating a directory on the server and uploading the file. The page template reads the directory structure and presents it to the user. It also presents a breadcrumb trail to show the user where they are within the structure of the site. It would be easy to open multiple windows to get different versions and forget where you are from page to page, so the path helps users find their place.

Overall, this "directory" approach to the archive manages the user's expectations. In many FTP sites, or other sites that allow mass download of files, a view similar to this often is employed. It indicates to the user that they are responsible for figuring out what to download based on directory structure and file names alone.

Clearly this isn't an ideal solution for the long-term, and many users have requested an index page that shows the version numbers, platforms supported, dates, and even size of archives. These same users also would like the ability to sort the pages based on any of these criteria.

The only thing that has really kept us from doing this is time. Not only would the entire site have to be catalogued, but all new browsers would need to be catalogued as well, and a method for allowing admins to catalog those attributes would need to be built. This has, however, been deemed a lower priority in the light of the other work that we hope to perform on the site, and the fact that people still seem to make use of the browser archive despite this failing. This is a case where we hoped that the need of the user would outweigh the less-than-ideal interface we've created.

Because the browser archive is generally a static set of pages that don't feed off the rest of the *evolt.org* sites, the sidebar navigation is non-existent. Part of this is a function of the physical location of the hardware, preventing it from sharing the same user and session information as the main *evolt.org* site.

members.evolt.org

Evolt.org is not just an informational resource. Thanks to some nice hardware and a desire to please, *members.evolt.org* came about as a playpen for members to experiment with new technologies under the *evolt.org* banner. Initially begun as a place for the more involved community members to keep e-mail or host a small web site; it's grown into a valuable development resource for over 1,000 web developers. In exchange for free hosting and access to a myriad of technologies, such as PHP, ColdFusion, and others, members display the *evolt.org* logo on their pages. No commercial hosting is allowed, and usage is monitored so that it doesn't turn into an MP3 trading ground.

Applications for space are restricted, so not everyone gets a spot on the server. About 65% of the accounts use between 8 and 15 megabytes, and about three dozen use significantly more for various projects. There are more blogs than you can shake a stick at, but they're all kind enough to use the *evolt.org* logo on their pages as support for their free space.

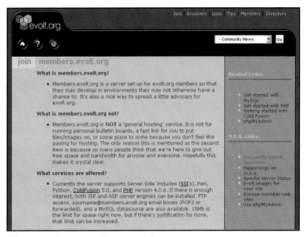

The members.evolt.org *main page.*

Overall, the only part of the site sporting *evolt.org*'s general brand and interface is the home page of *members.evolt.org*. All news about services or changes on the site is handled through the personal blog of Dan Cody, the poor guy who stays up late at night tweaking the hardware. While it was more than adequate to get the site up and running, there are plans to move the news off the site into its own place on the server, within the *evolt.org* branding and interface.

directory.evolt.org

A more recent addition to the *evolt.org* family of sites is the directory. With so many posts on the lists with addresses to wonderful web resources whizzing by, coupled with URLs strewn about articles and comments on the site, as well as nuggets of useful links hiding in `<tip>`s buried within the harvester, it's easy to lose track of all the places one can go to find information on web development.

One of the *evolt.org* members, Simon Coggins, who was not an admin, wanted to create a place to track all these links, so he approached us with the idea, and the code to build it. Otherwise, we probably wouldn't have thought to build one, and if we did, we might not have had the time.

The directory is supposed to help prevent all those URL gems from sliding by. Organized as a simple directory, and building on the model of Yahoo!-like directories, the site is broken into main sections, which are then broken down again and again within the site. Users can get to it at *directory.evolt.org*, or the shorter *dir.evolt.org*.

Each entry consists of a link to a resource, a title for that link, and a description. Every one of these entries is submitted by a members, so clearly streamlining the submission process is as much a factor as making the site usable.

Links on the directory site under the usability section.

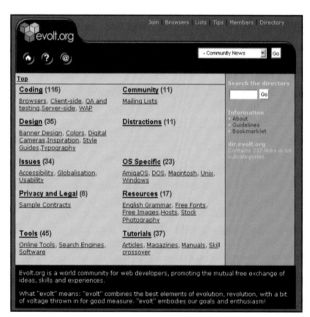

The directory.evolt.org *main page, showing the directory categories.*

Just as *browsers.evolt.org* offers a breadcrumb navigation trail to allow users to move back up the directory structure, so does *directory.evolt.org*. In this case, its location on the page is different, but it serves the same purpose. Unlike the breadcrumb trail, it allows the user to click on any word in the trail to move up to the directory a level at a time, making it more functional. The purpose of the site is otherwise generally clear to visitors, even though there is no initial explanatory text on the home page.

Submitting a link.

Users can submit links, as well as suggesting new categories. Since all submissions go through a review process, submission isn't restricted to just members. However, we found that users who find a new site worthy of inclusion in the directory tend not to surf to the directory and take the time to fill out the form. We needed a simpler submission process.

And so we came up with the idea of using a JavaScript-powered bookmark, or bookmarklet as they are often called (as they are on the site itself), to allow users to submit a site to the directory while they are still visiting it. This bookmarklet is linked from the sidebar, as one

of three links (the other two being an "about" page and a set of guidelines for submission).

In order for this to work, the user has to generate a custom bookmarklet at the *directory.evolt.org* site that contains their name and e-mail address. The user is informed that this information is required, so a bookmarklet that has no name or e-mail address may not be generated.

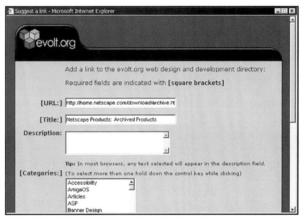

Using a bookmarklet.

With this bookmarklet in place, a user can visit a site, realize in a flash that it would make a great addition to the directory, and simply call a bookmark or favorite (or hotlist item, depending on the browser) to add it. The bookmarklet opens a window with most of the required fields filled out based on the name of the page and the address to the page being submitted. The username and e-mail address are pre-filled if the user submitted one during bookmarklet generation. All the user has to do is supply a brief description, and choose a category (or more). Once it's submitted, the window thanks the user and closes without fanfare.

test.evolt.org

All developers need a place to play – and a place to break things. We like to break things away from our production site, so we've created *test.evolt.org*. It looks like the main site in every way, except for any changes that are in development. For instance, the new rating scheme is still being modeled on *test.evolt.org*. Our author information blocks were tested on this site, as well as style changing capability, and nearly all of our other new features.

This site is not closed to the public, so at any time we can simply post a URL and get people's feedback. Members can even stop in to the site and leave comments on test articles, weighing in with their feedback early in the process. The site has become a very effective way to prototype and get immediate feedback.

Unfortunately, the test server sometimes appears in search engines thanks to links in our public developer archives. Every now and then I see traffic coming to my site from the aptly-named *Dancing monkey boy* article, where I was testing inline code samples. I can only wonder what people think when they stumble across these pages.

> *Don't web developers stay alive exclusively on Jolt cola and ramen noodles? We actually often mix the two.*

food.evolt.org

Of course many have the perception that web developers stay alive exclusively on Jolt cola and ramen noodles. This isn't quite the case. We actually often mix the two. For those who mix other, more palatable items, we've created a new site just for them.

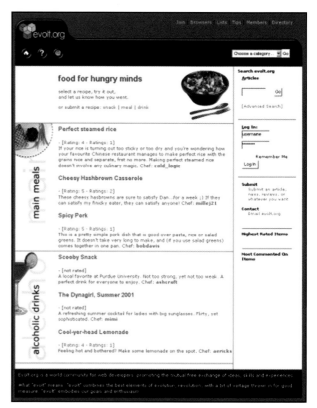

Mmmm... noodles....

food.evolt.org is a break from the web developer focus of the other sites. Its design is slightly different, but it uses the same interface for the most part.

Any member of *evolt.org* is automatically a member of *food.evolt.org*, and can participate in exactly the same way with the *food.evolt.org* site. Since the site is more of a novelty, more attention is paid to making it look nifty than making it function exactly as the other *evolt.org* sites do.

This site will also make it possible to see which *evolt.org* members can cook, and maybe even see who makes better meatloaf – designers or coders.

> *Have we got it right yet? Nah, but we're getting there. Most recently, evolt.org has opened up decision-making power to its membership.*

Who was Responsible?

There are many people who have had a hand in the old site, new site, and ongoing maintenance. Not to mention them would be a disservice since so many of them do so much for the organization. Each of them brought their experience to the table as not only a user, but a web developer.

These people include, but aren't limited to: me for the initial coding, validating, and browser testing. Dan Cody for helping to integrate all this with the ColdFusion templates and data sources. Jeff Howden for integrating some handy JavaScript and beating the heck out of ColdFusion to get it to work with our design. Isaac Forman for the initial design and helping ensure we stayed true to it. David McCreath and Elfur Logadottir, for updating the styles, the HTML, and working it into ColdFusion. Martin Burns for testing and pushing compliance. Marlene Bruce, for generally harassing us into doing something. Rudy Limeback for making me defend the structural appropriateness of practically every tag used. And '*thesite*', evolt's mailing list dedicated to discussing all the development on the site, past, present, and future.

The rest of the admin team handling so many of the updates to the sites, and pushing us forward to version 3, consists of Amanda Erickson, Ben Dyer, Bob Davis, Dean Mah, Garrett Coakley, Javier Velasco, Joel D Canfield, Madhu Menon, Matt Warden, Ron Dorman, Scott Dexter, and Seb Potter.

Conclusions

Hopefully those of you who use *evolt.org* might now see that we don't do everything in a vacuum. Granted, with only a few voices weighing in at times, it can certainly feel like a vacuum.

Overall, we've gotten very positive feedback from users. And as admins, we've worked very hard to address every concern brought to us. Sometimes, however, we'll dwell on minutiae, while larger issues fall by the wayside because some of us just don't have the time to devote to them. For *evolt.org*, site usability is one of our highest concerns, but sometimes takes a back seat to our jobs, our real lives (OK, except me), and even the day-to-day administration of half a dozen mailing lists and as many sites.

Have we got it right yet? Nah, but we're getting there. Most recently, *evolt.org* has opened up decision-making power to its membership. Previously, we had opened up site development to members, allowing them to weigh in on issues and even develop solutions. Now we've taken it another step and created a forum for the membership to help determine the direction of the entire community. This most recent shot of motivation has resulted in our survey, a number of changes to the site, and bigger and better plans for down the road.

Given the number of developer sites and reference sites that link to *evolt.org* as a resource, and how well-regarded we seem to be in the community (as overheard on other lists and sites), I believe we've done a very good job of providing a place for the talented developer to come to teach and learn.

But nothing brings home the success more than meeting with a friend in the industry who is excited over a new article they have found – only to discover it's one of your own. Somehow it feels we've come full circle at that point and sealed the deal.

Aardvark's Usable Design Gallery

My scooter – I can't skateboard or rollerblade to save my life, but that little scooter keeps the distant offices within a couple steps. It corners well, except on smooth floors, where I mostly fall down.

Microsoft™ Natural Keyboard – The first generation, where the arrows form an upside-down "T". Taught me how to type, keeps my RSI at bay, works quite well with a mouse for Unreal Tournament.

Also:

Duct tape – Didn't you ever watch MacGyver? Or have to hold a rusty exhaust pipe to the bottom of your car? Or need to hold a friend back while you...nevermind.

Hands-free phone for the house – While I don't get enough calls to warrant it, not shouting to a speakerphone or arching your neck to hold a handset is quite handy when doing the dishes. And it makes me feel important (too bad only my cat sees me).

My wallet – A lovely calfskin tri-fold that opens into an "L" shape, allowing me to quickly flip open my ID to bouncers or flip open again to pay the cover.

A towel – "Douglas Adams sums it up best, but I've found having one in the car can be quite handy for all sorts of things my mother would look upon disapprovingly."

Paperclip – Because sometimes a bent piece of metal is just what you need to eject a disk, open a lock, skewer a cherry tomato, pierce an ear, etc.

Swiss Army Knife – They come in nearly all shapes and sizes for nearly any function you could need. Even some you don't.

MetaFilter

adventures in zero budget usability

matthew haughey

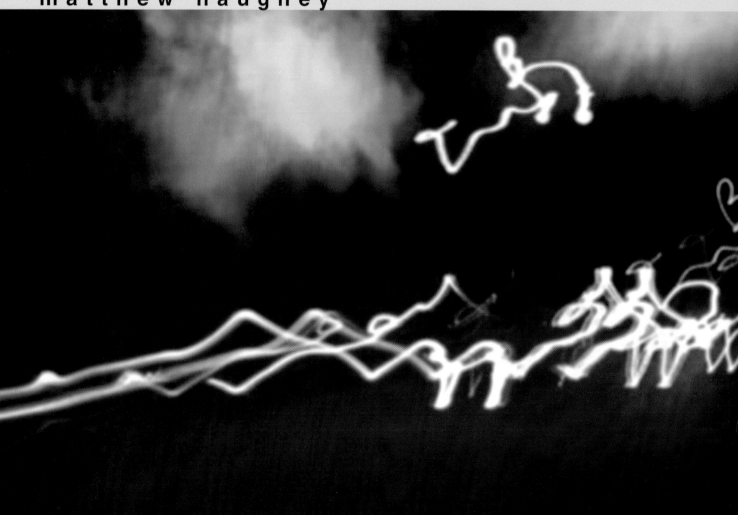

http://www.metafilter.com/
http://haughey.com/

Matt started building web sites in 1995, after playing with Mosaic in the college computer labs. He worked as a designer and developer in a university computer group at UCLA for a few years before moving to San Francisco to join the Pyra Labs team, helping to build http://www.blogger.com/. Since that time he's been at a number of other firms and completed a good deal of freelance work, ranging from interaction design and user experience to database programming and application server building. He's been nursing MetaFilter along for the past three years, keeping it up to date and easy to use.

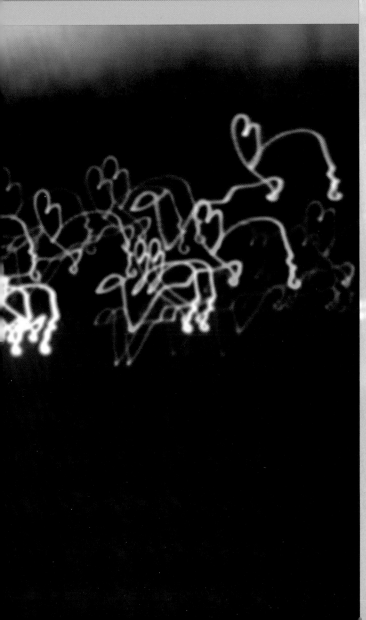

If you weren't doing this, what would you be doing?

Well, I was an environmental engineer when I got out of college, but I hated my job. If there wasn't a web developer/design role to keep me away, I would have either continued being miserable pushing pencils for environmental regulations, or quit and moved on to a commercial art/graphics design job, I suppose in print design.

Which living person do you most admire?

I should say "my wife" here. That'll score big points for all eternity. I admire anyone that stands by their convictions in the face of adversity, in my wife's case, that adversity is me.

On a scale of 1 (Amish) - 10 (Star Trekkie), how geeky are you?

I think I'm only an 8, at most. I don't have a computer science degree and I can't build robots that specialize in killing other robots. Once I attain that, I'll be a 10.

What's your favorite building?

While I admire the classic great buildings of the 20th century (the Guggenheim, Frank Lloyd Wright's falling water, etc.), I haven't seen any of them in person. I guess the last impressive building I saw and experienced in the flesh was the new Getty Museum in Los Angeles. It was an impressive building and incorporated into the landscape well.

What's your favorite book? Piece of music? Type of pizza?

For books, I can't really name a single favorite; they seem to correspond to my current age and moods. I guess Catcher in the Rye was the first book I loved, back when I was 16. It was Shampoo Planet by Douglas Coupland at age 22, Microserfs, also by Coupland at age 26, and A Heartbreaking Work of Staggering Genius by Dave Eggars at age 28. My favorite music would take a book to fill, as a lot of different types and styles float my boat. Favorite pizza? Anything interesting and vegetarian.

If you were a superhero, who would you be?

Cynical Man: able to stop evildoers with a single bad attitude.

What gadget could you not live without?

Tivo, easily. I could not live without my tivo, as it makes American television watchable. Over here, there are hundreds of channels of fluff, and with a tivo equipped with my preferences, all the crap of modern TV is squeezed down to a few hours of pure diamonds.

adventures in zero budget usability

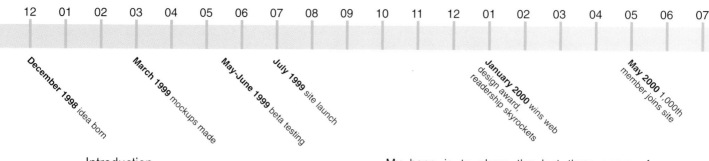

12   01   02   03   04   05   06   07   08   09   10   11   12   01   02   03   04   05   06   07

December 1998 idea born

March 1999 mockups made

May–June 1999 beta testing

July 1999 site launch

January 2000 wins web design award, readership skyrockets

May 2000 1,000th member joins site

Introduction

I started MetaFilter in the early part of 1999, not with the grand ambitions of garnering press, fanning flame wars, or sharing a site with thousands, but instead simply to create a site that let multiple users post links to interesting things on the web and discuss them among themselves. Since its meager beginning, it has grown by leaps and bounds, and over the past three years has been used, tested, broken, and fixed thanks to the input of thousands of people by various means.

> *My hope is to share the last three years of my experiences running a busy web site so that you can learn from my mistakes and gain from my tips, and ultimately to help you build the most usable web site you can.*

The site has always been a personal side project, so there has never been a budget for testing, usability labs, or formal user interviewing. For the most part, the site has been operated and adapted thanks to valuable user feedback. Over the course of this study, I'll impart to you how I captured that feedback and used it appropriately, share experiences I've picked up over the years, and show best practices and code examples of features I've implemented.

My hope is to share the last three years of my experiences running a busy web site so that you can learn from my mistakes and gain from my tips, and ultimately to help you build the most usable web site you can.

Why I Started the Site

Back in late 1998, a new type of personal page appeared on the horizon. It was far from the then-popular musician or artist fan page, or list of links typically found on homepages. It was a **weblog**, a chronologically based, sometimes personal, oftentimes humorous, and always engaging page of entries written by a single person. The first weblogs were primarily link-driven, with several posts a day linking to interesting sites the author had found, usually with some commentary about the site being linked.

> *Weblogs were revolutionary at the time because they didn't worry about "stickiness" or try to keep you on the site; the first weblogs did their best to move you off to other places, knowing that if you enjoyed the links, you'd be back.*

Weblogs were revolutionary at the time because they didn't worry about "stickiness" or try to keep you on the site; the first weblogs did their best to move you off to

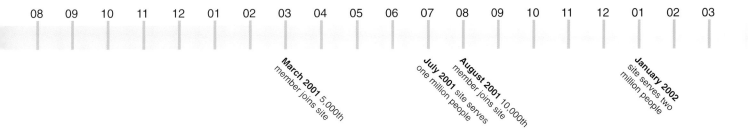

March 2001 5,000th member joins site

July 2001 site serves one million people

August 2001 10,000th member joins site

January 2002 site serves two million people

other places, knowing that if you enjoyed the links, you'd be back.

I had grown fond of these weblogs, and found them to be a fun diversion from my web developer day job. They were constantly updated so there was always something new to read. Many weblog authors were great writers, ensuring a steady stream of amusing and/or provocative things to read. I played with the idea of starting my own in December of 1998, and started mocking up some page layouts, created graphics, and worked on some names.

Forming the Vision

My first worry with starting my own weblog was finding enough compelling content by myself – typical link-driven weblogs of the day would have four or five links and descriptions to amazing things the owners had found each and every day. I had a knack for finding interesting things and e-mailing them to friends and co-workers, but it wasn't several gems a day, more like one a day at most. Then I had an idea: I thought having multiple authors would be the key to creating a good weblog. If I could find one or two links a day, perhaps having 4 or 5 others joining me would result in a fairly decent amount of content. I also figured that comments on posts would be a good idea, because the 4 or 5 other authors might want to comment on each other's work. What I envisioned was a site with a few contributors, a smattering of comments, and a sizable readership.

Some Goals for the Site (Choosing the Right Tool for the Job)

When I started the site, I had some simple goals in mind – the site should be:

- Updated regularly, at a greater recurring rate than any of my previous projects – it would need to be designed with this end in mind, and include some automated tools for making it easy. I wanted all the tedious, busy work to be eliminated from the workflow, so I could concentrate on the content.

- Easy to use by everyone involved, including features to allow posting of new threads, and especially to allow members to comment if desired.

With those technical goals in mind, I began to hunt for software and plan the site's backend architecture. I first surveyed existing community tools, since they were designed for use by multiple contributors. In early 1999, there weren't too many options. I mainly looked at **Ultimate Bulletin Board** by *InfoPop.com* and **Slashcode**, the open source package found behind *Slashdot.org*. Each had its strengths and weaknesses.

227

Ultimate Bulletin Board

I took a liking to the open source, Perl-based **Ultimate Bulletin Board (UBB)** at first, as I had seen UBB-based communities springing up all over, but the strong categorization didn't meet my needs. I disliked the fact that it forced users to first choose a path down a specific area before seeing new content. Another bad mark against the software was the interface presented to users reading and posting comments. It's got a lot of what I like to call **formjunk**.

> *Forms are tedious, confusing, often poorly designed, and most people equate their use with things like paying taxes.*

Of all the HTML elements on a page, forms are probably the least desirable things you'll have to deal with as a designer. They vary widely in their look, depending on the browser and operating system, and **Cascading Style Sheets (CSS)** offer some, but not total, control of their appearance. Forms are not only visually unpleasing, but by their very nature, they imply work on the part of the user. If you asked the average person what their first response would be to the phrase "fill out this form", I have no doubt that your findings would be overly negative.

Forms are tedious, confusing, often poorly designed, and most people equate their use with things like paying taxes.

Couple the implied work of a form with the lack of visual control over the elements between browsers and platforms, and you have something that is bound to create design problems and cause friction with users. I try to limit the use of forms as much as possible in my applications, making them as small as possible, or hiding optional longer forms in "advanced" preferences sections.

UBB posting forms are clunky, offering either too many options, or options that are rarely used (see figure). A quick look at the back-end revealed those options couldn't be turned off readily, and my lack of Perl programming knowledge meant I couldn't tweak the code myself. Since I had fairly specific needs for my site, and I couldn't get exactly what I wanted out of UBB, I decided against using it.

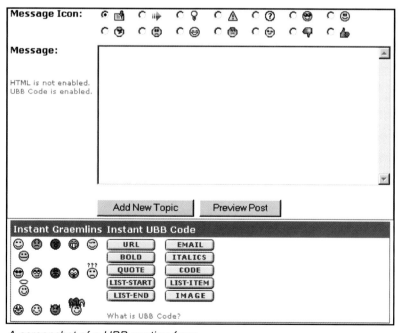

A screenshot of a UBB posting form.

Slashcode

In a way I patterned MetaFilter after *Slashdot.org*, and took a look at the free software behind it, Slashcode (*www.slashcode.com*) as well. I knew MetaFilter might share some visual and format similarities with Slashdot and I was reluctant to copy its code anyway, but what drew me away from using its software was interface issues. I'd been a longtime member of the community and was experienced with the toolset, but there were a lot of things I didn't like about it. Every new post, carries with it a lot of customization baggage. Below each post, and before the comments begin, the user is presented with **six** form elements (see figure), which allow for several different sorting options.

I knew MetaFilter might share some visual and format similarities with Slashdot and I was reluctant to copy their code anyway, but what drew me away from using their software were interface issues.

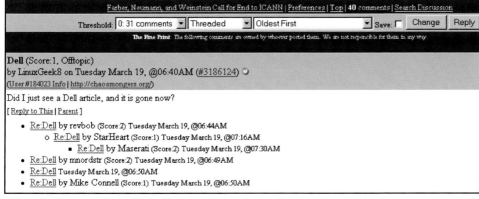

Slashdot comment page, beginning with sorting option interface.

The comment sorting options themselves are useful, and essential when a site gets very large and very busy. They were developed for Slashdot after the site had grown so popular that skimming through the ample comments was a hassle. Once in a while I come across a newly minted Slashcode site, and the plethora of customization options look downright silly when there are only a handful of comments (or none as is most often the case with new communities). Although Slashdot and the Slashcode software are designed to help create a peer-reviewed and commented community, I disliked the editorial layer that was built-in. There were user accounts, but the users couldn't directly post to the front page of the site – there was an upper layer, of editors, that had to review each submission. Slashcode is also organized around categories, which I didn't want when I first started my site.

The default views for comment sorting are set in the *Preferences* link for logged in users, but the other sorting options are also shown on every page, with no preference to turn them off. It would be a simple matter to streamline the interface, letting registered users set their preferences then hide the options from view after setting, since frequent users rarely change their sorting options.

adventures in zero budget usability

Rolling My Own

After reviewing community software packages and comparing them with my specific needs, I decided to program my own from the ground up. Weblogs had a definite format, and the various community tools out there didn't really address the needs of a weblog specifically. There weren't any tools available to create them automatically, so I had little choice but to go it alone with my own software.

On the positive side, taking this path would ensure the application was built to closely match the audience and would allow interfaces to be completely customizable and streamlined. Normally programming your own system is a major step, adding hundreds of hours of development time to the building process, but luckily for me, I had the opportunity to implement and learn a new programming language for use at my workplace.

With my ideas for MetaFilter and new tools at my disposal, I used the project as an excuse to push my ColdFusion and SQL database programming skills – that was the real motivation behind the initial coding.

ColdFusion

ColdFusion is a great way for designers to get into programming easily. It shares syntax with HTML, and feels familiar to anyone that has ever hand-coded a web page. It has its limitations – the server and studio packages are quite expensive, and ColdFusion isn't known for scaling well to large loads of visitors. On the bright side, you can find a low cost host that offers ColdFusion support and database hosting, author code in any text application, and tweak your code logic as your audience grows. ColdFusion serves as a good introduction to web programming and is easy to pick up for technically minded designers. For the database side, I created my first test applications in Microsoft's Access, because it was easy to use and well integrated with ColdFusion's studio environment. Since I knew MetaFilter would require a more robust database, I chose the big brother to Access, Microsoft's SQL Server, to handle the data on the site.

About two months before I began working on MetaFilter, I got the go-ahead to take an intense multi-day course in Macromedia's ColdFusion scripting language, and by the end of the short course I was building simple database-backed web applications. Based on HTML syntax, ColdFusion was at once easy to understand and use. After the training, I had a pretty good background on what the language could do and how to do it. After returning to work to implement my new-found knowledge, I realized my employer's applications were all quite simple on the surface and I should use ColdFusion in an extra-curricular site if I wanted to really stretch my knowledge.

With my ideas for MetaFilter and new tools at my disposal, I used the project as an excuse to push my ColdFusion and SQL database programming skills – that was the real motivation behind the initial coding.

The Intended Audience

Initially, weblogs appealed to the highly web-savvy. Among the 30 or so weblogs in existence at the beginning of 1999, each author seemed to be "one upping" the others with their search engine expertise, and skill at finding links to the most obscure sites online. I wanted MetaFilter to attract these more web-savvy users as well (so that some assumptions could be made – I wanted to design for a set baseline of intelligence), and I didn't want to see links posted that everyone had already seen before. I knew it was a tall order, and I can't say I'm surprised that only a handful of people besides myself posted new threads during the first six months of the site being live.

> *I made a few design choices to reinforce the appeal to experienced web users at the expense of usability.*

I also preferred the well-seasoned web veterans as the target audience to leave comments, as I'd had some experience with USENET and remembered that the more technical or cryptic a newsgroup's subject was, the better your chances were to find intelligent conversation.

Early on, I made a few design choices to reinforce the appeal to experienced web users at the **expense** of usability. In a way, these choices acted as a filter for people that didn't bother to read the about page or guideline page or click around and discover what they were looking for. To post a thread or comment on an existing thread on the site, you had to be a registered member of the site, which required a user to fill in a short form of basic login information. The only link to the signup was in the navigation, and was only referenced elsewhere on the login page (if someone didn't have an account they could find a link to the new-user page).

A year later, I made the process easier, adding indications of whether or not a person was logged in, with a link to the login page and new-user page at the bottom of every page on the site. I found that although it made it clear to users, many more people signed up than usual, so much so that I quickly changed back to the more concealed new-user page. There were also other things to consider: sudden influxes of new users present a problem to the community, as new users occasionally go against the grain or stray outside the accepted limits of the established audience. The simple filters served to keep community growth rate steady and low, and to encourage the more experienced web user that wasn't afraid to dig for information to sign up.

Also, being a community site, there is always a potential problem with scalability issues when adding new users. The site had been programmed to add more options, and therefore be more resource-intensive for registered users when compared to unregistered users. Throughout the remainder of the chapter, I will do my best to explain where and when a design choice was made at the expense of usability, so you can see why and how exceptions are made. Generally speaking, it's always best to design interfaces that are usable to the greatest percentage of your audience, but there are always exceptions.

> *Generally speaking, it's always best to design interfaces that are usable to the greatest percentage of your audience, but there are always exceptions.*

adventures in zero budget usability

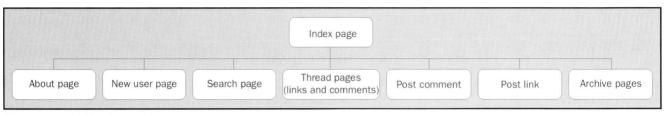

The proposed MetaFilter sitemap.

Pre-launch Interface

Once the time came to begin building the site, I started by first producing a plain text, style-free version. The reasoning was simply to get the very basic functionality built up first, focusing on the programming side, before proceeding on tackling the many presentation issues that were to come. Using Microsoft PowerPoint's simple flowchart tool, I came up with the following site map (shown above), and created pages for each.

> *Throughout the text, I may refer to the main content aspects of MetaFilter as posts, threads, or links – keep in mind they are interchangeable – posts=threads=links. Pages for each post will always be referred to as comment pages.*

The basic page interaction design was laid out. The *Index* page would be a listing of the past seven days worth of posts, and each post would link to a page of comments. There would be an archive for older posts. Creating a new post or comment required registration, so there needed to be a new user signup page and a *Login/Logout* page for those already having accounts. A *Search* page would allow users to scour the database for exact matches submitted, and an *About* page was necessary to explain who was behind the site, what the purpose of the site was, and the particulars about the server itself. Since it was a community site, driven by user submissions, a loose *Guidelines* page was created and linked from the new post page, and from the about page. In total, the site began life as a mere eight page templates, with the majority of user interaction occurring on two types of page – the *Index* page and the *Comment* page.

Initial Interface Decisions

Once the basic guts of the site were built, it was time to start thinking about the user interface. A good deal of thinking went into the initial design phase, based mostly on my own years of web user and builder experience.

For the site's first interface, I tried to:

- Incorporate tips from the dozens of articles I'd read on user experience

- Build on the collective knowledge of thousands of e-mail discussion list messages I'd read

- Use the lessons learned from dozens of web developer sites I'd encountered before (such as
  http://www.webmonkey.com,
  http://www.evolt.org,
  http://www.alistapart.com, and
  http://ahref.com, among others

Since I was an independent web designer building my own personal project, I crafted the initial interfaces very much in a vacuum. I had to start somewhere, but thanks to valuable feedback from a variety of sources, the site improved. Aside from the graphics, colors, and major layout, only a few remnants of the original design remain.

What kind of usability book would this be without some wild chest beating and mantra decrees shouted from atop my ivory tower of design?

The Design Approach

First off, a mantra is necessary whenever beginning a project that involves a new type of design or attempting to sound like an industry pundit. What kind of usability book would this be without some wild chest beating and ideological decrees shouted down from atop my ivory tower of design? My mantra for this project (and every other project I've done, incidentally) was the following:

Design all interfaces as simply as possible. Add complications only when absolutely necessary, and over time, as needs dictate.

From that mantra, everything followed. The choice between using an existing software package and creating new software from scratch was made based on this decision. However, the lack of interface control in existing software made the choice to code from the ground up necessary. When determining how much information to display on the front page, and on thread pages, following this mantra dictated that simplicity should reign supreme, and that the least amount of information needed should be shown to reduce screen clutter as much as possible.

When you break down the site's interaction with users, there are two distinct tasks: reading the site, and contributing to the site. Based on this approach, the design of each task was handled carefully and separately from the other. Let's have a look at them now.

The Reading Interface

The page most likely seen by both first-time visitors to the site and existing users is the index page, with the past few days of posts and pages of comments linked immediately off each post (these would be the second most likely pages to be seen). Both are focused on reading information, and were designed to make that process as easy as possible.

On the *Index* page, the posts are grouped by date, with the month and day showing. The year was unnecessary, as there would never be more than one year showing, except of course during the last half-week in December – but it seemed obvious that a December 31-January 1 week referred to one year that followed the next and didn't need to be explicitly stated.

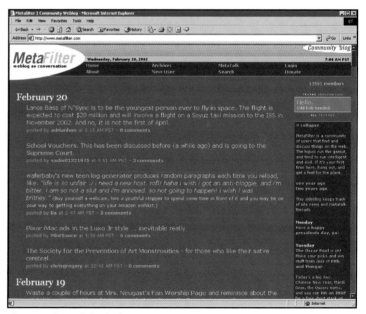

Screenshot of the index page.

Each post then comprised the following parts:

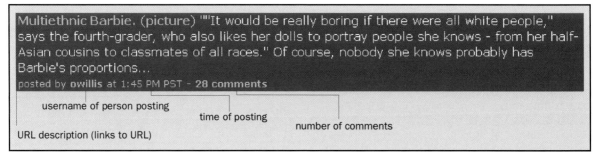

Breakdown of a post.

The URL and URL description began a post, but were optional, as long as the post description contained a link offsite. Below the post, a minimum of metadata was shown:

- The username of the person making the post

- The time at which it was made (unfortunately only shown in Pacific Time at first – it took me two years before I learned how to create custom time zones and query the data correctly)

- The number of comments already made about the post, with a short "post a comment" link

> *I noticed that users that were disliked by other users would have their posts filtered out by their detractors, on seeing their names. I didn't want this type of activity to occur on MetaFilter.*

The post itself contains links offsite to the actual article, but the metadata is linked internally – for example, the username linked to the user's profile, so people could see their previous contributions easily. In addition, the comment number links to the comment page, which showed a record of comments made in regards to that post. The "post a comment" message linked initially to a comment page that had a contribution form, which required registration to view (this will be explained in the next section on contribution interfaces).

The posts and comments were the most important part of the reading interfaces, and were shown clearly in high contrast white-on-blue text, at a full body font size. Metadata was shown in lower contrast light gray text, at a small font size to decrease both its visual importance and clutter. The layout of contribution above metadata was deliberate. I'd found on other community sites that sometimes the metadata (including a person's username) was shown above their contribution, and I noticed that users that were disliked by others would have their posts filtered out by their detractors, on seeing their names. I didn't want this type of activity to occur on MetaFilter. A person should be judged by their words first, before any preconceived opinion is attributed to them. I felt the **contribution-above-metadata** design best allowed for a user to be accepted or at least read, no matter how reviled their presence became, and hopefully would allow a user to change their ways, and still be judged on their contributions fairly.

The Contribution Interface

There are two main contribution interfaces used on the web site, the "new post" page and the "new comment" page. The page devoted to taking new post contributions was a bit of a challenge. It needed to be as simple and streamlined as possible, taking five basic bits of information (username, password, URL, URL description, and post), but also conveying the importance of what the user was doing. This interface allowed users to change the index page of the site, something that is both drastic in terms of potential, and extremely trusting on my part as the site owner and on the part of the community as a whole. The new post interface had to be easy to use but also remind users what they were about to do.

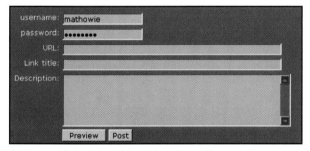

New post interface at the site's inception.

The comment posting interface was simpler, with just the pre-filled username and password, a large comment box for typing into, and a submit button below.

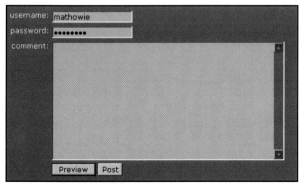

Comment interface.

It is worth noting that on the contribution interfaces, an extra step of registering with the site and logging into the site (done automatically after registration) was considered more important than an easier-to-use interface that might allow anyone to submit a post or comment with simply an e-mail and display name supplied (no painful registration step necessary). Since it was a community site, I was aware early on that accountability was important and that in order for people to trust what others were saying, there would need to be some level of security in the knowledge that if "John Doe" said something about music one day and something about news the next day, they were in fact the same person. I was also aware of reputation management that helps engender trust in the community at places like eBay™, where it is an integral part of the site. If I ever wanted to build real reputation tools in the future, I would need personal data on each user, so that also favored mandatory registration. At the beginning though, I wanted it to be clear that everyone owned their words, and their words represented them on the site. Keeping track of everyone's contributions allowed other users to look back at any user's history, creating in a sense, a low-tech approach to reputation on the site.

adventures in zero budget usability

Separation of Style and Content

Special care was taken when determining how the site's visual interface would be coded. Since it was appealing to a more technical audience and the site wasn't a business venture, I decided it was OK to use up-to-date technology to ensure the best user experience on the site. The content is entirely text-based, so I wasn't planning on any multimedia interfaces, but I did make an effort to incorporate Cascading Style Sheets (CSS) as much as I could in the design.

There were many benefits to such a CSS approach. The major deciding factor was load time of the site for users. Since the site's content was served dynamically from a database, I was aware early on that it would induce a processing delay while the server fetched data and sent it to the browser. To offset this delay, I looked for ways to speed the load time of the site as much as possible. The biggest way to save load time (in some cases up to multiple seconds) was to eliminate the use of HTML tables as containers. In every browser I've used (all versions of Netscape 1.1+ and IE, on Windows, Mac, and Linux), a page loaded with text information contained within table cells will delay loading until the last of the data within the table is fully delivered to the browser. The effect can be seen on sites such as *http://slashdot.org* – the top banner graphic loads almost instantly, while the day's content takes up to several seconds to load up in a white table. On e-commerce sites especially, this results in slow loading pages that can cause a loss in sales as visitors leave the site due to frustration. With MetaFilter, I knew a community site would be taxing on a server, and the action of multiple people requesting the same page every few seconds would slow load times considerably. Displaying content in tables would worsen the appearance of a slow loading site.

If you can remember the early days of the Web (or if you can't), there weren't any tables to deal with, and content flowed down the 14.4kbps and 28.8kbps lines as fast as the server delivered them. On content-rich sites, this meant your browser would fill with a screen-full or two of content fairly rapidly, and the rest would fill in eventually. Often I'd find myself reading paragraph after paragraph of a page that ended up taking more than a minute to fully load, but I could begin reading the page seconds after I initially requested it. After web designers began to use the `<table>` element for layout purposes, the delay in load time on content-rich sites was apparent and still exists to this day.

> *After web designers began to use the* `<table>` *element for layout purposes, the delay in load time on content-rich sites was apparent and still exists to this day.*

Cascading Style Sheets eliminate the need for tables by offering very specific layout rules for content display. Instead of building multi-column tables with transparent `.gif` file spacers, page margins can be set with CSS precisely, without negatively affecting load times. A major additional benefit of using CSS is the separation of style and content. A specific CSS file can be built for specific browsers or platforms, and applied to content. If the data is independent of any presentation code, a developer can support as many different views of the data as they want to build CSS files for. This allows them to create the best possible presentation of the site, so that it can be viewed successfully in the latest IE release on a high-end PC, as well as in a text reader by a visually challenged user, and on a handheld device such as a palm pilot. This can be accomplished by switching to appropriate stylesheets, based on browser sniffing done on the server side with whatever language you've built your application in, or on the client side with JavaScript.

Therefore, after exhaustive experimentation with test files and consultation with other web developers on places like e-mail-based discussion lists, I came up with a subset of CSS that would work with the two biggest portions of the audience, while being backward compatible so it wouldn't negatively affect the experience of those using older browsers.

The use of CSS was limited to two aspects of the site: positioning of content and font styling of content. The CSS positioning support varied widely at the time (and still presents major problems across browsers today) but my needs were limited to margins. On the main index page of the site, I wanted the top portion of the

CSS, A Brief History

Although CSS was delivered to the world by the **World Wide Web Consortium (W3C)** in late 1996 as a recommendation to browser makers, even the latest browsers (such as Netscape and IE 4) that existed in early 1999 while I was building the site didn't have much in the way of CSS support. This meant that of the extensive standards for CSS written in 1996, only a small subset was correctly implemented in browsers and could be used on a site without alienating everyone who didn't have the latest browsers, or having vast differences in the appearance of the site among users. Now in 2002, browser support for CSS1 (remember that it was unleashed in 1996) is finally approaching 100% in the very latest browsers, though given the proliferation of older browsers still being used, a developer today still isn't free to exploit all the benefits of CSS without losing some significant portion of the population, even if, like me, they stick with CSS1 only, to minimize this problem as much as possible.

page to butt up against all edges of the browser window, but I didn't want the text flowing below to hit the sides. I created zero margins with proprietary body tags (still there for Netscape 4 users, replaced with CSS for all others), and contained the main logo graphics and site navigation within a table in the top 100px or so (CSS couldn't be used for such a complex layout back then). Below that, I wanted a nice comfortable gutter of 50 pixels on each side, to keep the text away from the browser's edges. I wrapped a `<div>` around each post, and gave it two declarations in CSS: `margin-left:50px;` and `margin-right:50px;`.

For comment pages, I wanted an additional margin to set the comments apart from the original post, so I created a visual indent of another 20 pixels by wrapping a `<div>` around comments with this declaration: `margin-left:20px`. Since it was already in the main `<div>`, it created a total indent of 70 pixels. The term "cascading" in Cascading Style Sheets comes from the behavior of nesting data in such a way that style "cascades" down, where children of parent declarations inherit the styles of their predecessors.

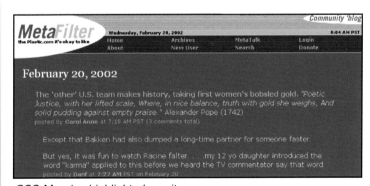

CSS Margins highlighted on site.

The styling used for fonts allowed virtually all presentation code to be eliminated from the presentation layer. Instead of using font tags of various sizes on each page, I could instead wrap standard descriptive header tags around date headings, and paragraph tags around content, then simply create

CSS declarations for each, specifying what face and size should be displayed and where the placement of those fonts should be in relation to other content chunks. This not only lessened the code required to build each page, it allowed me to stick to basic standards while still allowing for a rich, graphical view by those with the latest browsers. An additional benefit of using CSS to describe font display was that it allowed me to customize the site easily, even offering the chance for members of the site to declare their own personal fonts for the bulk of text content on the site, without having to change dozens of font tags.

By using CSS to produce margins for the page, I eliminated the use of tables on nearly the entire site. Even with all the content being served by the database, pages loaded quickly, filling the screen with content as fast as the database server could respond. The use of CSS to describe how fonts would look and be placed around the page allowed for custom displays in the latest browsers, while still offering a readable site in other devices, as we can see:

Initial Testing Phase

My initial testing occurred in my office, soon after getting everything laid out and programmed. I began posting to the site, testing the tools out, and getting a feel for how I used the tools. From this initial testing, I refined the layout of items, tweaked the CSS, and altered the new post pages. I found out very early on that mistakes were easy to make, and more thought would have to go into the "new post" page. To minimize mistakes by other users, I added a screenshot image of a sample post, shown below the posting interface, with each portion of the interface clearly labeled and shown properly filled in. I also realized a preview option was needed, in case users wanted to check their work before making it live, and changing the front page of the site.

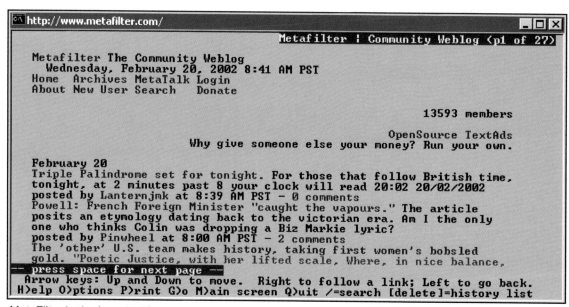

MetaFilter in the Lynx text browser.

I made a decision at this point to disallow comment or post editing. The requests for edit controls have come early and often, but I'd been a part of online communities that allowed changes and it too often led to bad results. In heated disagreements, things often went like this: people would sometimes use strong language or make assumptions about others. Numerous comments would follow as others debated the finer points or asked for clarification from the original post. The original poster would come back to see fellow community members had shot holes into aspects of their argument, and would promptly edit their original post or delete it entirely. I found that behavior such as that could ruin a community, by invalidating previous efforts by other members, and making old, edited threads lose context.

> *The request for edit controls has come early and often, but I'd been a part of online communities that allowed changes and it too often led to bad results.*

I realized that sometimes people make spelling errors or grammatical mistakes worth editing, but given the negative effects I'd seen rampant editing cause before, I instead chose to allow users to preview as much as they liked but, once they posted, it was set in stone. I knew that someday, someone might say something in the heat of the moment that they wished they could take away, but I felt that editing could be worse, allowing users to re-edit their history on the site, selectively removing negative aspects of their involvement. In a community, people are defined by their words and I felt strongly that if they could change their words, it harmed the formation and trustworthiness of everyone's reputation, potentially giving a false perspective of people's personalities.

> *They knew me well enough to take the request seriously and put some thought into their feedback, but they weren't so close to me that they were afraid of hurting my feelings.*

Beta Testing Among Friends

At this point, the site was now online, but few people knew of its existence. I knew that before I began promoting it or showing it to a wider audience, more extensive testing was required. I started the next testing phase by crafting an e-mail of several paragraphs in length, describing the site and its intentions, and asking for feedback on the interface. I explained what typical content would be found, and asked testers to try posting a new thread and leaving a comment or two, then e-mailing me back any feedback they had. I chose a group of about 15 people to do the testing, mostly acquaintances from mailing lists and colleagues with opinions I regarded highly. It seemed to be just the right balance between complete strangers and really good friends. They knew me well enough to take the request seriously and put some thought into their feedback, but they weren't so close to me that they were afraid of hurting my feelings. When I sent this request out, I had no idea if it would help, or if the feedback would be useful.

It was late July 1999 when I sent the e-mail out, and within a day I began seeing new contributions and an inbox filled with feedback. It quickly got to be so much that I created a new subfolder in my e-mail to sort MetaFilter-related messages into. The testers quickly found paths that lead to server error messages I hadn't caught. They made a point of notifying me when their expectations weren't met (for example when they expected clicking a button to result in some site behavior, but found that something different happened instead). They immediately began asking for new features or refinement of existing features. It was a tad overwhelming, but all of it was very valuable, and I thanked everyone who gave feedback. I took the time to return each e-mail message with my thoughts on the error or suggestion made, and an estimate of when and what I would do to change things as a result of their feedback. This e-mail feedback phase went rather well, and a few testers hung on and continued to occasionally participate in the site from that day forward.

Beta testing the site with a group of trusted peers was incredibly productive, resulting in a great number of improvements in a short period of time.

With an inbox filled with valuable feedback, I opened up a coding window and began going through each message carefully. I made the easy changes wherever I could, and I distinctly remember holding off on the more complex requests, due to my relative inexperience with programming. One such request, that of allowing for custom user time zones, was something that eluded me until very recently. Some requests asked for preset options instead of free form areas, like the user option that allowed for a user's custom font name. Instead of a blank input that accepted any choice, I could have also offered a drop-down element describing a handful of common, suggested fonts. This would have made for an easier-to-use customization page, but I lacked the programming knowledge to figure out how to handle

the submitted form. I patched the errors that I could reproduce, and refined the logout and login process.

If you can't round up a group of peers, the next best thing is to use interested strangers.

Beta testing the site with a group of trusted peers was incredibly productive, resulting in a great number of improvements in a short period of time. Since I launched MetaFilter, I've used the same technique on other personal projects. In the absence of a budget allocated for such testing, I've found that an e-mail beta-test request to peers finds most bugs and interface hang-ups. If you can't round up a group of peers, the next best thing is to use interested strangers. Put a request out on a mailing list devoted to the subject your new site covers, or just put a request up on the site itself. If you haven't launched the site yet, you can entice users to beta test by simply offering an early glimpse at the site, in exchange for feedback.

Permanent Cookies

To further entice users to contribute, I revised the login process as well, to attach permanent cookies that allowed people to remain logged in. I'd interacted on other community sites, and noticed that, where I was already a member of the site and wanted to make a comment, I often skipped it if I had to log in each and every time I visited. With MetaFilter, once you log in you're kept logged in until you purposely log out. It did create some minor security worries in that people using public or shared computers might accidentally remain logged in, but the benefits more than made up for it.

The Site's First Year

From its launch in mid-1999 through spring of 2000, the site went from a handful of registered users to a couple of hundred. The more people saw the site, the more feedback was generated in response to it. I made an effort to include my e-mail address in any error page served to the user. If I'd had the necessary programming expertise back then, I would have coded automatic e-mails to myself with all available environmental variables. I put my e-mail address in the footer of every page, and went out of my way to solicit feedback on the *About* page of the site, as seen here:

A lot of effort was made in gathering and acting on feedback.

During this time, many great ideas came from occasional users. From the beginning, when you clicked a link on the *Index* page to go to a comment page, the page to contribute comments was an additional link away. At the time, I programmed it this way because I could easily check to see if a user was logged in before showing them the comment page. When someone e-mailed me to suggest that forcing an additional click was both a waste of time and would inhibit comments, I agreed, and instead moved the behind-the-scenes login check to the public comment page. If a user was logged in, the comment form would appear automatically, ready to accept their contribution.

Several users that liked to write at length wrote feedback requesting a larger text area for comments, or asking for different size options in their preferences. I found with a little experimentation that the size of a `<textarea>` predicted how people would contribute to the site. The larger it was in both width and height, the more people tended to write. I found that an average good contribution was a paragraph or two in length, so I set the comment box `<textarea>` big enough to contain a paragraph of normal text, about 400 pixels wide by 200 pixels tall.

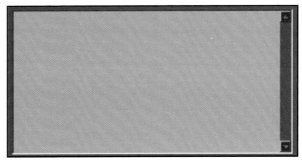

The final comment box dimensions.

I found with a little experimentation that the size of a `<textarea>` *predicted how people would contribute to the site. The larger it was in both width and height, the more people tended to write.*

Cross-Browser Issues

Once the site was open to the public, the most popular feedback seemed to be browser-related. I only had occasional access to a Macintosh for testing, so I would often modify layouts or put up new features without thoroughly testing them on a Mac. I quickly learned that Netscape and Internet Explorer browsers handled things like forms differently, and that the difference between platforms could often be even greater. Mac Netscape 4 displayed forms at about half the width of Windows Netscape 4. Wherever I could, I set form elements to exact pixel widths (by adding code such as `style="width:300px;"` to `<input>` and `<textarea>` elements). This worked in IE 4 and all browser versions 5 and up; for Netscape 4 I left mid-range values that worked on both the PC and Mac versions.

Fonts varied a bit in how they were handled on each browser and platform, but since the site's font settings were customizable, it didn't present much of a problem. I chose to use points as the display size, which allowed for browser resizing of text between "smallest" and "largest" controls within the browser. I found that a lot of feedback came from non-registered visitors to the site, so I decided to go against using fixed sizes in pixels, which rendered font control of browsers useless, and stick with points. It should be noted that going with points meant a fairly sizable difference between Mac and PC views of the site, regardless of browser. On a Mac, displays are 72dpi (dots per inch), so 1 point is the same size as 1 pixel, while windows monitors display information at 96dpi, so 1 point is actually 1.25 pixels. This meant that setting the default sizes on the page of 12 point and 10 point fonts resulted in 16 pixel and 12 pixel tall fonts on a PC, while Macs displayed them at 12px and 10px. I tried my best to accommodate both Mac and PC versions of Netscape and IE, versions 4 and above, and let older browsers deal with a not-as-nice view of the site.

Form Behavior

The behavior of forms, and how browsers dealt with submitted information was also a good piece of e-mail feedback that resulted in a major re-coding of a site feature, to avoid loss of user-entered data.

As it stood, the *Comment* and *New Link* pages would have forms ready for a user's input. Below the forms were two buttons, *Post* and *Preview*. The *Post* button immediately sent the information to the database and refreshed the page to show the new information, whereas the *Preview* button jumped to a preview page, which showed how the final page would look after submitting the user input, along with a *Post* button below, to allow for final submittal. If a user was unhappy with the previewed contribution, they could simply hit their browser's back button, re-edit, and repeat.

> *You haven't created a truly usable site if a user is forced to use their browser's navigation buttons (for example,* Back *and* Forward *in IE) to move about the site or out of a dead end.*

However, what users often found was if they worked on a comment or link for a significant period of time (anywhere from five minutes to fifteen minutes would set off this behavior), going back with your browser's back button would wipe out the previewed comment. It seemed that different browsers cached information differently, but after a period of time browsers just "forgot" what you had submitted. To rectify the situation, a preview system was built that allowed for users to preview again and again, without having to use their browser buttons, to ensure that information would never be lost due to a browser cache expiry. The new system meant that the *Preview* page not only presented contributed information as it would appear on the site, but would also repeat the same information below, in the same editable forms interface the user created the preview with – a *Preview* button accompanied the *Post* button. Therefore, you could *Preview*, edit an entry below, hit *Preview* again, and repeat until satisfied, before hitting *Post* to save the information to the site.

When designing site navigation, I've realized you haven't created a truly usable site if a user is forced to use their browser's navigation buttons (for example, *Back* and *Forward* in IE) to move about the site or out of a dead end – browser-based interaction like you find on MetaFilter should never rely on browser buttons if you want to be able to limit problems in the application and present a predictable user experience.

Another major problem on the site that came from widespread use and feedback was that of how to handle user input. Although the interface of MetaFilter was built in HTML, member contributions were allowed to include HTML. From time to time, the interface itself could be changed or damaged by someone's submission. After some significant testing, it was found that the use of `<div>` elements as containers seemed to "confine" code submitted by users, and prevented changes in margins or line spacing. When the site first launched, users often added line breaks themselves, by inserting paragraph tags or line break tags. Browsers treat paragraph tags differently, usually adding some sort of vertical margin above and below each insertion. I didn't want to force users to know HTML in order to create paragraphs, and I also wanted to keep as much of the submitted data in the database as free of HTML display code as possible. The remedy was to search for hidden line break characters in a post, and when displaying data from the database, simply do a search and replace, adding line break tags in place of the hidden carriage returns. The example code below illustrates this:

Example Code

```
This is an example post. This is the second sentence in the first paragraph.

After hitting return twice, in the textarea, I created this second paragraph that
I'd like to add a sentence to. When displaying this data, as user, I would expect
it to look exactly like the way I submitted it, in distinct blocks of text.

I don't want to have to insert HTML myself to do it, and I would hope to see three
paragraphs after I hit the post button below
```
Multi-paragraph sample post, as submitted in a form

```
This is an example post. This is the second sentence in the first paragraph.<br>
<br>
After hitting return twice, in the textarea, I created this second paragraph that
I'd like to add a sentence to. When displaying this data, as user, I would expect
it to look exactly like the way I submitted it, in distinct blocks of text.<br>
<br>
I don't want to have to insert HTML myself to do it, and I would hope to see three
paragraphs after I hit the post button below
```
Multi-paragraph sample post, as delivered to a browser

By searching for hidden carriage return characters in the database (in this case, they can be selected by searching for ASCII characters 10 and 13 successively), and replacing them with two `<br />` elements, users of a site don't have to know HTML and will see their contributions as they submitted them, without having to muck up the data with presentation code.

Beyond the First Year

In spring of 2000, I had been working on the site for over a year, and the membership was now in the low thousands. Many members were web developers themselves, and offered plentiful advice and feedback, but also requested many features. I would often get vague bug reports like "a page gave me an error" without good descriptions of where they were, what they were doing, and what they were using to view the site. My "feedback" folder was full in my e-mail program, and I'd often devote a weekend to working on the site, but I could never keep up with all the requests or bug reports. New features were constantly being dreamt up by users and e-mailed to me. Often I'd get three identical suggestions in the same week, and I'd have to tell each person individually if it was a good or bad idea and if I could work on it. I started to notice people making new comments on the site itself, in threads that had nothing to do with interface issues. I began to realize that I needed to add something to the site to keep track of bug fixes or feature requests, and give people a place to voice their concerns. There were only so many free hours in my day, and unless I found a way to manage all the feedback, I would be overwhelmed.

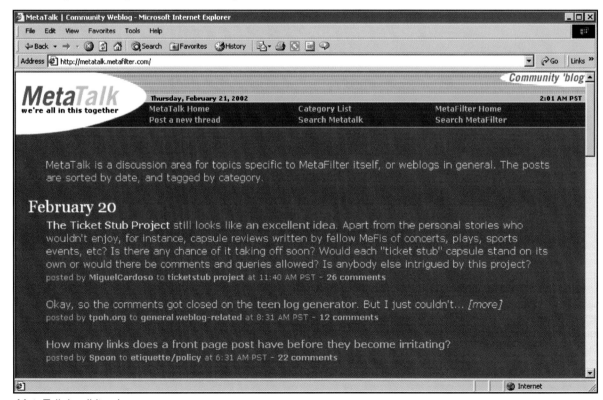

MetaTalk in all its glory.

Over the course of a weekend, I programmed a new section of the site devoted to issues specific to the site itself. Since the site was already called MetaFilter, I decided to call the new section **MetaTalk**, to imply it was for talking about MetaFilter.

I built a system like MetaFilter, with threads and comments, but I added strict categories to the posts, to better manage the information. The categories were:

- Bugs

- Feature requests

- Etiquette/policy

- MetaFilter-related (a catch-all for other MetaFilter matters)

- General weblog-related for more general questions about the format itself

The new section started off slowly, but quickly became a better way to manage my feedback. For bug reports, people could report errors they found, and if I requested more information, others could see what types of helpful feedback got bugs fixed the fastest. It also meant I wouldn't get three copies of the same bug, and I could gain more information as others would try to figure out the problem and do additional testing for me. Instead of bug reports being user-to-developer, they were now largely user-to-user, and others could offer solutions or workarounds to common problems.

The feature requests worked the same way. Someone would suggest a new feature or way of doing things on the site, and I and others could debate whether it would help everyone. I could ask what type of interaction they would expect from the new features, and I could even ask for advice or help in coding the new features. The etiquette/policy section worked well, as people could report misbehaving users or could openly debate the site's policies. Since it was a community site, and my first community, I was always open to new voices and

perspectives. Nothing on the site occurred in a vacuum now – users could help make the site error free, they could suggest and discuss things they'd like to see, and participate in discussions about changes to the site. Whenever I finished a new feature, I would always announce it early in MetaTalk, where the frequent users of the site visited. I would make a new post, with a link and information about a new feature, and request feedback. Within hours, I'd often have over a dozen beta test reports, with detailed descriptions of each person's browser and OS, how it worked or didn't work for them, and what they liked and didn't like about it.

With these new tools at my disposal, I could accomplish more than I could alone with private e-mail feedback. By involving the community in the maintenance of the site, I could share the burden of developing and testing the site with others. Whenever I had free time to kill, I could go to MetaTalk to see a nicely sorted and discussed list of things to fix and things to work on. Overall, it worked beautifully, and saved my sanity early on in the site's rise in popularity.

> *I could go to MetaTalk to see a nicely sorted and discussed list of things to fix and things to work on. Overall, it worked beautifully, and saved my sanity early on in the site's rise in popularity.*

Could you create such a public feedback area on a business site? Any site used by thousands, with an enthusiastic user base could implement some public forums for dealing with technical problems or new feature requests. It would require an open philosophy, one where a company openly asks for features or beta testers, and doesn't prefer to code in secret to hide bugs from the world. I've witnessed many small companies benefit from user-to-user forums. With a staff of only a handful of busy people, the only way a small company can compete with a large corporation is to offload some of the support costs to feedback forums. A small company with a public support forum doesn't need a team of support specialists working a bank of phone lines 24 hours a day, seven days a week. Public forums also help a company's marketing activities. An enthusiastic group of users can often help sell products if there is a site somewhere where prospective buyers can witness users singing its praises. In lean times, for small companies, and for forward-thinking corporations, a public feedback forum can be a valuable asset.

> *I've witnessed many small companies benefit from user-to-user forums.*

Usability Improvements Garnered from Feedback

With the new section of MetaFilter in place, I could alter the site more quickly and easily, and manage a great deal of feedback. Suggestions could be discussed, revised, and tested by the users, saving me a lot of time and effort getting things right. Improvements to the site occurred all over.

The posting interfaces became more useful after I'd heard a lot of feedback suggesting the comment and link page <textarea> was too small. Users noted the *username* and *password* fields were largely extraneous and pre-filled out, and I realized the only reason I put them there was because it was easier to code the site initially by passing information in form elements. The *username* and *password* fields were also inputs, but pre-filled out with information stored in a user's cookie, so they weren't really requiring any input at all – I remedied any possible confusion by removing them

from the interface. The same cookie data could be stored in hidden form elements, or queried from the cookie the moment a submission is made to the database. This allowed me to streamline the posting interfaces to the point that they were merely a <textarea> and a *Preview* button on the comment interface, and a <textarea> and a *Preview* button on the new post interface page. Given my own aversion to "formjunk" and needlessly complex interfaces that force many form elements on users, I was happy to simplify the interfaces as much as I could.

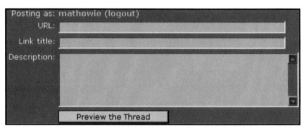

Before feedback.

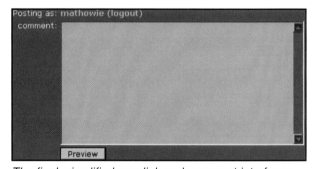

The final, simplified new link and comment interfaces after incorporating feedback.

> *Given my own aversion to "formjunk", I was happy to simplify the interfaces as much as I could.*

I found that patterns emerged in user behavior, and feedback from users describing how they used the site supported them. Avid users would revisit the site often, and the most valuable piece of information for them was to figure out how much had changed since their last visit. With a combination of stored timestamps in the database and session variables on the server, I could keep track of a user's last visit to both MetaFilter and MetaTalk. At first I was only able to provide a count of new posts and comments since a user's last visit.

Feedback quickly suggested that more information was desired. It was as if I was teasing users, telling them that there were five new comments, but it was up to them to find the comments. The next step was to enumerate how many new comments were in each thread, so that a user could see that there were two new comments in one thread, but three in the other. The final new activity interface improvement, and one that was only possible thanks to help from a member who happened to be a database expert, was to select the first of the new comments in a thread, and link the indicator of new comments as a target to the first new comment in a thread. This meant if a post had four new comments, the database query would select the ID number of the oldest, or first of the new comments. The comment pages all had "permalinks" or targeted links to the precise location on the page where a comment was located. Since all the comments and threads have unique IDs given by the database, it is possible to create a permanent hypertext location of a specific comment on the site. These are built automatically by putting the unique ID of the comment in a name attribute before each comment like so:

```
<a name="23675"></a>
This is a comment on a long thread, but if
you look at the source code, you can
figure out how the permalinks work, and
why they come in handy on a community
discussion site.<br>
posted by username at <a
href="comments.html#23675">12:30 PM on
March 1</a>
```

Simplified source code of a post, showing how targets are used on comments and permalinks

With the <a> tags, name attributes, and targeted links like those in the figure above, clicking on a "*4 new*" comments indicator could load the appropriate comment page, and auto-scroll down to the first new comment of the four. This allowed people to read longer threads, and revisit them more often by simply skipping to the new activity. I should mention that the permalinks weren't initially added for this specific purpose. They were added earlier on to allow people to reference other comments. With a unique hypertext address for every post on the site, you could make a permanent link to someone else's contribution, to highlight it, refute it, or use it to support an argument.

Creating Usable Forms

One day a user suggested that the search form would be easier to use if the cursor focus was automatically set to the *search* <input> form element. This would allow you to hit the *search* page in the navigation bar, then simply start typing as soon as the page loaded, saving the step of clicking into the input with your mouse. Sample code is shown below:

```
<body
onload="searchform.searchme.focus();">
   ...
  <form name="searchform"
action="search.html">
    <input type="text" name="searchme">
<input type="submit">
  </form>
```

Simplified code listing for form auto-focusing

It may sound minor, but it goes a long way to creating a site that is more easily and efficiently used by everyone.

I've been a big fan of JavaScript-powered image rollovers since they originated in 1996. They provided a great way to give important visual clues to users, letting them know visually that something is a link. With the adoption of CSS, I found similar value in the `hover:` pseudo-class, allowing a user to know they were hovering over a link by its highlighted state.

A fairly simple bit of code utilizing the `onfocus` and `onblur` events provides much of the same visual feedback to form elements in IE and Netscape versions 5+. When a user clicks into a form input, or tabs into it, it changes color, and when they leave it, it changes back. This provides a nice visual indicator of where a user is in a form, especially useful for long forms that contain many elements. The code is shown below:

```
<input type="text" name="username"
style="color:#ccc;"
onfocus="this.style.background:#eee;"
onBlur="this.style.background:#ccc;">
```

Form highlighting code

The `<label>` element is part of the HTML 4 specification, and is interpreted by IE and Netscape browser versions 5 and above and effectively ignored by earlier browsers. It provides for both increased usability and accessibility of form elements. On the usability side, it allows for much larger clickable areas for things like small form elements such as radio buttons and checkboxes. Once it has been implemented, descriptive text next to a form element can be clicked, much as in desktop applications most personal computer owners have been using for years. The `<label>` element also allows forms to be parsed and used by screen readers, so people who are visually impaired can know exactly what text applies to each option on a form. The code is fairly simple:

```
<input type="checkbox" name="email"
id="email">
<label for="email">Show email on user
page?</label>
```

Example of the `<label>` element in use on a checkbox form element

In addition, each form element needs an `id` attribute unique to the page, so if you've got a long form, try to add a number or unique name to each form element. The next step is to wrap `<label for=" ">` tags around descriptive text that is associated with the form element. A final interface improvement to give users visual indications that this feature is available, before they click, is to add this additional CSS:

```
<style>
label
{
    cursor: pointer;
    cursor: hand;
}
</style>
```

CSS code to provide quick visual indication that a labeled element is clickable

This provides the following visual clue:

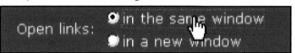

Label code and CSS in use on a web form.

Putting these minor form enhancements together, it became possible to create a truly useful form and give very specific and helpful error pages. On a page asking for input on multiple forms, I typically do server-side checks to make sure the required elements are filled in, and if not, return the page as they left it, with the missing elements highlighted in some way. In the past, I might have displayed a short message such as "you must add an e-mail address" and made the label for "e-mail address" red and bold, so it stood out. What I found by combining the previously described form usability enhancements was that it wasn't necessary to force the user to hunt around for the missing information on their form. It was now possible to physically put the cursor in the empty or error-filled form element and highlight the form element by changing its background color, in addition to changing the form's label to indicate where the error occurred. The technology required isn't too difficult to implement – after server-side checks for submitted form elements are done, the previous page can be returned to the user with a custom form focus in the <body> tag, which would also highlight the form element, as long as the onfocus code was added to all form elements. Also, remember to send back the data that was submitted before the error check, so a user never "loses" their work. If they filled four out of five things correctly, give them the error page back with their four pre-filled replies, and the fifth properly highlighted and described, so they can solve problems quickly. Screenshots showing an improperly filled form before and after submission are shown here.

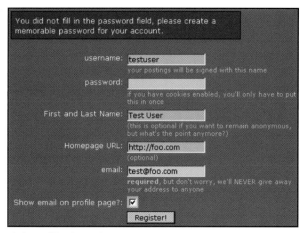

A form filled out, but returned, with a required field missing.

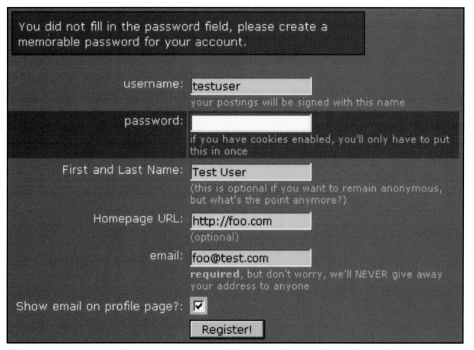

The same erroneous form returned, but this time with the missing form field described and highlighted in a different color, with the focus automatically set on it, as well as different shading round the whole entry.

adventures in zero budget usability

Unintended Usability

Some design decisions were made with little forethought, and surprisingly turned out to be good choices worth sharing. Each decision presented in this section was completely arbitrary, and even though some early feedback advised against them, I stuck to these choices and eventually the site and community benefited from them.

I'm a big fan of lower contrast on visited links. Since a user has already been there, they should mix into the background slightly, and the unvisited links should "pop" out a bit.

When I first designed the look and feel of the site, it was during a time where everything on the web had a white background, and usually default blue and purple links. The World Wide Web was deeply entrenched in "portal-itis" (where everything was an information portal) back then, and anything remotely corporate had to have a white background with black text. Most personal sites were anything but white, and with that in mind my early mockups were all shades of either gray, green, or blue. I eventually chose a muted medium blue background with an unusual yellow-green as an accent color because they seemed to be uncommon colors on the Web, which made my site stand out from the rest. The pages were text heavy, and I set all text in white, with the yellow-green used for unvisited links, and a lower contrast, less yellow-green (almost tan in color) as the visited links.

I'm a big fan of lower contrast on visited links. Since a user has already been there, they should mix into the background slightly, and the unvisited links should

"pop" out a bit. This becomes almost a requirement on MetaFilter, where a page can often contain dozens to hundreds of external and internal links. I don't know why I stuck with the blue background at first; maybe it was because, in the back of my mind, I likened the white text on blue backgrounds to old WordPerfect terminals I would write papers with when I was a student. Early feedback asked for custom colors and user-switchable stylesheets, and I only balked because I didn't know how to approach adding that functionality into the application. After a couple years, everyone became accustomed to the colors, dubbing it "MetaFilter blue", and in a weird way these things work: a valid explanation was put forth by Derek Powazek in an article critiquing MetaFilter's design (see *http://www.designinteract.com/insights/022201/*). He basically stated that because the site is often so reliant on outbound links, the characteristic-on-MetaFilter-but-uncharacteristic-on-other-sites blue was a brilliant way to differentiate the outside linked sites from MetaFilter. If you were to quickly glance at an active member's desktop during their morning visit to the site, you might see a smattering of browser windows, and it'd be easy to spot the blue MetaFilter one underneath most others. I don't know if I completely agree with the conclusion, as I never put much forethought into it, but the dark background-light foreground text makes for comfortable reading and is easy on the eyes. On a text-heavy site, comfortable reading is a key design goal.

On a text-heavy site, comfortable reading is a key design goal.

Un-Threaded is Good!

When the site first launched, the pages for comments on the posts were shown in a flat, un-threaded format. The person posting the fifth comment could be responding to the second one or the original post, and the person below them could be referring to other comments as well. It sounds a bit chaotic, but seeing everything on one page allows users to follow more easily, and offers the only way to see everything on the site without forcing much effort on the user. I had a good deal of experience with other community systems, and they all were based on the newsgroup metaphor. For every post, there could be a reply. Below replies, there could be deeper replies, and to those replies, even deeper levels of responses could be made. This architecture results in finely sorted, mass communication in a community, but on the web, where each page load can take 1-20 seconds due to traffic, server load, or page size, it quickly becomes exhausting to keep up with every thread, sub-thread, and sub-sub-sub-sub-thread. An example screenshot of a deeply threaded message board is shown next:

- I love my free software by doubtless (Score:1) Sunday March 17, @11:03PM

    - Re:I love my free software by Anonymous Coward (Score:-1) Sunday March 17, @11:07PM
        - Re:I love my free software by Anonymous Coward (Score:-1) Sunday March 17, @11:10PM
        - Re:I love my free software by doubtless (Score:1) Monday March 18, @12:16AM
            - Re:I love my free software by Anonymous Coward (Score:1) Monday March 18, @12:36AM
                - Re:I love my free software by SerpentMage (Score:2) Monday March 18, @06:58AM
    - Re:I love my free software by kz45 (Score:1) Monday March 18, @12:13AM
    - Re:I love my free software by I.T.R.A.R.K. (Score:-1) Monday March 18, @12:30AM

- Wide pages are still here! by Klerck (Score:-1) Sunday March 17, @11:05PM

    - you're not a real troll by ArchieBunker (Score:-1) Sunday March 17, @11:11PM
        - Re:you're not a real troll by Serial Troller (Score:-1) Sunday March 17, @11:15PM
            - info on klerck by Anonymous Coward (Score:-1) Sunday March 17, @11:58PM
                - Re:info on klerck by Serial Troller (Score:-1) Monday March 18, @12:03AM
                    - Re:info on klerck by Anonymous Coward (Score:-1) Monday March 18, @12:10AM
                    - Re:info on klerck by Anonymous Coward (Score:-1) Monday March 18, @12:15AM
                        - Re:info on klerck by TurboRoot (Score:1) Monday March 18, @12:48AM
                        - Re:info on klerck by Serial Troller (Score:-1) Monday March 18, @01:16AM
                        - Re:info on klerck Monday March 18, @01:15AM
                        - Re:info on klerck Monday March 18, @01:27AM
        - Re:you're not a real troll by Anonymous Coward (Score:-1) Monday March 18, @12:09AM

Deep threading in a message board requires many pageviews to unveil content.

adventures in zero budget usability

The design of flat comment pages on MetaFilter was in fact deliberate. I experienced the exhaustion of trying to keep up with busy community threads and hated losing track of sub-threads on other sites. I also realized that even though most community software depended on the threaded newsgroup design metaphor, heavily used programs like desktop e-mail applications seldom did. Even though almost every e-mail you send or receive sticks to an agreed upon standard with reply history and status, most users choose to read e-mail in a flat, time based format. Among my group of highly experienced, Internet-using friends, only one or two went to the effort of locating and configuring an e-mail client that does true threading (on subject).

What wasn't deliberate about the flat comment page design was the way it affected future growth and user interactions on the site. Early on, the geekier users often requested the ability to view comments in a threaded format, and again, my then lack of programming experience made it impossible for me to even offer it as an option. But as time wore on, the flat comment views turned into both a useful way to view the site, and a good way to keep the community members civil towards one another. Even on a busy

Social Community Aspects of Usability

Some aspects of a community's usability are more social than technical in nature. A pet peeve of mine is the spontaneous creation and mass adoption of jargon. Jargon, by its very definition describes words or phrases not used or understood by those outside a specific group. It makes those new to a community feel like outsiders, and those using it appear self-absorbed. It's strange, but I've witnessed a small group of enthusiastic participants come up with new acronyms, new in-jokes, and non-sequiturs seemingly out of nowhere, and watch others quickly adopt them as an often-used phrase. I think those creating such jargon almost always do it unintentionally; it's usually a form of shorthand, a new abbreviation done to save typing. What's odd about it is seeing others read it and begin using it. Jargon ends up serving almost like a "secret code" that puts those more active on the site above those that visit or read on a more infrequent basis. It conveys the message that "if you don't know what the abbreviation stands for, you can't be reading the site enough". By the use of

etiquette discussion areas within MetaTalk, I've been able to actively discourage most forms of jargon on the site, and together the community has come up with an accepted glossary of common terms, kept because they're mostly obvious even to new users.

When dealing with a large community, perceptions of anonymity can also lead to unfavorable behavior on the part of users and make for both an unfriendly atmosphere and an unfriendly web site. Among the current 13,000 or so users of the site, about 3,000 actively visit each and every day. Among those, a few hundred contribute to the site in some way. It's a sizable group, but once it gets big enough, the constant streaming of new names will eventually leave everyone as unrecognizable members of a crowd. Once that happens, social pressure from others diminishes and you get a higher incidence of unruly behavior. You'll never hear news of mass rioting and looting in a small farm village, but you'll be sure to hear about the same crimes committed someday in a major metropolitan area for much of the same reasons.

day, it was possible for most users to simply click into each post's comments page, and see everything said in response to it. I found it easier for me to keep administration tabs on things, by being able to view everything going on with a single page. The lack of sub-threads hidden behind links meant that people couldn't "hide" things like nasty comments in places few saw (only those following all the way down would see them). With a flat system, everyone is out in the open. Those wishing to call others derogatory names or make wild accusations are instantly seen by everyone else and are quickly dealt with. Much of the site works on the fear of embarrassment from messing up in front of everyone or shame brought on by nefarious deeds witnessed by all. I never knew it would still keep the discourse civil and intelligent to this day, but I'm very glad to have stuck to my guns with my choice of simple views of comment postings.

Dealing With Trolling

A similar result on the social dynamics of the site has been the lack of a feature often seen on community sites; that of user scoring and filtering of other users based on score or name. "Trolling" is the classic act of saying obnoxious things in a community setting with the knowledge that you will disrupt the proceedings. It's a form of heckling, done for kicks by those wanting to start shouting matches between other members. On many community sites, trolls are dealt with in one of two ways. You can either hide users from view by their name (imagine buttons marked "never show me posts by *crazyheckler2000* again"), or you can score their contributions, then allow users to set filters (don't show me anything scored "-1" or below). The short-term solution leads to long-term problems with the very people these tools are set to eliminate.

> *What results in practice is a quick way to root out bad behavior.*

By creating a permanent place for trolls to reside, they stick around, goofing with people until they get the -1 score, but they often leave their mark and drag other members into pointless arguments before they're hidden from view. A regular feature request early on was the creation of such tools, but although I probably could have programmed the functionality, I knew even at the start they were problematic in their effects on the social interactions of the community. With MetaFilter's flat view, everyone else sees every user's contribution throughout the site. Every user is also linked to their entire history on the site, acting as a record of their previous behavior. What results in practice is a quick way to root out bad behavior, with appropriate action (anything from a polite e-mail reminder of their wrongdoing up to banning the account from posting or visiting the site ever again). This creates a highly visible, close community that reinforces good behavior in others, and makes for a pleasant place to visit overall.

Usable Advertising

Since the inception of MetaFilter, self-promotion by members has been actively discouraged to eliminate "conflict of interest" problems. As people use the site to post interesting links, one of the few rules to observe is that people shouldn't link to their own works, for the simple reason that it may be interesting to them, but not to others. As the site has motored along, the occasional self-promotional link would slip through, and some members took it upon themselves to go to great lengths to prevent their discovery – almost like a kind of secret society! During the Fall of 2001, I had grown tired of going through increasingly intensive investigative lengths to research overly optimistic posts, and while discussing my frustration with Derek Powazek, a fellow community site owner, we came up with the idea for self-serve advertising for the site. Since it wasn't ever going to go completely away, an advertising outlet on the site would hopefully funnel all those looking to trick the audience into seeing their site, and also bring in a small revenue stream to an otherwise completely non-profit site. I was a big fan of Google's self-serve AdWords system (see *https://adwords.google.com/*

AdWords/), due to its simple setup and maintenance. Large banner graphics wouldn't have to be created, checked for size, and approved for content by me. A self-serve ad system based on simple text form fields could almost run itself, so I dubbed my new creation **TextAds**.

MetaFilter's technically savvy user base tends to dislike rampant advertising on the web, so the choice of text-only advertising was a careful and deliberate choice. Google pioneered the unobtrusive design qualities of its site, its search results and its keyword advertising. I patterned TextAds on that, limiting the displayed advertising on the site to a small box built in CSS, with a text link and short description below. The box matches the site's color palette, with a lighter background color to make it stand out a bit.

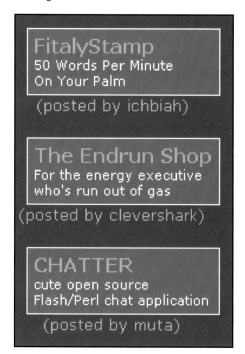

Some TextAds.

I would consider TextAds usable advertising because they go against the last few years of online advertising trends. As users have grown blind to the standard banner, commercial sites have resorted to changing ad sizes, adding multimedia banners, separating content pages with forced viewing of intervening ads, and most recently it has become common to see full screen motion graphics on large, high-traffic sites for big budget products and services. It is almost as if advertisers have declared war on users and are developing and stockpiling new weapons in their quest to get paid information in front of users at any cost. The best interests of users have been lost in all this, as advertisers seek to broadcast their messages at the expense of a site's readability.

The text-based advertising of Google and MetaFilter is the anti-banner, as it sits peacefully off to the side, reminding only those that glance over at it that there's another site they could view if they chose to. It could be said that text advertising is downright respectful of the user, remaining unobtrusive as the user goes about their business on the site. It is prone to the same "banner blindness" as more conventional ads, but doesn't seek to intrude upon user behavior. It remains relevant or successful by a combination of targeting and good writing. On Google, the targeting is obvious as ads are tied to requested search keywords, but on MetaFilter, the targeting isn't so strict, but tailored to the audience, usually placed by members of that audience. MetaFilter exists mostly to show you interesting sites at other places, and the TextAds seek to do the same. They retain higher click-through rates than banner advertising by simply remaining relevant to users, instead of traditional online advertising's continued evolution to invent newer and better ways to be hostile to users.

Text-based advertising on MetaFilter has been highly successful, meeting both the goals of eliminating self-promotion on the site and bringing in a steady level of income. It's not enough to pay a full-time salary, but it is enough to deal with minor monthly maintenance on the server. The self-serve aspect of advertising is indeed a new direction, and the typical advertiser is either a small business owner or a member of the site looking to promote their own work to their peers. The pricing is kept purposely low ($1 per thousand impressions currently with a $10 minimum) to further encourage members of the community itself to advertise their works to other members. So for example, with the index page of the site showing up about a million times each month, that means I can sell a maximum of $1,000 per month, which isn't enough to live on, but helps defray hosting and server maintenance costs.

Without having any experience in advertising sales, I can run a self-serve system that doesn't require me to seek out large corporations for their support for more costly traditional advertising methods. Since the inception of my TextAd system, the model has been copied across multiple community sites, a few enterprising folks have built central services that allow you to run ads on your site from their system, and one person has even developed an open sourced, free self-serve text advertising system that can be integrated with almost any site – see *http://textads.sourceforge.net/*.

Future Improvements

Given all the ways MetaFilter has grown in terms of usage, audience, and features, there always remain ways for it to improve. Since I created the site myself, the only limits on my adding any features are my time, programming knowledge, and energy. The following are a few blue-sky things I've been thinking about adding to improve the site.

As the sheer number of participating users has skyrocketed, this has exposed the limits of the reading interface. The easy-to-use flat comments page allows you read everything everyone has said in a single page load, but on a busy post, it also leads to two problems. It inhibits others from posting because it looks like everyone has said everything already. Everything probably wasn't covered already, but after looking at a page of eighty comments, someone with something to say when they first see a post may not feel like sharing it after spending the next few minutes reading everyone's earlier responses. The opposite problem the busier site creates is that there are so many comments that users neglect to read any of them, instead scrolling down to the comment box immediately and writing their response. This behavior tends to end up producing threads where dozens of users seemingly shout their opinions from the mountaintops, without interacting with one another. In the future, something will have to be done, because even on the slower days, the 20-30 new posts generated on the site will frequently average well over 50 comments each. Few people, if any, can keep track of a full day's activity, which may approach 1,000 comments, site-wide.

To help deal with the site's content there are a few options that would make it easier for users to read and keep up with everything. **Comments could be limited to a per user, per day basis.** Instead of hundreds of comments happening each day, if a person were limited to say, five comments a day at most, they would have to pick and choose what they said, and hopefully reduce the number of new comments added to the site. This might have a side benefit of improving the quality of comments, as users would be forced to think before speaking, given the limits. Another way to deal with the problem would be to add user moderation to the site. If users could rate comments by others based on quality, other users could limit their views to only the highest quality comments. This would act to "bubble the good stuff to the top", and allow people to view only a few dozen comments per day, site-wide, and only the highest quality comments at that. Moderation data could be used along with some simple collaborative filtering mechanism to show you things like "if you liked this comment by this user, you might also like this other highly rated thing they said." The large number of users on the site can either be routed around, and limited to keep the site readable, or they could be harnessed, to help filter the site as much as possible, reporting errors, making necessary edits, and filtering low quality contributions from view entirely.

One improvement I'd like to make is the ability to truly quantify usability on the site – every usability-related lesson I've stated here and learned from the site has been largely qualitative. "Streamlining the comment forms to a single box and single button leads to an easier-to-use site" would be impossible to really quantify without gathering actual data on users. I could devise an experiment where a group of users are shown a link and some comments and asked to post a comment. I could then test a similar, though untested group on the same task, but give them a more complex interface, and measure their success rate. Given that I don't have the time, money, or other resources to run such tests, the next best thing I could do is compile data on the server. Instead of building and maintaining a real-life usability lab, I could run tests on the live site, using members as participants in various tests. In the future, whenever I want to make a drastic addition or change to the interface, I could elect to show it randomly to a subset of the site's users, then compare to a control set of users on the unchanged interface.

For example, if I wanted to add subject lines to every comment, much like in e-mail, but was concerned with the added complication on the comment form, I could run a simple test to measure the effects on the users. I could elect to show all even numbered userIDs the subject form field added to comments, and keep it from being shown to users having odd numbered userIDs. I could run the test for a day, and count the number of actual comments made by each group and compare. I could even go so far as to compare the data for statistical significance by running statistical relevance tests on the data. The separation of test subjects, data collection, and compiling of statistics are all fairly simple to do programmatically, and I'm confident that with a few weeks of work I could build a live "testing engine" that could run on top of the site's code and allow me to test every new feature for a few days before either implementing it site-wide or killing it depending on what the data revealed.

I've noticed a recent trend towards better quantification of usability data, especially since much of the hype and money has left the Internet industry. **In the post dotcom explosion era, a usability specialist increasingly has to justify their work in economic terms.** If you find your recommendations lead to an "easier-to-use site" you'd have a tough time relating that to how much money the company saves or new revenue it creates by implementing it. If you instead quantify usability in real terms, you could say something like: "75% of subjects bought our product from the test site using our new one-click buy feature. Without the feature, only 25% did, so the company stands to triple sales if we added the feature to the site." Usability is a real science, and can only stand to benefit by the collection of actual data before forming an opinion of what works and what doesn't work online.

The only constant on the web is change.

Conclusions

Over the course of this chapter, I have charted the history of the site and lessons I learned from running it. I have described how I collected feedback and made changes based on that feedback. The interface and usability of MetaFilter has evolved over time, due to a handful of factors. Below I will summarize the lessons I have learned – they are universal, and can hopefully be used on any site you work on in the future.

Remember that the only constant on the web is change.

1. Pick the right tools for the job.

Figure out your specific needs, and if you can find a software package that meets them, by all means use it. If, however, you can't find anything that specifically does what you'd like, or is flexible enough for your needs, don't be afraid to code your system from scratch. Using your own in-house system means you will always be able to change anything you like, or add new features as necessary. There is a logical mid-point between using an off-the-shelf tool to build your site, or building it completely from scratch. You can build on the work of others if you find a tool whose source code is available and easy to understand. You won't have to reinvent the wheel, but if you have to get under the hood to add a new feature or streamline an existing one, you can. When I couldn't find adequate community software, I built my own. There were drawbacks to taking that path, especially early on when my programming expertise was limited. Lately, I've used existing code where possible, building on the work of others and integrating it into the site's existing code base.

2. Tailor your site to your intended audience.

There are times when a choice must be made between usability and functionality. In the best circumstances, an interface can both be easy to use and do amazing things, but be aware of your audience, and don't be afraid of making choices at the cost of usability or ease-of-use if the situation warrants it. With MetaFilter, I wanted technically savvy users and wasn't afraid to introduce artificial barriers. If you're building a site that sells high-end audio equipment, make the process of purchasing items as easy as possible, but don't be afraid to show full technical details about products to users, much more than the average store might, to reflect the nature of audiophile customers.

3. Make interfaces as simple as possible and add complexity as needed.

Nothing sends users or customers away from a site more quickly than a difficult interface. Eliminate frustration in users by starting out simple, and only adding additional features and complexity when needed. When possible and applicable, allow interface complexity to be turned on and off in preferences or settings, so those not needing those features can hide them. In MetaFilter.com, the reading and contributing interfaces are as simple as I could make them, and a great deal of planning and testing goes into changing any interface or making an addition to existing interfaces.

4. Don't be afraid to take advantage of beneficial technology.

The benefits of using CSS on the site outweighed the problems of compatibility at the time. Content could be effectively separated from presentation, allowing it to be modified for different uses and devices. There are all sorts of ways to improve user experience by utilizing the latest technology. If you could cut the download size of a movie by offering it in a new format, it may be worth asking users to upgrade if you can demonstrate the benefits to them. There are new Internet standards coming out every day, and although application support often lags behind, in the cases where you can present a sleeker appearance or increased functionality by relying on new features, don't be afraid to give them a go. MetaFilter would suffer from unbearable load times and be impossible to customize the look of for users unless I chose to use CSS.

5. Test early and test often.

As soon as you have the most basic functionality ready for your site, give it a whirl. You'll often find major oversights or the need for major modifications after taking your site from "planned on paper" to "working in a browser".

6. Friends and colleagues make great (and cheap) test subjects.

It doesn't take much effort to conjure up a group of people you know to test out your new site and give feedback. Most often, you'll find that people love to see new sites or test new interfaces and will jump at the chance to play with your latest creation. I found that even after testing on a small group, I received enough feedback to last several weeks of fixing bugs and adding features. After testing your site by yourself, the first logical step is to show it to others. Your friends and colleagues make for good, willing participants and will probably give you more in-depth and valuable feedback than the average anonymous user.

7. Make it easy for users to report feedback about your site.

Once you launch a site, put a feedback link in the footer of every page so people can report errors or comments. In the section of your site explaining what the site is about (usually an *About* page), explicitly state that you'd like to hear questions, comments, or problems with the site and link to an e-mail address or comment form.

8. Create public feedback forums when possible.

If possible, a public feedback forum can often be more helpful than simply an e-mail or feedback form on a site. If a user is frustrated and can't find a page on your site, they could e-mail you or leave the site and never return (which happens more often than them leaving feedback). With a public feedback forum, a user might benefit from user-to-user help, or find someone else that has already reported the problem and found an answer for it. With a public feedback area, you will be less likely to have to answer the same question as many times as with a private one, and you will be more likely to benefit from the effects of the community, by users helping each other and letting users test new features before others.

9. Improve user interaction wherever possible.

After using the site for about a year, watching the patterns of others, and talking to some users about how they used the site, I found I could improve the way users found information by doing some significant enhancements to the site's back-end programming. Be aware of use patterns on your site, use the site as much as possible yourself, and solicit feedback from users about how they use the site.

10. Advertising can be usable.

By respecting the user and providing advertisements that don't interfere with the user experience, the annoyance of advertising can be avoided. Target audiences precisely to keep ads relevant to users.

Be aware of use patterns on your site, use the site as much as possible yourself, and solicit feedback from users.

11. Sometimes your first choice was the right one.

When you first create a site, there are often a lot of interface choices to make, and you probably make them based on your first instincts. Those instincts might be the best ones, so don't wipe all your initial work until you've adequately tested it out. If you change everything based on new user expectations, you may lose potentially characteristic features before they have a chance to prosper.

12. Always think about the future.

Even an excellent site can always be made better. Always try to stay on top of how people use the site and where problems occur, and note patterns that may point to larger issues that a simple interface change can't solve.

> *Good luck with your next project, and remember to make it as usable as you can.*

I think that about sums up the things I've covered here, and I hope you can take something useful away from my shared experiences. Remember, just because you don't have a budget for conducting intense, full-fledged usability studies doesn't mean you can't have a highly usable site. There is a lot of published information (like this book) and many helpful e-mail-based discussion lists to learn from, and testing sites yourself and among friends can go a long way towards improving usability. If you make it easy for users to leave feedback, you'll continue to improve your site as a result of feedback. If it becomes too much to manage, you might want to try giving public forums a try. Good luck with your next project, and remember to make it as usable as you can.

Matt Haughey's Usable Objects of Desire

Tivo – Making a very powerful computer based system incredibly easy to use, and changing the way people use television.

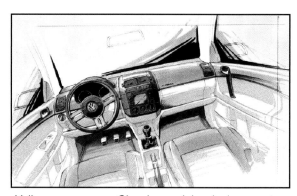

Volkswagen cars – Classic, modular design creates a design vocabulary that allows the passat to share interiors with the beetle and with the jetta.

*The Titanium Powerbook –
Lightweight, beautiful, and functional.*

Courtesy of Apple.

The Blogger.com interface – Simple enough to allow anyone to create web content, powerful enough to change the Web.

Sydney, Australia – The city is elegantly designed, signage is clear and easy to read, plenty of transportation options.

Also:

Oxo™ cooking utensils – Making human factors design beautiful.

Fleece clothing – Soft and comfortable, non-cotton and flexible enough to keep you warm on your couch at home or on top of Mount Everest.

Lego™ bricks – Simple binary building blocks can be used to build anything, by people of any age, 2 year olds to adults. A toy that teaches.

Index

A Guide to the Index

The index is arranged alphabetically word-by-word (so that New York would sort before Newark). An unmodified heading represents the main treatment of a topic. Acronyms have been preferred to their expansions as main headings, on the grounds that they are easier to recall. Any comments or suggestions specifically about the index would be welcome at *billj@glasshaus.com*

index

index

index

index

M

index

index

index

index

glasshaus

web professional to web professional

glasshaus writes books for you. Any suggestions, or ideas about how you want
information given in your ideal book will be studied by our team.
Your comments are always valued at glasshaus.

Free phone in USA 800-873 9769
Fax (312) 893 8001

UK Tel.: (0121) 687 4100   Fax: (0121) 687 4101

Usability : The Site Speaks For Itself – Registration Card

Name _____

Address _____

_____

_____

City _____ State/Region _____

Country _____ Postcode/Zip _____

E-Mail _____

Occupation _____

How did you hear about this book?

☐ Book review (name) _____

☐ Advertisement (name) _____

☐ Recommendation _____

☐ Catalog _____

☐ Other _____

Where did you buy this book?

☐ Bookstore (name) _____ City _____

☐ Computer store (name) _____

☐ Mail order _____

☐ Other _____

What influenced you in the purchase of this book?

☐ Cover Design ☐ Contents ☐ Other (please specify):

How did you rate the overall content of this book?

☐ Excellent ☐ Good ☐ Average ☐ Poor

What did you find most useful about this book? _____

_____

What did you find least useful about this book? _____

_____

Please add any additional comments. _____

_____

What other subjects will you buy a computer book on soon?

_____

What is the best computer book you have used this year?

Note: This information will only be used to keep you updated
about new glasshaus titles and will not be used for
any other purpose or passed to any other third party.

Check here if you DO NOT want to receive support for this book ☐

glasshaus

web professional to web professional

Note: If you post the bounce back card below in the UK, please send it to:

glasshaus, Arden House, 1102 Warwick Road,
Acocks Green, Birmingham B27 6HB. UK.

Computer Book Publishers